MASQUES III

Books by J. N. Williamson

Fiction

The Black School
Shadows of Death
Noonspell
The Longest Night
Ghost
The Evil One
Death-Coach
The Banished
Babel's Children
The Houngan
The Ritual

Nonfiction

New *Devil's Dictionary: Creepy Cliches & Sinister Synonyms*

Edited by

How to Write Tales of Horror, Fantasy and Science Fiction
Masques
Masques II
The Best of Masques

MASQUES III

ALL-NEW WORKS OF HORROR AND THE SUPERNATURAL

EDITED BY
J. N. WILLIAMSON

ST. MARTIN'S PRESS / NEW YORK

Short Story Index
<u>1989-1993</u>

DESIGN BY GLEN M. EDELSTEIN

Library of Congress Cataloging-in-Publication Data

Masques III : all-new works of horror and the supernatural / edited by
    J.N. Williamson.
        p. cm.
    ISBN 0-312-02948-9
    1. Horror tales, American. 2. Horror tales, English. 3. Supernatural—Fiction.
    I. Williamson, J. N. (Jerry N.) II. Title: Masques three. III Title: Masques 3.
    PS648.H6M35 1989
    813'.0873808—dc20   89-35106
                                                                                CIP

First Edition

10 9 8 7 6 5 4 3 2 1

CONTENTS

INTRODUCTION   xi

STORIES FOR ALL SEASONS   1

DRIFTER   *by Ed Gorman*   3
REFLECTIONS   *by Ray Russell*   17
THE HAPPY FAMILY   *by Melissa Mia Hall and Douglas E.*
     Winter   21
DEW DROP INN   *by D. W. Taylor*   33
REFRACTIONS   *by Thomas Millstead*   45
THE SPELLING BEE   *by Adobe James*   57
BETTER THAN ONE   *by Paul Dale Anderson*   67
EVER, EVER, AFTER   *by Graham Masterton*   75
PROMETHEUS' DECLARATION OF LOVE FOR THE
     VULTURE   *by Alan Rodgers* (poem)   99

THE "NEW" HORROR   103

LONG LIPS   *by R. Patrick Gates*   105
SINNERS   *by Ralph Rainwater, Jr.*   115
SUNDAY BREAKFAST   *by Jeannette M. Hopper*   123
THIRD RAIL   *by Wayne Allen Sallee*   131
COOCHIE-COO   *by Mark McNease*   137
THE WULGARU   *by Bill Ryan*   145
THE LUCKIEST MAN IN THE WORLD   *by Rex Miller*   155
THE BONELESS DOLL   *by Joey Froehlich* (poem)   166

CONCERNS OF THE MIND AND SPIRIT   167

THE SKULL   *by Diane Taylor*   169
ON 42ND ST.   *by William F. Nolan*   181

SAFE   *by John Maclay*   193

ALL BUT THE TIES ETERNAL   *by Gary A. Braunbeck*   199

POP IS REAL SMART   *by Mort Castle*   211

WHEN THE WALL CRIES   *by Stanley Wiater*   215

RETURN TO THE MUTANT RAIN FOREST   *by Bruce
    Boston and Robert Frazier* (poem)   227

CREATURES OF TERROR   233

THE WILLIES   *by James Kisner*   235

THE DRINKING PARTY   *by K. Marie Ramsland*   245

CHOSEN ONE   *by G. Wayne Miller*   255

THEM BALD-HEADED SNAYS   *by Joseph A. Citro*   265

MOTHERSON   *by Steve Rasnic Tem*   275

KILL FOR ME   *by John Keefauver*   285

SHAVE AND A HAIRCUT, TWO BITES   *by Dan Simmons*   293

THE ORCHID NURSERY   *by Amanda Russell* (poem)   312

OF ABSENCE, DARKNESS, DEATH: THINGS WHICH ARE
    NOT   *by Ray Bradbury*   315

ACKNOWLEDGMENTS

The people cited here include not only the ones who helped to make the present anthology possible but some of those whose co-operation, affection, or imaginative suggestions led to the development of *Masques* as an open-ended series. For my own reasons the list begins with Mary, my wife; followed by John Maclay, publisher of the first two *Masques* anthologies, and his wife Joyce; Dean R. Koontz; Ray Bradbury; David Taylor; Lori Perkins, my agent; editors Stuart Moore and Gordon Van Gelder, St. Martin's Press; and the late Milton L. Hillman, whose title for this series continues. Alphabetically but with similar gratitude I wish to acknowledge the following individuals: Hugh and Peggy Cave; Irwin Chapman, *2AM;* Don Congdon; Michael Congdon; Richard Curtis; Norman Curz; Reid Duffy, WRTV, Indianapolis; Editorial Consultants International; William J. Grabowski, *The Horror Show;* Charles L. Grant; Allen Koszowski; R. Karl Largent; Barbara Lowenstein; Wiescka Masterton; Rex Miller; *Mystery Scene;* Barbara Puechner; Katherine Ramsland; Ray Russell; Alan Jude Suma; Uwe Luserke; Robert and Phyllis Weinberg; and World Fantasy Conventions 1985 and 1988 Awards Committee.

INTRODUCTION

"Fear sells," critic Stephen Schiff wrote in *The New York Times* (March 6, 1988). But concerning "the Gothic short story," he added, "Serious people don't take it seriously anymore."

He then lumped together in one "horror chamber" such disparate bedfellows as best-selling novels, the virgins and rascals of romance fiction, pulp magazines, comics, and the movies. A mistake. One might just as fairly combine with the Olympics the ancient Mayan basket-sport that demanded the winners sacrifice their lives. Or confuse the song of whales with that of Michael Jackson, church choirs, Frank Sinatra, and the Beatles. Then throw in Pavarotti and any author in this book who vocalizes in the shower!

Schiff did argue, however, that if horror fiction—he persisted in using the term "Gothic"—is to survive, it can't "rely on plot twists and shockeroo endings alone." Agreed. It must "haunt and tantalize" the way "well-wrought prose" generally does.

Agreed, once more. And each of the brand-new tales and poems in this book is the work of a *very* serious person who has also set out to entertain and quite possibly scare the hell out of you into the bargain. Tantalizingly. Hauntingly.

There appears to be a lot of sudden concern going around about the matter of horror's survival. Yet, curiously, this sudden solicitude is being expressed at a time when both the most and the best of this fiction is being written and published. And it's a time when we *need* to be entertained, and we *need* to have the hell scared out of us. Because, I think, we cannot afford to give hell a free ride much longer.

You're about to enjoy exceptional encounters with many old favorites of fright in new disguise—ghosts, vampires, nameless terrors prowling the streets or lurking at the pastoral fringes of town—but you're also going to run headlong into shockingly contemporary beings and circumstances. Material for the first *Masques* anthology was selected during the year and a half before release in 1984, and many of the recurring fears human beings now experience have mutated, or shifted in emphasis. Whether they are greater or lesser in fact, we are today more haunted than ever before by the spectacles and specifics of apathy, poverty, disease, ill-used surplus. And by negligence of God and ever greater deceits and conceits; by the abuse of such divine indulgences as parenthood and other basic, obvious human obligations.

Writing independently, the authors in this anthology mirror a point in history when acronym and euphemism attempt to replace apology, action, grief; when definitions with real meaning are more brutally twisted than our characters. We are poised on the brink of another century, and the writers in this anthology seem to be wondering if it isn't the seventeenth century, or the first, that we're leaving! It's clearly time to jettison surplus cargo before venturing ahead. But some of these writers appear to suggest we may want to rethink the situation and reach out, hastily, for the baggage we must not pitch—even at times when the craft might seem to be going down.

The idea for a certain kind of anthology was born in the brain of former publisher John Maclay. The onetime Baltimore ad executive felt his life was missing something central without a more active participation in writing. Then the writer of quietly disturbing limited-run works concerning the unwise replacement of grace and style in architecture with gross commercial structures, Maclay wished to recapture the concerns and elements of the science fiction anthologies he'd read as a boy, but in the modern horror/supernatural genre. We discussed it over the phone repeatedly, at length.

Maclay's concept was to publish original fiction without a primary intention of either shocking or preaching—but fiction that *said* something about the way people are at heart. And the frights *we* become whenever we meet the bad guys and bad things without trying to do something about them. He hoped I'd seek writers with a feeling of awe and wonder who created yarns with style and grace. With the sweep of imagination often discouraged editorially, there was a place for humor, gore, the experimental or outrageous—and for the sort of subtlety readers understood only much later. There'd be tales that scarcely fell within conventional descriptions of the genre, but that furnished some horror; of disturbing (haunting) reflection; tantalizing glimpses of the reality of the victimized, and of the mad. We viewed short-shorts as a lost art—welcome—but plots were essential.

It was one of my tasks to locate and introduce the gifted new writers—and some thirteen writers have made their first professional fiction-writing appearances in the three *Masques* anthologies. At least twenty writers have been published for the first time in these hardcover books. Many have sold their own first books of fiction (R. C. Matheson, Wayne Miller, Alan Rodgers, Dave Silva, Steve Tem, Doug Winter, Jeannette Hopper, and John Maclay among them) since appearing in these anthologies.

When *M III* was conceived, I meant to continue things basically as John Maclay envisioned them. Then, when most of the material had been chosen, I happened upon a remark by Ed Bryant in the December 1988 *Twilight Zone* that illumined the creative process exercised in assembling an anthology. It led to the format for these new tales and verse. Bryant, a fine writer, said, ". . . no single anthology has yet captured in one volume the full panoply of talent and amazing energy presently propelling the horror boom toward its inevitable peak." Commenting on an anthology other than mine, he observed that it comprised work by many "of the top rank, *at least saleswise . . .*"

He noted, as well, that it included no female contributors.

The remarkable energy Ed correctly celebrates is, I think, in a constant state of flux, of growth. Whether anything like a "peak" is "inevitable" is debatable and in any case may suggest a pinnacle that, once attained, necessarily implies imminent decline.

With all due respect, I deplore such attitudes. I believe that the same variety of literarily homicidal and suicidal prophecy doomed mystery and science fiction to previous declines, that such predictions were fundamentally self-fulfilling, and that there are ways to wage a holy war against such sophistries.

The first battle begins with the will to resist falling into the trap of trying seriously to approach Bryant's "full panoply." No individual writer can unfailingly sustain the same level of excellence from work to work. The more we write, the more we may be published, and the less easily we become motivated by "invitations" to any published works—unless we *want* to write on a particular theme or for a particular publication.

It seems to me an unacknowledged fact that, in the case of many of our best-known writers, their finest work either was created at a time when their first encouraging successes came along, or that it was their best work that actually *made* them famous—at a time when they were neither well-known nor affluent. The moon moves, planets shift, loved ones fall ill or quarrel, and the famed author may discover he has made commitments beyond the time or energy allotted him or her. On the other hand, productive newer writers sometimes craft stories that fairly bubble off the page. When they are amenable to editing, their fiction tends to charge an anthology with electricity, with fire; to balance it.

So, stratagem two is seeking the ideal blend from a variety of writers. "Levels" or "kinds" of writer shouldn't be determined either by affluence or lack of financial success but by the degree of individual creative talent—and the particular material the writers submit for consideration. If there's one place left where we should not make either celebrity or economic status our first criteria, it's in what we *read*.

Bryant is right. There should be women among the concerned human beings crafting our fiction and verse. And newcomers writing because they're scared stiff by what they see around them; and alarmed, outraged pros. Gays, other minorities. Troubled single people, anxious parents—all the "kinds" of writers there are as people, identifiable only (if then) as an afterthought to the enjoyment of their work. Horror and other genres should reject the star system the way it was done years ago in films. To the degree that publisher profit will not suffer needlessly, all fiction should do so.

Genres peak or dip for numerous reasons, but writers of talent must have a marketplace in which to sell their wares censor-free, creating their work in their own best ways, not in imitation of their predecessors. Whether they are household names or not, they should be expected only to satisfy the primary standards and tastes of the editor—who never, surely, makes selections without surmounting his or her own prejudices. It is exclusively in what the editor creates himself, or herself, that a right to advocacy is permissible. Anything less is story-ordering and not story-finding, and selection; anything more can become didactic, dictatorial.

Horror and the supernatural come in many forms. Most of them now await you. And the fiction will go on selling, even "booming," when editors remember they are really "first readers." Surrogates for those who buy the publications. Horror fiction *is* energetic, and the talent producing it *does* represent a panoply of passions, aspirations, and terrors. If it has freedom to develop, it will be haunting, it will tantalize.

But horror will only truly "peak" when we can agree that *people* have done so.

Let the masque begin!

> J. N. WILLIAMSON
> Indianapolis

STORIES FOR ALL SEASONS

IN this volume of *Masques*, the writing—all of it new—is conveniently gathered under four hard-thought subsets or finer groupings. With the first of them, it was tempting to call such stories (and the poem) "traditional." And my Roget's didn't help much when I looked for a term that was less likely to carry connotations of old-fashionedness. It mentioned "standard," "elegant," and "custom-bound," terms both close to what I mean and *far* from it! "Standard" sounds as trite as "customary," and "elegant" could imply pretentiousness.

I almost called this group "time-honored," since Stephen King and Dean R. Koontz write time-honored fiction, just as did Charles Beaumont and Fredric Brown. None of these writers would create stories that are either hard to understand or done "by the num-

1

bers.'' Rather, in the tradition of great writers of the past, their work is so readable that it can be enjoyed decades or centuries later. Their subjects, concerns, settings, and styles are widely, enduringly familiar.

But such stories are also, obviously, tales for all seasons of people's thinking, people's fears and worries. Enjoying yarns such as theirs—and those in this group of stories—triggers a feeling that they have *always* been around, somehow. That they were plucked magically from some collective, fictive cosmos with merely the *help* of writers who, in the cases of artists such as Brown and Beaumont, may merely *appear* to have been gone from us for decades. They frighten today, would have frightened a hundred years ago, and they will frighten one hundred years from now.

Then these particular tales will be time-honored as well.

Ed Gorman

DRIFTER

ED Gorman, who writes original and laconic horror novels under the pseudonym Daniel Ransom, won a Private Eye Writers of America nomination in 1987—for Best Novel—with his gripping *The Autumn Dead* (St. Martin's Press). *The San Francisco Examiner* called it a "serious novel" with "a wonderful writing style" allowing Ed to "say things of substance in an entertaining way." He does a lot of that, also, as co-publisher (with Bob Randisi) of one of the most readable writers' mags ever, *Mystery Scene*. As a postscript to that, *MS* is also for horror readers; among the periodic contributors are James Kisner, Dean Koontz, Charles de Lint, and Richard Laymon. It's worth noting that Ed is also the editor of two *Black Lizard Anthologies of Crime Fiction* and is working on a third.

As Ransom, Gorman's *The Forsaken* and *Night Caller* displayed writing that was "strong, fast and sleek as a bullet," according to Dean, "lean and mean and red-blooded," according to Joe Lansdale. This new yarn by that nice guy happens to exemplify all those qualities.

DRIFTER

Ed Gorman

for Michael Seidman

THE DENVER RIG DRIVER DUMPED ME fast when he caught me trying to stuff a pint of his whiskey down the front of my pants. I'd figured that with the dark and the rain and the way even this big mother was getting blown around on the two-lane blacktop, he'd be too busy to notice. He flipped me his middle finger as he pulled away.

So I landed around seven o'clock that night in some town named Newkirk ten miles south of the Nebraska border, with half a pack of Luckies, two Trojans, and maybe three dollars in change to my name. I had a pocketknife, one of those babies that will do the job but that the law can't bust you for in most states, and a backpack filled with my one change of clothes, which was exactly like the ones I was wearing except they were more or less clean.

Newkirk had a single main street three blocks long. In the October night only two lights glowed, one for a DX station, one for Chet's café. No doubt about which one I needed first.

The kid at the DX station was trying real hard to grow a mustache—you could almost *hear* him trying to will that sucker into existence—and he had already grown an attitude.

"You ain't got no car," he said when I asked him for the restroom key.

"So?"

"You're some stranger and you ain't got no car."

"I need to pee real bad, friend. I figure you'd like me to do it in your rest room rather than your street."

The kid had spooked blue eyes. "Strangers never been good for Newkirk. Just last year—"

I interrupted him. "Friend, if I was a bad sort, I would've already hauled out my piece and stuck this little joint up. Ain't that about right?"

He relaxed, but not much. Over his grease-stained coveralls he wore a brand-new high school letter jacket. He probably had a girlfriend with a nice creamy body and they got to spend a lot of time in front of the TV, out of the wind and cold, watching horror flicks and having the kind of sex only teenagers can have. At thirty-one, I felt old and envious. I also felt filthy. It had been four or five days now. I said something I rarely do. "Please, friend. Please."

I put my hand out and he filled it with one of those keys that are attached to two-pound anchors so you won't steal them.

"Thanks, friend."

He didn't say anything, just sort of nodded.

October had stripped the trees and put a coat of frosty silver over everything. The cold only made the dimly lit rest room smell all the worse. It was more in need of a cleaning than I was. The mirror had been shattered by somebody's fist and I saw myself in a dozen fragmented pieces. There was a brown lump floating in the john. I didn't need to ask what that was. I flushed the john. Or tried to. It didn't work.

Laid over everything was this sickly sweet smell from this black-and-white air-freshener deal hanging off the edge of a condom machine. The air freshener was in the shape of a cute little skunk.

I got to work. On the road this way—the last real job I'd had was back in Cincinnati just before the '82 recession, when I'd been working construction—you learn how to sponge-bath yourself fast. You take a rough paper towel and you soak it with cold water (they never have hot or even warm water) and then you soap it till it's nice and silky almost like a real washcloth and then you do your face first and then you do under your arms and then you do down in your crotch and then you do down in your behind and then you take the BIC and you careful-like shave your face. I say careful-like because the road leaves you looking rough enough. You don't need any help with cuts on your face.

I finished off by combing my dark hair and brushing dust from my denim jacket and dousing a little Old Spice on the collar of my black turtleneck. There'd been a time when I'd done all right with the ladies and, looking at myself fragmented in the shattered mirror there, I thought about those days as the wind screamed outside and the light in the small, filthy rest room wavered. I used to always think, You're a long way from home, sonny boy. But lately I've realized I was always kidding myself. I wasn't a long way from home—I'd never *had* a home. Never.

I was two steps out of the rest room when I saw the guy. I should have known what the kid would do. Small town, distrustful of strangers, me walking in out of the night.

He wore a kind of baggy dark suit and a gray business hat like they always wear in '40s movies. He had white hair and a nose that looked almost proud of how many times it had been broken. The only thing different about him from any other cop in any other town was his eyes. You rarely saw cops with eyes sad as his.

He came right up to me and said, "I'm afraid I'm going to have to ask you for some identification."

I shrugged. "Sure." I pulled out my wallet and showed him my driver's license.

"Richard Anderson. Six feet. One hundred fifty-two pounds. Blue eyes. Black hair. Place of residence, Miami." As he read each of these off in the light on the drive, he'd look up at me to verify that what the license claimed was true. "You're a long way from Miami."

As if to prove what he'd said, a dirty truck filled with bawling cattle on the way to the slaughterhouse went rumbling by.

"Miami was a long time ago," I said.

"You doing anything special here?"

"Thought I might get something to eat."

"And then?"

"Then push on, I guess."

"That'd be a good idea." He handed me back my wallet. "I'm Jennings, the Chief of Police."

I wanted to laugh. The Chief? How big a force could he command in a place like Newkirk? People's fondness for titles always gripes me. It makes them feel like somebody. Me, I know I'm nobody and I've learned to face it.

He made a big production out of looking at his watch. "You see Chet's over there?"

Chet's was the diner. From here you could see a counter and a row of seats with only one guy in a Pioneer Seed Corn hat sipping coffee and forking off big chunks of what looked to be apple pie. Other than that the place was empty.

"Yep," I said.

"Good. You go over there and you tell Mindy that you're a friend of mine and that I told her to give you the special tonight— that's Swiss steak and peas and mashed potatoes and apple pie— and let me tell you, Mindy's apple pie is a pisser—and then I want you to have her put it on my tab."

"Hey," I said, "that's damn nice of you."

He stared at me with those sad eyes of his—so sad they made me a little nervous—and then he said, "Then I want you on the road. You can pick up the highway about a quarter mile east of here and you can get a ride in no time. You understand me?"

"Yes, sir."

He was just about to say something else when a pack of kids, dressed up variously as Freddie in *Nightmare on Elm Street*, Darth Vader, Spock, and several others I didn't quite recognize, pushed past us.

"Hi, Chief Jennings!" several of them called. And then, "Trick or treat!"

They encircled him.

From his trouser pocket he took a fistful of change and then, standing right there on the DX drive with gasoline fumes strong on the bitter night wind, he gave each of them a quarter.

He also gave them a small lecture. "Now you be sure to all stay together, you hear me? And I want you in by"—he glanced at his watch—"seven-thirty." He nodded to the one who looked like Freddie. "Walter, I'm making you responsible, you understand?"

"Yessir."

"Seven-thirty."

"Yessir."

Then they were off again, caught up in themselves and the chill night.

I saw how he watched the kids. He looked sadder than ever.

"You don't want to be a stranger in this town tonight, son," he said softly. He sounded almost as if he was going to cry. Then he corrected himself by clearing his throat and said, "You go have Mindy fix you up."

"Yessir," I said, watching him wave to the kid in the DX and then walk back to his squad car.

"Yessir," I whispered again.

I sounded like one of those kids he'd given a quarter to.

The food was just as good as he'd said it'd be: big chunks of Swiss steak floating in tomatoes and so tender you could cut it with a fork, whipped potatoes with big yellow pats of butter, and some juicy green peas; all capped off with a wide wedge of apple pie and a cup of fresh coffee. It was one of those moments when you didn't want to leave, when you wanted to freeze the world in just one place, when you regretted things you'd been and done, and never wanted to be or do those things again.

The place smelled pleasantly of frying grease and cigarette smoke as I sat there finishing up my after-dinner coffee and talking some with Mindy, a short woman with unnaturally red hair and a grease-spattered pink uniform and horn-rimmed glasses that kept slipping down her nose.

She was saying, "You sure can't beat the Chief now, can you?"

She wanted me to be grateful and a part of me resented that, but another part of me understood, so I said, "You sure can't. You sure can't."

I was about to say more when the door opened up and two farmers leading a bunch of kids got up in Halloween costumes came in. They all took over the place instantly, some of the kids to the johns, others sitting along the counter or at the tables.

I'd been planning on shooting the breeze with Mindy before taking off. I knew she figured me for scum, just another drifter, but it was just one of those times when I needed some conversation and I didn't much care about what or who it was with.

In lieu of talk, with her making a big fuss over all the cute little kids, I pointed to the coffeepot, and she nodded and even gave me a little smile, and then I had me some more java and another Lucky and took to staring out the front window.

Which was when I saw the little red VW bug all shiny sitting just outside, with the young blond girl—I figured her for eighteen or so—sitting there and staring inside Chet's. She seemed to be staring at me, even though I knew better. She was just as shiny as her car and there was no way she'd be looking at me.

Then she sort of grinned and took off. But her image stayed on the night air—her blondeness and her quick girl grin—long after she was gone.

I finished my coffee and Lucky and got up to go. Mindy was so busy with the kids that all I could do was kind of wave and mouth a big thank-you. She nodded back to me.

One bite of the cold night and I was right back to being me again. My heels crunched through ice as I moved down the street, hefting my backpack, heading for the highway.

I walked from one streetlight to another, and in between it was as dark as nights ever get, and for a minute or two I felt like a kid, sort of scared of how vast and black the night was. I touched the pocketknife in my jeans.

I had just reached the highway when I heard a familiar straining engine noise. I'd just come up a steep grade and the motor was laboring to climb the same grade. Tiny VW engines always make that particular sound.

She whipped across the center line and pulled in right in front of me, cutting me off.

She rolled down the window and said, rock 'n' roll blaring on the radio inside, "You look just about as lonely as I am."

"You don't look like the kind of girl who has to be lonely if she doesn't want to be." Up close she was even better-looking. The only slightly disturbing thing was that she looked familiar some-how.

"The men around here are strictly dull."

I smiled. "I guess we've all got our crosses to bear."

She said, "What's your cross?"

There was something serious in her question, and again, for a reason I couldn't explain, I felt disturbed. I shrugged and said, "I ain't got it half as bad as some people I know. It just gets a little wearying sometimes."

"You going to get in?"

"Can I ask you a dumb question?"

She laughed. "People ask me dumb questions all the time. Why should you be any different?"

"You legal?"

"Huh?"

"You legal? Age, I mean."

"You asking if I'm jailbait?"

"Yeah."

She laughed again. She had a real nice laugh even above the loudly idling engine. "Honey, you do wonders for a woman's ego. I'm twenty-four years old."

"Oh."

"So get in."

"Where we going?"

"How's my place sound?"

"Right now that sounds about as nice as any place in the world."

She lived in a trailer court out on the highway, in one of those long silver jobs that was now almost white with frost in the cold moonlight.

The last stragglers of Halloween ran up and down the dirt roads between the trailers. Hers was set off from the rest by a good city block, over by a grove of elms forming a windbreak.

I know it's not supposed to happen this way but it did. We went inside her trailer and she didn't even turn a light on. We just stood there in the moonlight coming through the window and she put her arms around me and kissed me with a mouth that was warm and tender and frantic, and it had been so long for me that I nearly went crazy.

It didn't take long before she was undoing my shirt and leading me back to the bedroom.

We were spreading out, getting ready, when I said, "You smoke
cigars?"

"You're so romantic," she said, reaching behind her with
slender graceful arms and undoing her bra.

"I mean it smells like cigars in here," I said.

"My dad's. He comes over sometimes."

"Oh."

"Why? Who'd you think they'd belong to?"

"I wasn't sure. I mean, this . . ." I paused.

"This what?"

"Well, this sort of makes me nervous."

"Why? I thought you'd be having a good time. *I* am."

"So am I. Just . . ."

"Just what?"

"Well. Why would you just sort of—"

"—pick you up?"

"Yeah. Pick me up."

"Because today my divorce from Larry is final and I need to do
something to make it real and I don't happen to want to do it with
anybody from Newkirk. If it's any of your goddamn business, I
mean."

"I didn't mean to make you mad."

"Well, you did."

"I'm sorry."

She was naked from the waist up. She sat there in the moon-
light, letting me look at her, and believe me, I did look at her.

"You don't like guys or anything, do you?"

"No. I just kind of wanted to know where you were coming
from," I said.

"Well, I guess you know now, don't you?"

"I sure do," I said. "I sure do."

The funny thing was, the first part of it was as sweet as doing it
with your girlfriend back in high school, you know, when you
really love somebody and do it as much to convey your feelings as
to get rid of your needs. Her hair there in the darkness smelled
wonderful and so did her perfume, and her flesh was soft and
beautiful and there were nooks and crannies in her body that al-
most made me cry, they were so wonderful, and we went very

slow then and her breath was pure as a baby's and her fingers on the back of my neck were gentle as any woman's had ever been, making me feel wanted and important and somebody.

And then, just as we were rolling over to the other side of the bed, she said, "Now I'm going to ask you to help me."

Something in the way she said it made me real nervous. "Help you?"

In the shadow I saw her nod.

I tried to make a joke of it. "And just what if I don't help you?"

She didn't move or speak. I saw the lift of her breasts as she sighed. "Then I'll kill you," she said. "And you'll be dead, just the way I am."

He came home, just as she said he would, ten minutes later. Now I knew who the cigar smoke belonged to.

She had the tape recorder set up for me and she had me set up in the chair next to the recorder. She also had a .38 Smith and Wesson, a policeman's gun, to put in my hand.

I sat there in the darkness listening to the gravel crunch as his heavy car pulled up to the trailer. The car door squeaked open and a big engine trembled into silence and then his shoes snapped through ice and then he put a key in the door and then he came on inside and turned on the light and then he said, "Jesus Christ! Just who the hell are you?"

He was a big guy, six-five maybe, and fleshy. His face was mottled from drinking. He smelled of cold and he smelled of booze. He wore a cheap rumpled sport jacket and cheap rumpled pants.

"I want you to sit down over there," I said.

"You a thief, or what?"

"I want you to sit down over there and tell me about the night you and your friend Frank Campion raped and killed the girl two years ago tonight, on Halloween."

"What the hell are you talking about?"

"You know what I'm talking about."

"I never raped no girl."

I pointed the gun at him. "*She* put me up to this."

"You're crazy, mister. You some kind of dope addict, or what?"

"She put me up to this. The girl you killed. Meaning, she's controlling my hand. Anytime she wants she can force me to pull this trigger."

"You really are crazy."

I shot him in the leg.

He looked totally surprised. I guess because of the way I'd been talking—crazy and all with her controlling me—he'd started to feel as if he were in control of the situation, that he might have some kind of chance of getting the gun from me.

But she was in my mind now, and she eased my finger back on the trigger.

"I want you to tell me about that night, everything you did," I said.

He was crawling backward and shouting for help. He kept looking at his leg as if he hoped it might belong to somebody else. "I didn't rape no girl," he said.

I shot him in the arm, the right arm.

This time he vomited. I'm not sure why. Maybe fear.

But it worked. He started talking.

"We was drunk, Frank and me," he said, and then he said it all and it was pretty simple, really right up to and including how they'd buried her at the bottom of a grain elevator, where nobody would ever find her.

I turned off the tape recorder and let it run back and then I tested it and his voice was good and loud and clear. She had what she wanted.

He was crying, the big guy was. He was bleeding a lot and getting weaker and crying.

He said, "I can't even shout no more. You call an ambulance, okay? Okay?"

I got up and went to the phone and picked up the receiver. I started dialing, but then she turned me around abruptly.

As I realized what was going to happen, I jerked the gun to the left so that it misfired into the wall.

She came out of the bedroom and he saw her, and he started screaming louder than anybody I'd ever heard.

She tore the gun from my hand and walked over and stood above him. She fired four straight shots into his face.

When she was finished, she threw the gun to me and I caught it from reflex.

Down her cheek ran two tears like drops of mercury.

Then she was gone, the trailer door flapping in the wind, with her disappearing over the edge of the hill along the line of moonlit horizon.

I stood staring down at the corpse on the floor, the gun grasped in my fingers, as the first neighbor peered into the cabin and said to the second neighbor, "*Look*. This man shot John!"

The Chief made sure that nobody else rode back with us to the jail.

I'd told him everything that had happened, the girl and all. I knew better than to expect he'd believe me.

The funny thing was, as he listened, his sad eyes got sadder. He said, "I figured she'd be back tonight."

"You knew about her then?"

He looked over at me. "She was my daughter. I knew those two men raped and killed her but I could never prove it and I could never find where they'd buried her. Last year she used another drifter the same way—that's why I warned you to get out of town. He killed Campion, except Campion didn't confess before he died. So I figured she'd use another drifter like you to get the second man." He sighed. "And she did."

"Where's this other drifter now?" I said.

He shook his white head. "Death row. Tried and convicted of first-degree murder."

For the first time I saw what had happened to me. What had really happened to me.

"But if you tell them the real story, they'll believe you, won't they?" I said, sounding like a little kid, all pleading and desperate.

The Chief's car shot through the chill darkness. I could still see her in bed. Feel her . . .

"Son," he said, "that's why I warned you about being a drifter in Newkirk on Halloween night."

He shook out a cigarette from his pack and offered it to me.

"Son," he said. "I like you, so I'm going to do you a favor. I'm giving you a half-hour head start before I come looking for you."

"But . . ."

He looked at me with those sad eyes and I knew then why she'd looked so familiar from the start. She'd had the same sad eyes.

"Son," he said, "they're not going to believe you any more than they believed that other drifter." He paused. "You know what it's like on death row—just waiting?"

Twenty minutes later I was on the highway headed north. Three trucks rushed by, nearly knocking me over with their speed. A couple of carloads of kids came by, too. They just saw me as somebody to have some farm-boy fun with—calling me names and flipping me the bird and challenging me to a fight.

Then they were gone and there were just the unending prairie darkness and the winter stars overhead, and the lonely crunch of my feet on the hard ground.

I kept thinking of her, of how good and loving she'd felt in my arms, even though all the time I held her she'd been . . . dead.

I don't know how long I walked or how many cars and trucks roared by. After a while I faced frontward and just started walking, forgetting all about thumbing.

Then I started thinking about my own life. The years being raised by my uncle in a one-room apartment in the city. And the wife who'd dumped me for a grinning young Marine. And the years of drifting after that . . .

I heard it from a long way off. It came up over the sound of the wild abandoned dogs roaming the night, of the distant train smashing through the darkness of the distant prairie, of the crunching sound of my feet . . .

I recognized it immediately, that sound.

A slightly laboring VW engine.

At first I was scared and started running along the shoulder of the road, my backpack slamming against my shoulders. But the faster I ran, the closer she drew . . .

When she got alongside me, I decided there was no use fighting it anymore. Chest heaving, warm now from sweat, I turned and looked at her there inside the red VW.

She leaned over and rolled down the window. "Would you like a ride?"

"Just leave me alone, all right? Just leave me alone."

"If I didn't like you, I wouldn't have come back. When we were making love, I realized how lonely you are . . . being a drifter and all, and I thought I could help you." She smiled and held her hand out to me. "I thought I could take you with me."

I didn't want to hear any more. Throwing my backpack down so I could run better, I set off, trotting back down the road, away from her as fast as I could get.

For a long time I could hear the VW sitting there, engine idling, but finally I heard her grind the gears and set off over the hill, leaving me alone.

The blackness again; the sound of my own heart racing; the texture and smell of my own sweat.

I stopped. She was gone. I no longer needed to run.

And then I saw the headlights headed toward me and heard the engine with the idle set too high, the laboring VW engine.

As I watched her come closer, an exhaustion set in. All I could think of was the time I'd had mono. For three weeks I hadn't even been able to walk down the hall to the bathroom . . .

She pulled up. This time she opened the door for me.

"I'll drive around till you get used to the idea," she said. "So you won't be so scared, I mean." Blond hair hiding part of her face, she said, very gently, "It's really what you want, you know. No more bitterness . . . no more pleading . . . no more pleading."

The door opened wider.

"We can drive these highways all night and look at how beautiful the forest is on the hills, and by then—"

"—by then I won't be scared."

"By then," she said, "you won't be scared."

"My backpack—"

She smiled again. So soft. "You don't have to worry about things like that anymore. I'm going to take you with me."

She put out her hand once more, her warm, tender hand, and I took it and let her draw me inside her car, the red VW that set off now into the unceasing black prairie night.

And it was just like she'd promised. I didn't worry about anything.

Not anything at all.

Ray Russell

REFLECTIONS

IN 1987, St. Martin's Press unleashed the funniest novel in years, *Dirty Money*. For decades Ray Russell has been one of the most original, literate, and versatile writers alive, and the fact that he is one of the nation's wittiest authors will come as no surprise to anybody who has read Russelino's "God Will Provide," "The Hell You Say" (previous clever shortshorts), or the hilariously horrific "American Gothic" in *Masques II*. (Or *M 2*, as Ray would have it.)

A key to the success this first executive editor of *Playboy* has enjoyed with very brief stories is the particularly skewed view he holds on our times—a singular eye that sizes up what's already been done with various icons of horror (or SF; or fantasy; or anything). Ray hones in on elements no one else has even noticed, including an icon as familiar as that which you'll find in his newest story . . . dead ahead. Nobody else could have written it but the author of *Sardonicus* and *Dirty Money*.

REFLECTIONS

Ray Russell

THIS TIMEWORN CITY OF OURS IS a place of many shops. I have often reflected that they are like voluptuous sirens, luring us with the enticing wares that beckon from behind the shining panes of their windows. A person could stand—as I stood last night—outside Alecu's pastry shop, and simultaneously see the mouth-watering cakes and tortes as well as one's own face, licking one's lips at that delectable display. At certain hours, when the light is right, the windows of those shops are as good as any looking glass. Frequently, with their aid, I have straightened my hat or smoothed my mustache before going on to keep a rendezvous with my beloved.

Last night, I waited for her in front of the pastry shop. It was closed—dark inside, each windowpane a perfect black mirror. I could see myself, lit by the combined rays of the street-corner lamp and the full moon: the respected physician, elegant host, pillar of society. All those qualities and attributes seemed to be reflected there. I fancied I could see them clearly.

But would I see *her?*

I feared that I would not. I feared that my most morbid suspicions would be confirmed. I shivered, and not only with the cold. Soon I would know the truth. I had set a trap for her and had asked her to meet me in front of the shop at midnight.

Somewhere, in the chill darkness, a distant bell tolled that hour, and at the same time I heard the delicate click of her approaching heels. I turned away from that sound, to face the shop window. The click of her heels drew nearer . . .

And then I saw her beautiful reflection in the glass. I was filled with a welcome warm flood of relief.

"Good evening, Ioan," she said in that sable voice.

I turned to her. "My dear . . ." I began to say, but my voice faltered.

"Is something wrong?" she asked. "You seem ill at ease."

"I am an ingrate and a fool," I replied. "I misjudged you. Can you forgive me? I actually had come to think that you were—"

"A vampire?" she said, as her lips stretched wide in a ghastly smile, revealing hideous fangs.

I recoiled, in disbelief as well as horror. "No!" I cried. "Impossible!" I gestured wildly toward the window. "Your reflection . . ."

"Ah yes," she said, admiring her lovely image in the window.

"A vampire cannot be reflected," I pointed out. "Everybody knows that."

"You are a famous scholar of the healing arts, Ioan, but I am afraid you have not studied the lore of my kind closely enough."

"I have," I insisted.

"If indeed you had," she replied in a mocking tone, "you would have known that our forms, even as yours, can be reflected in many things—in water, in windows, in gleaming china . . ." She began to move closer to me. "But not in silver, or in mirrors backed by a coating of it."

"The killing power of silver bullets is known to me," I murmured, "but . . ."

"Silver," she crooned, slowly moving ever closer, "was the coinage paid to Judas for the betrayal of your Lord. And the old legend has it that, to compensate the spirit of that metal for the base use to which it had been put, it was forever granted the power to repel evil. Hence, when a creature of my sort stands before a silvered mirror, the glass refuses the reflection. But a shop window, with no silver behind it . . ."

"I understand," I said.

"You understand too late, my poor Ioan."

Baring her fangs again, she moved quickly toward me. From under my cloak I drew the syringe. It was filled with glittering fluid.

She laughed. "Poison? That will avail you nothing."

"Not poison," I said sadly. "Medicine. We prescribe it in cases of epilepsy."

"I do not suffer from that complaint," she said, and laughed again.

"No, my dear. Your affliction is far more terrible. And this will cure you."

She lunged at me like a panther. I sank the needle deep into her smooth white throat and pressed down the plunger. *"Argenti oxidum,"* I whispered, as she fell dead at my feet. "Oxide of silver. Farewell, my love. And may you rest in peace at last."

The shop window reflected my anguished face and my tears.

Melissa Mia Hall and
Douglas E. Winter

THE HAPPY FAMILY

MELISSA Mia Hall's fiction, she writes, "has appeared in a variety of anthologies"—edited by Charles Grant and Jane Yolen, by Kathryn Ptacek, Marty Greenberg, and Joe Lansdale. A book critic and photographer too, Hall created, produced, and directed "a short film entitled *Manikin*" rising from a "certain fascination" she has with mannequins. "Especially," she adds, "the human variety."

Doug Winter, saying he can "count at least one mannequin among my personal friends," was editor of the prestigious *Prime Evil;* before that, he was a chronicler of horror fiction in general, S. King in particular. His story "Splatter," from *Masques II,* was nominated for a World Fantasy Award. He's also the collaborator—with Grant—on a novel, the lawyer's first, titled *From Parts Unknown.* "The Happy Family" is the second part of a proposed tetralogy of stories by Hall and Winter. It *is* a story for all seasons, but might just as easily have slipped into any of the other categories of this anthology.

THE HAPPY FAMILY

Melissa Mia Hall and
Douglas E. Winter

SKIN SO PALE AND BODY pencil-thin. Hard. Cool to the touch. Put your head against that unmoving breast and hold tight; everything's going to be all right.

She stares blindly at the track lighting of the department store. Her arms are crossed protectively in front of her, as if she's embarrassed by something he said. There's a slight arch to her back, and she's too tall, her legs long and bare. She is modeling lingerie, or a swimsuit that could pass for lingerie. A bicycle leans against the Plasticine rock behind her. Two steps to her left, another mannequin, not as fetching or desirable, scans the distant menswear section, as if she's lost a boyfriend to the racks of disconsolate ties.

Walter stares at her and thinks about the movie where a mannequin turns into a girl. A real-live girl.

That is not what he wants. He just wants her.

There is something special, something right, about this mannequin. She is so much like the others, the ones he has collected. They wait for him at home, perfectly coiffed, perfectly clothed, perfectly arranged down in the den.

Rachel doesn't particularly like them. Neither do Laurie or Rob, his children. Laurie seems afraid of them. He can never understand why. She always liked playing with her Barbies.

Walter pats his pocket to make sure that he brought his checkbook. He'll have her. Somehow he will have her. All you have to do is name the right price to the right person.

But there's no rush. She's not going anywhere.

He smiles crookedly, amused with himself. No one at work thinks he has a sense of humor. His secretary walks on eggshells around him. She's afraid of him. But the name partners of most blue-chip Dallas law firms tend to be frightening, don't they?

There aren't many shoppers this early on a Saturday. Give it an hour and that'll change. He savors the silence, marred only by the throb of rock videos warming up in the junior department. At least that's what they used to call it. Now it's something like "Connections" or "Upbeat." Laurie once liked to hang out in those places, but now she seems to prefer the same expensive boutiques as her mother.

Walter has always loved department stores. He liked them when he was a kid and Sears was top of the line and Penney's just for window-shopping. He never thought he'd marry a woman who would consider Saks Fifth Avenue slumming.

Her arms are crossed so tightly.

Walter turns to watch a grim-faced clerk march past, his arms filled with pantsuits. Then he looks back toward her.

Her wig is styled in a short, punkish bob, laced with spiky curls that dance on her forehead with comic intensity. He'll take the wig off. Let her go bald.

Her eyes are blue. A beautiful blue, wide and watery bright. Her nose slices the air. Imperial. Her cheeks are hollowed as if she were sucking air, preparing to say how lost she is, how defenseless. Her skimpy pink underwear would make anyone feel defenseless. Who could ride a bicycle like that? She's not even wearing decent shoes, just flimsy white sandals, half-on, half-off.

She's so scared.

He'll buy her. He has to save her.

He wonders what to name her. Amy? Leigh? She doesn't have a name. She doesn't have anything, really. She is penniless. Her friend, over there by the bicycle, could care less. She's alone—

except for me, he thinks with a curious satisfaction. And she's not going anywhere unless I take her with me. And I will. I will buy her; but not now. Later.

She's not going anywhere.

He walks away from her and wanders over to the menswear department, with its shirts and slacks and jackets, wallets and belts and ties. He never buys ties. His secretary buys ties. The receptionist buys ties and the receptionist's secretary buys ties and the secretary's receptionist buys ties. Even his wife buys ties. But he does not. His partners—and even, on occasion, his associates—say that he fancies himself as the Don Johnson of north Dallas. It's true that, in the summertime, he does not wear socks at home or on the golf course. Or on the *Fairweather*, his boat—or, as Rachel calls it, his yacht. But he doesn't look like Don Johnson. He shaves everyday. And he doesn't feel like Don Johnson. Women don't hang on his every word and he's never been in *People* and he's never been on TV (well, maybe once), and he's never cut a record. Not a record record, but he has cut some record-making deals.

He looks in a mirror, holding a red necktie against his chest. It's silky and shiny and absolutely uncouth. He tells the bored clerk he'll take it and tucks the package under his arm. The paper crackles reassuringly. He doesn't like the plastic bags that most stores are giving out these days. Nonrecyclable. He thinks of all that plastic still lying around, long after he's dead and gone. It bothers him.

He gazes into the distance and sees the two mannequins in their "Sportif" ensembles. The bicycle gleams. She could ride away in a minute, if she wanted. If she could. But it wouldn't be long before they were together again.

These things are inevitable.

He suddenly wants to walk away. Especially from her. She's so vulnerable, so needy. Rachel was like that once. He'd believed her. It was only later that he discovered it had all been an act; but by then he had also discovered that it didn't matter. Or he chose to believe that it didn't matter. He's still uncertain; perhaps she simply changed. But Rachel is a good woman. Patient. Understanding. Demure.

He does like Florida. On occasion. The right occasion.

And he likes the song that Don Johnson sings. He has heard it on the radio, on MTV. Something about a heartbeat. Looking for a heartbeat.

The multilevel mall opens before him, vast, impersonal, glittering, and real. So real. Rob's favorite word is "real." Everything's "real"—like real radical, real stuff, real right, you know? *Real.*

Walter's hair is going silver at the temples. Terry Bragg accused him of coloring his hair, because it was just too distinguished-looking to be real. Really real. He charges down the mall, taking huge strides, burning calories, being aerobic, healthy, stirring the blood.

People are pouring into the mall now. It's like an awakening beehive. They all look so wonderful. The men purposeful and fatherly. The women smelling of perfume and money. The children circling and laughing, circling and laughing. He finds himself smiling again.

He pictures Rachel and Laurie somewhere in the crowd. They're pretty, Rachel and Laurie: Rachel's fair hair with its faint reddish streaks, Laurie's redder hair catching and holding sunlight until her head looks as if it were on fire. They both have green eyes and a dusting of freckles across their perfectly matched noses. Both are petite and slender, their breasts like half-opened buds. Short and flashing-quick on their feet, their hands sporting the fingernail polish of the week, Laurie's showing signs of teeth marks.

He stops in a bookstore and heads for the magazine section. Tchaikovsky is playing over the sound system. This bookstore sells music, videos, calendars, postcards. He glances through the array of foreign publications that marks the stand as an upscale, trendy sort of place. A lovely girl holds a *Madame Figaro* closer to her face. She's obviously pretending to read it. She squints at the French and then notices that he's watching her. She blushes and puts the magazine back.

"Hello," Walter says. He has no intention of carrying this further, but she looks so innocent and sweet. Like the mannequin.

"Hi," she says and blushes again. She's about average height, with brown hair and hazel eyes—or are they brown, too? Her clothes look old but clean. Her sandals are worn. She's not as young as he thought at first. There's gray in her hair. Maybe she's over thirty.

"Ever been there?" he blurts out, gesturing toward the magazine.

She glances at him, uncertain. "To Madame Figaro's?"

"No. To France."

She tugs at her shoulder bag. One of the straps is splitting. She shrugs.

He has lost count of how many times he has been there. To France. But never to Madame Figaro's. He visualizes a comfortably fat woman wearing a lace shawl and holding a wooden spoon, red with tomato sauce, in her hand. A good name for a restaurant or a fortune-teller. But for a fashion magazine?

"I've been to France lots of times."

"Great," she says coolly, as if she were unimpressed; but her eyes seem wider. Perhaps she is envious. Perhaps not.

"You read French?" he asks her as she picks up the *Madame Figaro* again and heads for the cashier. She glances over her shoulder at him and says, "A little," and then pays for the magazine. She's ignoring him. She doesn't want to talk to him. It makes him angry. She's a nothing. She's just a woman he doesn't know. It doesn't matter.

Why would a woman who doesn't read French buy a French magazine? But she said she could read it. A little. She was probably lying. Probably she has fifty dollars in her checking account, if she has one at all. Maybe she doesn't even have a car. Maybe she rides the bus. Is there a bus stop near here? He thinks of the mammoth parking garage and of all the cars on the expressway girdling the mall.

He finds himself following her. She looks so old-fashioned, wearing her faded black pants and her faded black shirt. The amber necklace was probably plastic. Or was it carnelian? She couldn't afford carnelian. Glass?

She's almost five stores ahead, but she's walking slowly. He catches up to her in no time. She turns and enters a chocolate shop. There are small tables and chairs out front, so that patrons may watch passersby as they eat. She comes out and sits down, clutching a small bag of truffles. A plastic bag. She eats a truffle and, when the waitress arrives, orders a cappuccino. She glances up and sees him. She looks trapped. Captured. He sits down across from her.

"Do you mind?"

"I guess not," she says, but he can see that she's scared. He finds this oddly thrilling. The waitress comes back and hands him a menu. He orders chocolate ice cream with almonds.

"My name is Walter."

He waits for her to tell him her name. She just stares at him.

"So?"

He wishes that he could think of something witty to say. He feels very young and very foolish. He hasn't felt this way in years.

"So. I'm a lawyer."

"Okay."

"What do you do?"

"Whatever I have to do to get by," she says. The waitress brings their orders. She stirs and sips her cappuccino without looking up.

"I find you fascinating," he says.

She says nothing. She won't look at him. Her body, he realizes, is like white enamel. Porcelain. The only place with color is her cheeks. They bloom like pink roses.

"You don't get out in the sun much, do you?" he says.

"I burn easily," she whispers.

"What's your name?"

"Look, pal, I really don't know you and I don't think—"

"I don't mean any harm. I'm not a mad rapist or anything."

Now she almost gulps her cappuccino.

"I just want to know you."

Is this love at first sight? Her hands come to rest on the sack with the French magazine. Her hands are beautiful. She doesn't wear any rings at all. Rachel wears a ring on almost every finger. She especially likes diamonds. This girl has probably never owned a diamond. He wants to give her diamonds, rubies, emeralds. But she probably wouldn't wear them. He sighs.

"I think I'd better leave," she says, half-rising. He stops her with an over-eager hand. She freezes; the fear turns into shock.

"Don't go."

She sits back down. Their eyes lock. She's not afraid at all. Walter glances around, checking reality. The sun slides through the glass ceiling. Shoppers whip past, and the plants seem to rustle in their clay pots. The noise escalates. A child screams and laughs with another child. A mother tells them to stop running. He glances back at the young-old woman and she's not there. The sack with the magazine is still on the table. She forgot it like she forgot him. He leaves the waitress an overlarge tip and takes the magazine.

His enthusiasm for his Saturday at the mall has waned. He heads for the exit closest to the parking garage where his Mercedes is parked. He does not even have the heart to go bargain for his mannequin, with her crossed arms and big blue eyes. The girl from the bookstore had big eyes, too; lost eyes. Now he feels lost. He knows he's being childish. Rachel will get a good laugh out of this.

For all her faults, Rachel usually understands. It all comes from being thirty-nine. He's going to turn forty next year. It's only natural to have days like this. But he has so much to live for. He's done so well. His father's proud of him. He's proud of himself. He has a good life, a happy family.

And that mannequin's not going anywhere.

He finds the exit. In a minute, he stands in the parking garage, looking for his car. He does this a lot. He's always forgetting where he parked his car. One time, he spent two hours searching for his car at the Beverly Center in Los Angeles. To this day, it has made flying to the West Coast a pain in the ass. He's always afraid it will happen again. Consequently, he never goes to shopping malls in California anymore. It's a matter of principle.

He is sweating profusely. Rob loves to say that, too: "sweating profusely." His face cracks into another lopsided smile. He walks past a Porsche, and sees her staring at him. The girl from the bookstore. It's her Porsche. He can't speak. She stares at him, crosses her arms defensively. As if he's going to attack her. As if he's going to grab her and hold her against his chest. Though he does want to do that. But she's gone and slammed the door of her Porsche and it's squealing past him. He catches one last glimpse of her startled face, her mouth open, a crack of red in her porcelain skin. He breathes in the exhaust and coughs. His Mercedes is right there, right next to the space where her car was parked.

Poor little rich girl.

He feels worse than cheated. He feels dumb.

Sighing, he sinks into his car and leaves.

*   *   *

Walter likes driving. He's got a sports car in the shop. A black Ferrari. He drives and drives and drives. He drives fast. See Walter go. See Walter go fast. See Walter get a ticket for speeding. It's no big deal.

Late afternoon in Dallas. It's been a hot summer. It's cooler right now, but not by much. He cranks up the air conditioner. He feels hungry—the ice cream went untouched—but he doesn't want to head for home. Not yet. His family is probably not there anyway. He can't remember, but he thinks they're gone. Somewhere.

Saturdays are always busy. Laurie had a dentist's appointment. A dance lesson. A friend's birthday party. Rob had a baseball game. A Scout meeting. A sleepover. Rachel had a date with the girls—or maybe, with the boys. He thinks she has lots of affairs of the heart.

That's what she calls them: "Affairs of the heart."

Has Walter had affairs? He doesn't think so. He has held a mannequin in his arms, but he's never screwed one. He wouldn't do that. That would be perverse.

Walter may be many things, but he's not perverse.

Not really.

It's almost twilight. The sun is watered down and mellow. Mellow-yellow, orange and red. He clicks a cassette into the tape player. The Moody Blues sing of nights in white satin. He's dated and old. Never reaching an end. Floundering.

The expressway is almost empty. Soon it will be overcome with exhaust and taillights. He's driving home the way he's always driven home from the Galleria. The light shines in his eyes. He might have a wreck. Just in time, the sun winks and is gone.

He's approaching an overpass. His favorite overpass, a sleek angle of white concrete and sunbaked steel. He sees something dangling in the shadows overhead. It looks like a body, hanging at the end of a rope. But it can't be a body. He puts on the brakes, and the Mercedes slides. He brings the car to a stop on the shoulder and gets out, gaping back at the body, twisting and turning above the highway. An eighteen-wheeler wheezes by. It doesn't stop. Another car passes. Doesn't anyone care? He's got to save that poor girl. But he knows that it's probably too late.

Why do people kill themselves? *Selves.* He sees a multiple image of himself trying on a suit. Did she plan this, or was it spontaneous? Panting and sweating—sweating profusely—Walter manages to scale the earthen bank. He boosts himself onto the pavement of the overpass. It would have been easier to move the car, but maybe she's still breathing. Maybe she's alive.

He carries a pocketknife in his jacket. His father always told him to be prepared. But he can't haul her up by the rope; he's not that strong. And if he cuts the rope, she may die from the fall. He pulls tentatively on the rope and discovers that she is not very heavy. She is not very heavy at all. He pulls the rope, hand over hand, and soon holds her in his arms. She does not breathe. Her heart is silent. He cradles her against his chest, uncertain whether to laugh or cry.

It is a joke of some sort, isn't it?

He hears a siren, and from the corner of his eye, he sees a police car's knowing lights. They're coming to get him.

He looks at her again and still can't believe what he sees. He knows this lady. But she's so far from home. It's Christine. The shaggy blond wig he had glued on her himself; he had glued it well. And dressed her in the silk Kamali blouse and sleek faded jeans. One of her spike heels is missing. He kisses her cheek and the policemen approach him carefully. There's a crowd gathering. The policemen may arrest him. They must not do that.

He is a lawyer. He can talk himself out of anything. He starts talking. The policemen listen. They listen as they finger the long rope, the thick noose. They listen as they go down to the patrol car. They listen as they escort him to the Mercedes. They marvel at the nut case—or perhaps it was a high school prankster—who planted the mannequin at an unusually busy section of the Interstate.

The policemen shake his hand. Walter says good-bye. He watches as they carry Christine to the patrol car. He checks an impulse to wave. He'll miss her. Did he do this? Did he hang Christine from the overpass? When could he have done that?

It is almost night. The cars zip by, one after another. Their headlights are bright, probing, like flashbulbs. If he didn't hang her, perhaps Rachel did. But how would Rachel know when he would pass? How did she know that he would be the one to stop? And why didn't anyone else stop to see if it was a real body? Real body. Real. His brain feels fuzzy.

Doesn't anyone care?

Rachel would not have done this to him. He's a good husband. A good father.

A Porsche drives past. The girl from the bookstore. He starts to follow her, but the car is white, and he knows that her car wasn't white. But it wasn't black. He thinks it was silver. Gray. He's not sure. Two Porsches in one day.

He sits behind the wheel of the Mercedes and cries. No one understands. No one cares. No one but Rachel.

Ahead, the highway curls into darkness. In the rearview mirror, he watches the shadows lengthen. And sees someone hanging from the overpass, twisting at the end of a rope. A trick of the fading light. He turns the ignition key, tries a new tape in the cassette player. But he doesn't listen.

He has decided to drive straight home. He follows the highway to the third exit. Turns right at the end of the ramp. Passes two traffic lights, then takes a left, another left, a right, another left. He's there.

All the lights are on. The station wagon, a Volvo, sits in the driveway. Maybe everyone's home. Maybe dinner is ready. Maybe a chilled Martini is waiting on the table. Maybe they'll play gin rummy.

Walter trembles as he slides the key in and out of the lock and walks into the living room. He clutches the sacks with the magazine and the red tie. Rachel prefers Italian fashion magazines, but she'll be glad he thought of her. They'll laugh about the tie. It's a joke, he'll explain. They'll laugh. He should have bought something for the kids. Of course, Laurie's not a kid anymore. She has a boyfriend named Chad.

They're not in the living room. He tries the kitchen, the dining room. He can't find them. The bedrooms. They're not there. He hears music coming from the den. With enormous relief, he heads in that direction. Down the stairs. They're safe. They've been waiting for him. All the lights are on. They're sitting on the couch, staring at the TV.

"Welcome home, Daddy," he says for them. He kisses Laurie on the cheek, scuffs Rob at the back of the neck. Then he sits next to Rachel, touches her beautiful hair, her eyes, her lips.

He loves her.

"We love you."

He pulls her to his chest. Her breasts are cool and hard. He listens between them for the sound of a trapped heart.

Maybe, someday and always.

He listens.

D. W. Taylor

DEW DROP INN

TOO often, teachers get a bum rap. Like second looies and mothers-in-law, only the shrill or grumpy are usually recalled. Yet if you like this anthology, you might pause to pay mental homage to ol' Ms. or Mr. So-and-So who made your joy possible. Other writer-teachers present here include Castle, Ramsland, Anderson, Kisner, and me, but the best "teach" I've seen, since Miss Jean Grubb personally taught me about deadline diligence and integrity, wrote the following story.

I had the chance to watch David Taylor and his Moravian College (Pennsylvania) students at work and formed an ameliorating impression that America's future is in good hands after all. Kids still read, write, have sunny smiles and manners—once they've listened to this passionate, patient, thought-provoking prof who really *sells* his love of good fiction and good kids. The husband of Diane Taylor, who also debuts herein, David is just short of forty summers and has written a first novel that achieves the impact of most horror writers' fifth novels.

You may recall Taylor's horror studies in *Horrorstruck*. If you've read his tales in Masterton's *Scare Care* or *Gorezone*, you *will* remember him. Such a fine, compelling story is "Dew Drop Inn."

DEW DROP INN

D. W. Taylor

TEN HOURS ON THE ROAD AND Rick couldn't remember it ever being day, the night thickening around the highway like grave dust and all he could think was move, move, move, eating up the road with speed. Jonesboro 46, take it; 35 more to Johnson City, maintain the strain. Yeah, this was how the truckers did it—lost in the rhythm of the road, on the move and in the groove. Sixty-five mph, seventy; the BMW was a silver bullet. Didn't matter. The cops were good ol' boys too. Besides, everyone was in a hurry. It was Christmas.

"I wanna hear Madonna. See if you can find Madonna." The irritation went through Rick like a jolt of current, settling right in the amalgams of his teeth. Chrissy had developed one hell of a whine this year. She and her little buddies in the second grade must practice it at recess, trying out different versions at home and comparing notes the next day—honing their art until they had developed the perfect whine, guaranteed to rattle fillings. Make a man do anything. He had seen the little devils giggling together triumphant, out on the Academy's playground. The *expensive* Academy's playground. And this was what he got for his money?

"Jesus, honey, do something to shut her up, will ya?" Rick glanced over at his wife. Mary Beth was just sitting there sliding the needle across the radio's dial, slowly, expectantly, deliberately, with all the patience of a goddamn saint.

"You always get to listen to what you want to. I *never* do." Absolutely perfect. Her child's vowels drawn out just so and blended with a touch of the nasal. A pitiful little singsong on the edge of tears.

"Mother of God, hurry up. She's driving me crazy." Still nothing but crackle and arruphs from the radio; voices from outer space. They were somewhere in the tip of Tennessee, that sawblade state on the road atlas with a blue stripe called Interstate 40 wriggling like a vein across its middle. Nowhere, man. In between Bristol and Knoxville it was just you and the hayseeds and the stars, good buddy.

All Mary Beth could get was some soul station with Ray Charles singing Christmas carols: "Shepherds quake—Oh, *say* now, can't you hear them quakin'—at the sight."

Rick knew it was coming.

"That's not Ma-don-na."

"Mary Beth, do something with your child. *Now.*"

She bent over into the backseat, her rear end kissing the windshield, and began talking in her Mommy Voice to the pouting face with its little conceited mouth all screwed up. "Daddy's trying to drive, honey, so we . . ."

God, whatever happened to the good old days? Just the two of them cruising down south to visit Mary Beth's parents for Christmas. Then maybe to Florida for a few days. They used to go anywhere they wanted, buy anything, anytime. Then the nightly DoveBars got traded in for an Aprica stroller. And ever since *it* was born, all Rick could remember was dirty diapers, sleepless nights, its constant presence, feeling manacled to it—*its* slave at home, at the law office earning money for *it*, watching Mary Beth do everything for *it*.

He even knew the precise instant everything changed: Mary Beth up on the delivery-room slab, legs in those stirrups, gown

pushed up to her waist. She was grabbing at his arm, her face
washed in sweat, eyes pleading. Then her mouth made that ugly,
grotesque oval of pain while everybody stared between her legs as
the plastic-gloved hand reached into her.

Something clicked, snapped, broke; whatever. But his Mary
Beth, the slim, sexy, long-blond-hair-on-her-shoulders Mary Beth,
the girl he used to wait for at the college dorm while she floated
down the stairs like an angel, the girl who took his breath away
when she walked into class that day—she was gone. Just like that.
She wasn't his anymore. The *it* took her away, destroyed her. And
now sometimes, only *sometimes*, mind you, he wished they would
both just go away. Just leave him alone. Silently, carelessly, at the
low brilliant stars littering the sky with promises, he intoned: "Star
light, star bright . . . I wish I may, I wish I might . . ."

"She can't help it, Rick. Ten hours. Why don't we stop for din-
ner? It's almost six."

"Terrific. Why didn't you say something before we got past Bris-
tol? We're in the middle of nowhere out here."

In the backseat Chrissy was singing to herself: "Like a vir-gin."
What did an eight-year-old know about virgins? He hadn't even
noticed that Annette Funicello had breasts under that Mickey
Mouse emblem until he was ten, much less speculated on her sex-
ual status vis-à-vis Frankie Avalon. What was the hold this
"Madonna" had on kids? His daughter looked like a miniature
bag lady with those droopy socks and fingerless gloves.

"Must have been subconscious," Mary Beth said. "I'll die if I
have to eat at another Pizza Hut."

"What's wrong with franchises? At least you always know what
you're getting." Rick realized his mistake too late.

"It's not the food, it's the people." Mary Beth launched into her
"They're-so-gross" speech—one of her specialties—describing
how the fat women lined up, haunch to haunch, at the all-you-
can-eat bar. How the men piled their plates like pharaohs building
pyramids, one of every topping, stuffing it all into their faces as if
they were scared of ever being hungry again. She added a seasonal
twist: "They make me *sick*, especially at Christmas."

He had her this time. "Okay, then, at what *new* place would you
like to watch the local yokels stuff their faces?"

But she had learned to ignore loaded questions during the cross-exam. "Look, we *have* to stop someplace. You promised to call your mom before they shut off the switchboard at seven. You know how she worries."

Obvious but effective. Rick imagined his mother in her room at the Bronxville nursing home, sitting hunched over in the wheelchair, staring at the phone, arthritic hands curled in her lap like twisted roots. A shy stab of guilt made all the lies troop forward on cue, defenders of the conscience: It was the right place for her. My God, the woman had rheumatoid arthritis so bad she could barely get in and out of the wheelchair or feed herself! And with him and Mary Beth both at the office all day, they'd just have to hire someone anyway. She was better off there with others like her.

Then he remembered the conversation by the Christmas tree the year before, his mother gripping his arm with her cold, gnarled hand, the same way Mary Beth had in the delivery room, making him look at her, making him promise never to put her in one of those homes. "Son, I'd go crazy. Son, *please* . . ."

"Rick, look. The Dew Drop Inn. What do you think?" Mary Beth moved to the edge of her seat. Chrissy popped up out of the back, instantaneously. "I wanna stop. Can we stop? *Ple-ease?*" Right in his ear. There went the amalgams again.

They had driven this route at least five or six times and he couldn't remember ever seeing a "Dew Drop Inn." But there it was, halfway up a dark hillside, red neon "Dew" and "Drop" and "Inn" flashing in tedious sequence. Obviously, Tennessee's terminal case of corniness had struck again. "Only because my ass is pleading its case for mercy," Rick said. "But don't blame me if the real name of this place turns out to be the 'Do Drop Dead' after we eat." Chrissy cheered when he took the exit.

No cars in the gravel parking lot, yet lights were on inside. Strange; usually every pit stop along I-40 was doing good business this time of year, jammed by station wagons with presents stuffed in the back, presents flowing out the windows and up onto the roof—the bounty of America runnething over.

"We must've missed the ptomaine warning on the radio. Everyone's left already." Rick was really getting into this. "Oh, look, it's built of logs, just like in the old days. Isn't that clever? Chrissy, I think this could be a valuable educational experience for you."

"Park it, Dad." The brat. He'd pay her back later. She was all business now, getting her bag-girl costume ready to impress any potential rival second graders. It would be so easy to show up these hick kids. They probably thought Madonna had something to do with Christmas.

Interior decor was definitely "Early Davy Crockett": oak barrels and fake log counters. There were racks of toy outhouses for sale with tiny doors that opened onto the best in scatological humor; shell ashtrays with a map of Tennessee painted in the middle; a bounty of corncob pipes and Rebel T-shirts. Expensive, classy stuff that you just could not *get* at Neiman Marcus anymore.

But Rick couldn't understand how, with no cars out front, there could be people dotting nearly every booth and table in the restaurant section. And they all looked like travelers, too—definitely not local yokels. There was a skinny brunette in one of those trim business suits that made any woman look like a schoolmarm, a salesman type in polyester, a dapper gray-haired gentleman, even a trucker leaning on meaty forearms over his coffee. No kids. Sorry, Chrissy. Just adults sitting quietly alone, one to a table, staring into space, speaking to no one. Not even to the dwarf waitress who waddled from table to table.

Rick smiled privately. The waitress looked just like Mother Teresa—an ancient angular face with great folds of skin, a wide trunk that seemed to stretch almost to the floor, definitely to her kneecaps. Her shoulders swayed up and down with each step. One stumpy leg was shorter than the other—Rick had it figured out by the time she did her little duck walk over to their booth.

"Evening, folks. What y'all gonna have tonight?" Her voice was low and full of gravel, making you want to clear your own throat. All three stared down at her, mesmerized. Her chin was exactly level with the table, which hid the rest of her, leaving just a decapitated head talking on top of the table. John the Baptist come back to life to scold Salome. Silence as she handed out the menus, her little hands brown and fragile as dead leaves.

"I'll be right back. Y'all take your time now and don't be in no hurry." She was saying the usual corny things, but the edge to her dry country-biscuit voice was somehow condescending—maybe even menacing. "That's a real cute outfit, honey," the turning talking head said to Chrissy, who started to smile but caught the dwarf's small sneer and stared quickly down at her children's menu.

All right! Rick thought appreciatively. Took the starch right out of those mesh stockings! He was beginning to take a shine, as they say, to this little table-waiting curmudgeon. Maybe he could learn a few things. One part churlishness and two parts sarcasm; he'd have to try her recipe.

"I hate her, she's ugly!" Chrissy blurted out after the dwarf had gone. She was almost beside herself, hurt and angry, the pout threatening to mutate any second into a full-fledged, scrunchy-faced bawl.

"Now, Chrissy, sometimes people don't mean . . ." Mary Beth went into her mother act about understanding others, how *some* people just *look* different, the need for tolerance, and blah blah. Did she really think it would do this kid any good?

Time for the payback. "Here's a quarter, honey," Rick said. "See if you can find any good songs on the jukebox." That should take her at least ten minutes of searching in vain for the one name he knew would definitely not, in this hick joint, be found alphabetically between *L*oretta Lynn and *M*el Tillis. Rick watched her wriggle her little butt across the floor. Too bad, Chrissy. No one else even looked up. They just stared at their plates or at the darkness pressed like a hand against the windows, their faces expressionless, as if in a trance, mouths chewing slowly.

"Can you believe that damn little witch? Saying something like that to a child?" A curse word! Saint Mary Beth must really be hot. "What was on her name tag—'Ida'? I'd a-like to trip her next time she goes by!" Not bad, not bad.

"What's really weird is the customers," Rick said. "Look around. Everyone's alone, no one's talking, no one's even leaving. And where are their cars? The lot was empty when we drove up." He leaned forward for emphasis. "This is *definitely not* the Pizza Hut."

Ida appeared suddenly at the corner of the table. These damn little midgets could really sneak up on you! The look on her face made Rick feel like a prisoner plotting an escape or something. Maybe she had heard Mary Beth. She looked directly at Rick, though, as if he were the only one at the table, and rasped, "Y'all know what you want yet?" Ah, that southern charm had returned.

Mary Beth said sharply, "Yes, we're having coffee—*to go*. Chocolate milk for my daughter. And please hurry." She slapped her menu down on the table as if she were playing a trump card and stared out the window. That was telling her!

"Uh . . . one more thing, if you don't mind." Rick just had to know. "Did I park in the right place? I mean, there are all these people in here but no cars out there. For future reference, you understand." He smiled. Funny how quickly you adapted. It seemed normal talking to a decapitated head with its chin on the table.

"Overnighters. Cars in the permanent lot. Cain't be too careful, 'specially at Christmas." She started to waddle off, her broad ugly shoulders dipping up and down, tilted slightly to starboard. Then she turned. "You folks welcome to stay, if you've a mind to."

"Gosh, right kindly of you," Rick said, hoping he wasn't being too obvious; but this one was for Chrissy and Mary Beth. "But we'd better be moseyin' on down the road a spell." The dwarf's old face lit up in a repulsive grin. She loved it! This was the kind of thing she fed on. You could never get to a person like that. The more you gave, the more they wanted.

Chrissy waited until Ida had disappeared before slinking back into the booth. Now she was really depressed. No Madonna in this place, only midget witches. While Mary Beth and Chrissy went to the rest room, Rick slipped a tip under his coffee saucer before leaving. Mary Beth would have said the second curse word of her life if she had found out—but, he told himself, you had to maintain your class around hicks. Besides, the old crone was a bit scary.

It was a relief to be back inside the BMW, the silver bullet of I-40, strapped in and ready for ignition.

Nothing.

He tried again. Still only that helpless sinking feeling in the pit of his stomach and a voice at the back of his head saying, "No, no, no!" as the engine growled over and over, lifeless, recalcitrant, inexplicable.

"Goddamn *son* of a *bitch*." Rick slapped his palm against the leather-covered steering wheel, took a deep breath, and tried again, telling himself this wasn't happening even while the engine kept grinding. "Come on, come on, come *on.*" Mary Beth and Chrissy, perfectly still—watching, listening, depending.

The grinding slowed as the battery weakened. And Rick finally gave in, slamming his fist against the padded dashboard above the digital AM/FM stereo cassette combination, throwing himself back into the anatomically contoured bucket seat and announcing to the dead cold silent night all around them, "This lousy piece of *shit!*"

Mary Beth waited until it was safe. "Rick," she said softly, ever so cautiously, "I think we might be out of gas. Look at the gauge." It couldn't be. He always filled up when it got just below half-tank. They'd had plenty of gas, pulling in here; he'd checked. But the little red stick was lying flat on its back under the big "E," asleep or dead. Same thing. He flipped the ignition switch off, and back on. Still no sign of life.

Dew Drop Inn. And they sure as hell had.

Rick shifted restlessly in one of the rickety beds; Mary Beth and Chrissy were curled up together in the other. He had been sleeping alone since *it* was born, but tonight, sleep wouldn't come because those damn faces were there, racing back and forth in front of his eyes like a film in continuous forward and reverse. When he'd walked back in—defeated know-it-all city slicker—every blank face from every table and booth had turned toward the door, given a collective suck of air, and stared in wide-eyed greater knowing, straight at Rick. Then there was the little hag's face from behind the register where she perched on her stool, her mouth twisted into the same wicked grin as before, victorious, eager for its pleasure.

Nope, fillin' stations done closed around here. Yup, might as well stay here till the mornin' and things open up. We'll take care of ya then.

God, what did these people have against vowels and inflectional endings anyhow? Like a mouthful of marbles! Why did everyone stare . . . Damn zombies . . . Ugly bitch . . . Early start . . . Tomorrow . . .

Blades of light from the closed venetian blind fell like prison bars across the room, casting a faint gray light against the walls, along the hardwood floor, and beneath the furniture where it was trapped in the tiny ghost balls of dust and hair that hid there, glowing dimly.

Rick pressed his fingers hard into his eyes and released, blinking as the bare room took shape around him—tan dresser and night-stand, wrought-iron beds, an old chifforobe that towered beside him like a guard. No ashtrays, no phone. Not even a Gideon's Bible in this hellhole.

And no Chrissy or Mary Beth.

Damn, it must be late! But they knew better than to awaken him. They were probably eating breakfast. Now he'd have to hurry around like a . . . what did Beth's mother always say, a chicken with its head cut off? How *utterly* charming. No, that was a cow. He absolutely had to get this farm talk straight.

Rick lifted one of the slats on the blind but caught only a glimpse of orange and white below before having to shut his eyes and turn quickly from the bright sun. Squinting, he edged the slat up and saw an ambulance backed up to the entrance, its rear doors flung open like two welcoming hands and the attendants lifting a stretcher into the back. The familiar, predictable lumps of a body pressed up against the heavy sheet that lay over it, head to toe. *Jesus, must be dead,* Rick thought.

Then he saw them next to the BMW: Mary Beth and Chrissy, shepherded by some tall, thin guy in coat and tie. He was carrying the goddamn suitcases. He said something to Mary Beth. She shook her head and stared at the ground. Chrissy looked up, to-ward the window.

Rick jerked down on the cord, sending the blind flying up, flooding the room with light. He grabbed both handles of the win-dow and pulled up. Stuck, of course. Again—this time with every-thing he had. *Damn* motel windows. By now the thin man was loading the *suitcases* into the trunk while Mary Beth and Chrissy stood by the car. What the hell were they *doing*?

Rick cupped his fingers and rapped his wedding ring against the glass as hard as he dared. But they just stood there, oblivious, casually glancing up at his face in the window, then down again. He shouted, "Mary Beth! Chrissy!" Nothing. They were watching the ambulance, waiting for something.

"They can't hear you, Ricky." The gravelly voice was a low,

patient growl rubbing against his back. He knew what he was going to see even before he spun around—the stump of a body covered in the white gown of Mother Teresa, twisted shoulders that loathed pity. "They can't hear you. Can't see you either." Ida's mouth curled into a vile sneer, not for Chrissy this time, all for him now.

"What the hell. . . ?"

"You know what they say, Ricky: 'Careful what you wish for— you might just get it.' " The hillbilly accent was gone. These vowels were round and cruel. And ancient.

"You bitch! Are you crazy? Let me *out* of here." He tried to move toward her but suddenly his chest was gripped by a hammering pain that spread like wildfire to his arms and throat, his whole body gnawed by an agony that lived and breathed. He opened his mouth to scream but could make only a small dry sound like a trapped animal begging to be released.

"How does it feel, Ricky? Does it hurt? Does it make you want to cry out to someone you love? Why don't they *come* to you?"

The pain released him as quickly as it had begun, leaving him bent over, eyes closed. He breathed in slow, deep, measured relief. "A heart attack is a terrible thing," she said in mock pity. "You were so young, so alone in your pain. You reached out but there was no one to take your hand."

Rick straightened, carefully, slowly, considered the hag's hungry face and smile. He turned away to the window and leaned heavily on the sill, weak from the pain but with something cruel holding him up, not allowing him to fall. He saw the attendants buttoning up the ambulance. Chrissy and Mary Beth were getting into the BMW.

"Please. Let me go." He was whispering now, pleading. "They're going to leave without me."

"Out of my hands, Ricky. I'm just the care nurse at this facility." Then irritation raised the growl a half octave. "What's the complaint, anyhow? Isn't this what you wished for? All alone, nobody to intrude on your little world?"

Now the mocking and sneering were back. "Don't bother even looking out the window, Ricky baby. There's nothing out there for you. You gave it up a long time ago." She was in heaven and used the word "baby" like a knife. "This is the world you wanted, what you and others like you have created, and it's my job to see that you enjoy it."

Still watching the two people that he loved now more than his life, two humans whom he wanted to hold and caress, to feel their soft hair against his face, the comfort of their arms, wanting all that at once and knowing it was lost forever, squandered, ground into dust beneath a boot heel, he said quietly, like a shamed little boy, "My name's not Ricky. Nobody calls me that."

The growl from the tiny body was now everywhere in the room, more real than the dwindling life he watched distantly through the window. "It's whatever I say it is—from now on." And those last words became three hideous things, set free, scuttling around the room, flying against the ceiling, finally lurking in the corner like enemies. *From now on.*

What he felt then was far worse than the burning and searing of before. He never knew pain could be so deep, the loneliness like drifting in a cold, faithless universe of night that swept across his heart as he watched his wife and precious daughter drive off into a wash of sunlight on Christmas Day.

He turned slowly from the window and knew that he would always turn in just this way, again and again, a motion as ancient as the planets and stars he had carelessly prayed to. And standing against the door, dressed in white, crooked shoulders and crooked smile, the face of eternity stared back at him.

Thomas Millstead

REFRACTIONS

WHEN an editor acquires a story that he can't talk about up front without ruining it, he must talk about the writer instead. With a lifelong friend, that's a joy. (It's happened a lot, editing *Masques III*.)

Millstead's the man who crafted the ingenious mystery novel *Behind You* (Dell) only a few years after Dial published his kids' novel that grownups loved—*Cave of the Moving Shadows*. Yet Tom's *first* novel, years back, was a Western called *Commanche Stallion*—and he's also versatile enough to have written the chapter on character-naming ("Oh, Just Call Me Cuthbert!") for *How to Write Tales of Horror, Fantasy and Science Fiction!*

Enjoy "Refractions"—and call Thomas Millstead a true original.

REFRACTIONS

Thomas Millstead

SHEILA DABBED A FEW TEARS FROM the corner of her eye. The new contact lenses bothered her, but she thought they'd be comfortable enough to leave in for the rest of the evening.

She felt a trifle self-conscious. None of the members of the Aura of Light had ever seen her without glasses before. At first she'd felt conspicuous, almost naked. Then she'd noticed herself in Millicent's mirror and liked what she saw.

Of course, she knew it was all psychological. She was neither more nor less attractive because of the absence of those heavy-framed bifocals. No sleeker. No younger. But the contacts had definitely given her an emotional lift.

"My dear, I never realized what lovely eyes you have!" Millicent—exuberant as ever—hugged her and introduced her to tonight's speaker, a Dr. Negruni.

"Lovely eyes, indeed." He stared intently at her, then bowed to kiss her hand.

She felt suddenly on the verge of giddiness. How long since she'd received a compliment? Of any kind? From anyone?

How long since Russell had last praised anything about her?

So very long. He'd seen her wearing the new lenses for the first time this afternoon, before he left for his overnight sales meeting. He'd puckered his thin, derisive lips and whistled mockingly.

"Whoa! Look at *this* hot number, would you!"

"Well, I'm not trying to look like a . . . a . . ."

"Hot number? I know. Believe me, I know."

Hurt, she'd turned away. "No. Not like one of those . . ."

"One of those what?"

"At your sales meetings. Those . . . women in the hotels that you pay to . . ."

"That I pay to what? Say it! It's a simple Anglo-Saxon word!"

"To . . . consort with."

"Consort with?" He laughed harshly, puffy jowls quivering. He slammed shut the lid of the suitcase. "God, is it any wonder you and I have *not* . . . 'consorted' for lo, these many years?"

Abruptly, his voice faded to a gruff whisper, more baffled than bitter.

"My God, the wonder is why I've put up with this . . . this *farce*. For so damn long! Why?"

And why have I? she asked herself as Millicent led the members of the circle into the evening's meditation period. Sheila concentrated on the question. All those hostile years. His infidelities. The occasional beatings. *Why?*

No answer emerged. It was time for their speaker.

Dr. Negruni had traveled widely and studied Eastern mysticism in India, Nepal, even Tibet. His voice was accented and soothing, rising and falling in gentle tones like the mesmerizing murmur of a mountain stream. He spoke eloquently of karma, of kundalini, of chakras.

What magnetism he exerts, Sheila thought. She could not imagine how old he was. But his age must be great, for many of his journeys dated to the early decades of the century. Yet he was vibrant, his face hardly lined. A small sparrow of a man, his skin was velvety olive and his eyes lustrous and penetrating.

Afterward, she clasped his hand and thanked him warmly. But she did not stay for the punch and croissants. Her lenses were increasingly irritating her and she did not want Dr. Negruni to see her squinting and grimacing.

On the sidewalk, as she sought a cab, she felt her forearm softly squeezed.

"Always it is such a pleasure to meet those who aspire to learn the secrets of the ancients," Dr. Negruni purred. "In all modesty, I have mastered more than a few. You know, it is the fusion of the Siva and the Shakti—the male and female principles—that generates prana. Which is the very energy of life. You are quite beautiful, if you permit me. In Western culture, mature beauty is not justly prized. Ah, here is a taxi!"

Idiocy! So stupid! At *your* age! Shameful!

Accusations raced relentlessly through her mind. But she smiled lazily in the darkness, her body glowing with a fulfillment she'd not known in—how long?

Never before, really, she admitted. Never, certainly, with Russell.

The sleep of satisfied exhaustion crept over her. But she fought to remain awake, to cherish every moment. To marvel again at the exquisite pleasures Dr. Negruni had awakened in her.

Drowsily, she reached out to slide her fingers once more over the silky, diminutive body beside her.

His arm was cold. She touched his chest. Icy, frigid. There was no heartbeat.

Panicked, Sheila bolted upright. She shook him, pounding his breastbone, desperately blowing breath into his sagging mouth.

It was too late.

She was stunned but she knew she must get out. This was ghastly, but there was no helping Dr. Negruni. She must not be found here!

She struggled to her feet, groping in the dark, unfamiliar room. Where were her glasses?

Then she remembered: contacts. She'd taken them out before she and Dr. Negruni . . .

Sheila scooped up her clothes, scurried to the bathroom. She flipped on the light and saw the lenses, hazily, on a tissue on the counter over the sink.

Now she was sniffling, sobbing. *Be calm,* she commanded. She dressed hastily, then wetted the contacts and, with trembling hands, inserted them.

She glanced in the mirror, briskly brushing her hair into place. It would not do to look disheveled when she slipped out of the hotel this time of night. She must *not* be remembered. Nor could she report this.

How would she explain it? Alone with a naked dead man in his hotel room? Her reputation! Her daughter Cindy in college! And Russell?

Would he merely smirk? Or come at her again with his hamlike fists?

One last tug at her blouse. But her arm froze in midair.

Behind her—she saw it distinctly in the mirror—stood a man. Only a few feet away.

It couldn't be! her mind shrieked.

At first, the irrational thought: Dr. Negruni!

But no. This man was tall, heavy, pasty-faced. Wearing a long, caped, Victorian greatcoat buttoned to the throat and carrying a small satchel. A black slouch hat was pulled low over his forehead, shielding his eyes.

He smiled at her.

She thought she couldn't move, yet instinct spun her around, to confront him.

She was alone.

Sheila fled.

She sank onto the chair in front of her own vanity. Her face was sickly pale as she studied it. "Shock, of course," she remarked aloud. Some hallucination. But predictably, after the trauma of tonight.

Once more her contacts were bothersome—gritty and grating. With her index finger, she stretched the skin of one eyelid, attempting to pop out the lens just as she'd learned. It remained nestled against her cornea.

Again she tried, with no success. Finally she was digging, gouging, and *still* the lens wouldn't budge.

She scowled, bent forward to the mirror. Strange: Her eyes looked brown. Yet—when she wasn't wearing glasses—the bright lights over her vanity had always brought out the vividness of her sky-blue irises.

She blinked. Brown? Yes. Deep, deep brown.

It came to her like an electric jolt.

These lenses must have been laid out beside hers at the hotel. Brown-tinted lenses. Dr. Negruni's.

Frantic, she pried, poked, squeezed. And could not eject them.

In her agitation she did not—for a few moments—perceive the large man reflected in her mirror.

He was still in his greatcoat, still clutching the satchel. A commanding presence; solid. He placed one hand on the back of her chair.

From under the wide brim of his hat, his eyes were barely visible. They locked on hers. They were a phlegmlike yellow, glittering, feral as a leopard's.

As in a trance, she half-turned her head to look behind her.

No one was there.

"Of course," she said matter-of-factly.

And buried her face in her hands, hearing high, keening whimpers she knew were her own.

Millicent, Sheila thought in the morning. She *must* see Millicent.

Millicent would be consoling. Millicent with her serenity and compassion. Not that Sheila would relate last night's circumstances. Not that she would compromise herself . . . or Negruni's good name.

But Millicent was uncanny about arcane matters. So wise and experienced. It had meant so much to Sheila—in the torment of her marriage to Russell—to be part of Millicent's circle.

She found it difficult to separate what had happened from what she must have imagined. Certainly she hadn't fantasized the death of that dear little man. Still, she wore his lenses, unable to remove them—and, it being Sunday, she could not seek help from her optometrist. But the other horror: that *creature* in the mirror . . .

Sheila nodded to the doorman at Millicent's apartment building, as she always did. He tipped his cap, as he always did. "How are you today, ma'am?" He was beefy, with the broiled-lobster flush of a heavy drinker.

A young woman in tight jeans sauntered past them, out of the building. The doorman winked at Sheila. "Just moved in," he said. He licked his lips. "Some hot number—ain't she?"

Rage exploded within her, a scorching flash fire of fury.

A "hot number?" *Russell*'s stupid words! Exactly the kind of filthy remark Russell would make! She had never before been engulfed by such a frenzy of anger. This damned *degenerate*! Sheila fumbled wildly in her purse; what could she use?

The manicure scissors—yes!

In Sheila's mind's eyes, she already saw the slice in this cretin's throat. How *jolly* that was—how *very jolly*!

She opened and closed the scissors convulsively, biting her lip to stifle her eagerness.

Wait! Someone—behind the doorman. Odd; she hadn't seen him before, the bearded man in coarse seaman's garb.

Never mind! Do them both!

Sheila's hand faltered. Suddenly she was shivering, drenched with fright. She flung herself through the door, into the lobby.

Merciful God, she prayed, *what was I thinking of?*

The elevator was ornate, paneled on three sides with mirrors bordered in gold leaf. Sheila held tightly to the burnished brass beside her, sucked in her breath.

The caped man was there with her. All around. He loomed above her in each of her three reflected images. He was so close that she might have smelled his breath.

She reached out her arms and swung them to and fro, touching nothing. Confirming—something.

"Who are you?" she asked softly, staring at one of the images.

His lips moved. Sensual lips, drolly amused.

She felt sound vibrations somewhere behind the back of her skull—as if from his voice. She tensed, listening. No; not his voice. Nor a whisper. More the shadow of a whisper.

Should've gone for the windpipe. Never a squawk out of 'im. Then into the carotid—and rip! Remember those bloody trollops? Oh, jolly!

With his left hand, the figure in the mirror brandished the satchel, laughing.

She squeezed her eyes shut and pressed her hands against her ears.

"Do have some tea, dear." Millicent smiled sweetly. "You seem distraught."

"Well, Dr. Negruni . . ."

"Yes, a terrible shock. I got the call this morning. Such a gifted man. So animated—just last night. But the transition was peaceful, I'm told."

"You'd known him long?"

"Eons, casually. He was away for years at a time. He'd made a fortune from his technological innovations, he was a genius in the field of optics. He could . . . well afford to pursue his passion for the occult." She tapped Sheila's knee. "Of course, you are upset. We all are. Yet it's merely a passage from one dimension to another."

Sheila sipped her tea, desperately searching for the right words. She must be discreet, but she had to have an answer. Somehow, Millicent would understand. She must!

"It's just that . . ." she began, but let her voice trail off. She nodded toward the corner of the room. She could not confide in the presence of a stranger. It was so unlike Millicent not to observe the social proprieties. Weakly, Sheila smiled at the woman, who gazed back at her.

"I don't believe we have met . . ."

"Who's that, my dear?"

"Your friend. In the beautiful sari."

"My *dear*." Millicent clapped her hands and chortled heavily. "How sensitive of you! Why, you surprise me."

"I don't understand."

"Dr. Negruni saw her, too! Last night—before our meeting. I haven't, unfortunately. But he had this rare ability—and now you. Remarkable!"

"Ability?"

Millicent's face radiated delight. "To see who we once were. In our last *incarnation*, don't you know?"

"Please. . . ?"

"I was a high-caste Indian woman, a teacher, in the early nineteen hundreds, Dr. Negruni said. The form . . . the identity . . . in which we last materialized—it clings to us, follows us, influences us. We carry with us the ghosts of those we were. He was often able to perceive those apparitions of our past. Something to do with his discoveries in optics."

The cup slipped from Sheila's hand, shattered on the floor.

Dr. Negruni's *lenses*.

Merciful God, that's *me* then . . . who I was, *what* I was. That abomination! That . . . *thing*.

Millicent talked on but Sheila couldn't hear for her throbbing pulse. It was like the crashing of heavy surf; then the waves formed words that were remote, blurred, insistent.

Remember? The nights? Whitechapel? The fog? The empty streets? Remember what they called us? The police, the yellow press?

It emerged, then—the recollection. As though a trapdoor had creaked open deep within Sheila. A dim memory, only fragments, sensations. But real.

As true as any other memory—of last week, last year, childhood even.

The bony faces of the prostitutes, petrified with terror . . . the dank midnight air. Echoes of boots on cobblestones mere yards away. The scalpel pulled from the surgeon's satchel . . . The uncontrollable orgasmic roar with the first thrust! . . . The *thrill!*

"My dear, what is it?"

Remember? They called us "Jack."

Gagging, Sheila stumbled from the apartment.

That evening she sat quietly before her vanity, wearing only a slip. Her mind was empty, drained. She looked steadily into the eyes of the other image in the mirror. She held a steak knife in her lap.

He was also silent; motionless. He hovered, erect, over her, returning her gaze with a kind of detached insolence.

Hours ticked by while they shared their wordless communion. A key rattled in the front door and Russell entered.

He dropped his suitcase loudly. By the stamp of his feet she knew he was very drunk.

When Sheila swung around to face him, her single thought was mild disgust. Now he'd had the effrontery to bring into *her* home one of those scummy tarts he patronized on his sales trips!

The girl looked cheap—Sheila was sure anyone Russell favored would be—her cheeks heavily, ludicrously rouged. And dowdy, with boxy buttoned shoes that were more like boots. Archaic, too, with a shapeless dress that fell to her instep, hair twisted into a crude bun.

She lingered in the doorway, partially hidden behind him, ill at ease, shifting nervously from one foot to the other. Russell ignored her, stepped toward Sheila.

"How's Miss Priss?" he demanded. His narrowed eyes roved over her, his voice dropped to a slurred, sarcastic whisper. "Damn if you don't look half appealing for a change. To a guy that hasn't gotten any—since last night, anyway!"

Sheila stared past him. Her heart began a trip-hammer beat. She'd *seen* women who looked and dressed like that. But in photos, faded, stilted photos of a time long gone.

That girl was *Russell,* she realized. Russell of the *past*—of a *century ago!*

Instantly, the roaring filled Sheila's ears, cascaded over her. She glanced in the mirror. Yes, *he* remembered this girl. He trembled, excited; one hand dipped into the black satchel.

Remember her? Liz Stride. Recall what we did to her? Recall that throat, ripped open and bubbling. . . ?

Sheila got slowly to her feet.

"Time we . . . consorted . . . again," Russell sneered, reaching for her. He whipped the back of his hand across her face almost casually, his knuckles bruising Sheila's jaw.

She brought the steak knife up for him to see. It was as if swarms of angry hornets buzzed within her veins then. A lust sprang to life; a clamoring. An awful appetite to be fed, so *long* dormant. Sheila's hand itched to lunge with the blade—to feel it slide in, penetrate flesh.

Now! Just as before . . .

Russell gaped, disbelieving. He threw up his arms to ward off the thrust.

Sheila struck, then crouched, waiting to strike again.

"Damn you!" Russell spat out, weaving from side to side, frightened and enraged. She had cut his shoulder and it was bleeding freely. Russell clutched his wound, reeled backward. "You bitch—this is what you *always* wanted!"

"Yes!" she shouted, exulting. And remembered the question she had asked herself so often—the one they had each asked, so often: *Why have I put up with this, year after year? Why?*

Now . . . she knew. Why they were irrevocably bound. Eternally linked.

He bumped the chair, fell. He sprawled against the vanity, brushing aside jars, bottles, brushes. She stood over him and read in Russell's face the cowering, gibbering horror she recalled so exquisitely well.

The horror in the waxen faces of all those women. Those pathetic, anguished women. As they stared up at the sight of the poised, glinting scalpel.

Now! Stab! Revel!

She shot a sidelong look into the mirror. The caped man wasn't there. No, he was *in* her now—squirming in spasms of rapture.

She saw him reflected in her own eyes—glaring and merciless. And in her own face, hot with delicious anticipation.

It was a face so hateful that she staggered backward at the sight of it. So repellent that she clapped a hand to her mouth, her entrails twisting repulsively.

No, she thought, screaming it inside.

She was *Sheila*—not *him*. Never again, dear God—dear God, let me be free of him. Let the damned debt be paid, forever!

Sheila hurled the knife to the floor.

Russell gave a sobbing sigh.

And *he* pounced on the knife, crying aloud with triumph. Then he raised it, studied the blood-flecked blade.

Through Dr. Negruni's lenses, Sheila saw the gawky, dowdy woman—that rouged harlot—drift forward until her body melted into Russell's.

Did *he* know? she wondered almost indifferently. Did he recall that life, long ago . . . how it had ended? Did he understand why vengeance was his at last?

Yes, she thought. His eyes were slits of searing, red-rimmed, wholly irrational hatred. But in their depths there lurked some wisp of . . . remembrance.

It seemed to startle Russell, to bewilder him. He paused.

You know why you must do this, she thought. *You know.*

She nodded, granting permission.

He plunged the knife home.

Adobe James

THE SPELLING BEE

ALFRED Hitchcock said world-traveler Adobe James was a "modern master and one of the very best story-tellers practising his craft today." He has published over five hundred short yarns, yet *I* didn't know his work! While I was editing a "how-to" book in '86, asking professionals to cite the great short horror fiction, they kept mentioning James's "The Road to Mictlantecutli."

While I was wondering who the devil Adobe James was, his agent sent along his first *new* short story since 1970! A reading reminded me that the sometimes seemingly diluted craft of marvelous, sheer storytelling is still being practiced. Then I *had* to correspond with "Adobe" himself, just to discover his true identity. He wasn't shy.

For fifteen years, Oxford scholar James Moss Card-well has been (simultaneously) the founder of the California Fire Academy; college coordinator for a commission on Peace Officer Standards and Training; and an instructor of creative writing, journalism, and psychology! Known as "Jamie McArdwell" for his "more lyrical tales," Adobe/Jim has appeared in the English *Vanity Fair* with six stories, all produced on BBC radio and TV. He has lived in Palma de Mallorca, Monte Carlo, Paris, Zermatt, Carmel-by-the-Sea, and was headed back to Oxford "to complete a suspense novel," *Death in a Walled Garden*, when we first corresponded.

"Because of encouragement by the editor of *M III*," Cardwell/James writes, "more original yarns are in the works." It may be that guy Williamson's great achievement. Judge for yourself after reading this astonishing story, "The Spelling Bee."

THE SPELLING BEE

Adobe James

GABE AND I WERE PLAYING CHESS in the garden when Peter, who serves as in-house security, put in an appearance. "Company," he said, looking troubled.

We glanced in the direction of his gaze and saw the dust cloud of the twice-weekly Greyhound bus creeping down out of the hills like a silver beetle.

The game was put on hold. I went into the shop to wait.

At the far end of Oasis's only street, which intersects the sun-bleached asphalt highway, the bus stopped and disgorged a tall, rather debonair, older man. He stood, motionless, until the bus headed back out into the desert. Then he began walking toward us. With the sun low in the late-afternoon sky, he cast a shadow thirty feet long that glided smoothly in front of him like a black mamba coming after prey.

Even though it had been a long time since we had last seen each other, when the bell tinkled and Trancredi walked into the shop, I knew instantly why he was there.

He made small talk while sizing me up. "You haven't changed a bit," he said. "Not one day older."

I refrained from commenting that the same could not be said for him; the poor devil looked as if he had gone through hell . . . a couple of times! Instead, I replied, "Is that so surprising? After all, Trancredi, look around you. Oasis is peaceful. No stress. No competition."

He merely smiled.

I waited. In a small town like Oasis, waiting was the one thing I did best. Next to spelling.

"You were number one," he said. He meant it. Because it was the truth, I accepted it without comment, even though his use of the past tense "were" was duly noted.

His eyes never left me; if he was searching for weaknesses or uncertainty, there would be no overt signs of it. Finally he asked, "You are prepared for a new challenge?"

"Do I have any choice?"

He snorted, then laughed. "Well, yes. Of course! The Committee simply names a new champion. You know the rules."

I knew the rules. Still, though, I hesitated. It had been years since I had last been in a real competition. I still kept my hand in with dilettantes, but without recent challenges from the professionals, I wasn't all that sure of my immediate readiness.

"How long," I asked, "do I have to prepare?"

He shrugged. "A week."

"A fortnight," I countered.

Trancredi smiled. "Ten days."

I paused again. Stalling, really. Ten days was enough time. You either remembered the words, the phonetics, the nuances, prefixes, suffixes, and origins—or you didn't. Finally I nodded my acceptance.

"Who is the challenger?"

"A girl. Fresh out of high school." His eyes became hooded. "She can spell anything." A slight smile, then his gaze met mine. "A natural. Like you. But better. And much younger, of course."

Now it was my turn to smile. "The last time you bet against my spelling, Trancredi, it cost you dearly."

"I plan to win it all back with the girl. All of it . . . with interest! I've waited a long time. She will depose you."

"It's possible." Like tennis players, politicians, movie stars, and gunslingers, we worry about novices; they are always a threat . . . always disturbing the status quo, dethroning acknowledged champions. To paraphrase something once said about history: "Competition is nothing more than the sound of newcomers' wooden clogs clumping up the front steps while silken slippers whisper down the back."

"So be it," I said.

"I shall notify The Committee that you have agreed to defend your title. Some of them"—he grinned nastily—"were sure you would resign."

"What? And not give you an opportunity to regain your very substantial losses?"

Trancredi closed his eyes slowly, then smiled, and laughed. He was still barking out his amusement when the bell tinkled to denote his departure.

You should know that the next ten days were not easy. I closed the shop; it was a necessity because so many new words had been added to our language during the last few years that I had to spend twenty-four hours a day reading and doing research.

Most competitive exhibitions have their legions of fanatics whose only standard of speech is hyperbole. Spelling is no different. A flighty female reporter, one of my supporters, from a magazine devoted to spelling, began her article with the statement, "The eyes of the universe will be focused on Oasis next week . . ." A bit of an exaggeration, but tame compared with the publicity from Trancredi's group.

When the evening of the contest arrived, I was ready. I drove to the announced site in my convertible, top down, enjoying the balmy desert air as the sun sank beneath the ridge of hills and one by one the familiar stars started popping out.

A large circus tent had been erected for the event, and a white banner bearing the words SPELLING CHAMPIONSHIP flapped listlessly in the torchlight.

Inside, The Committee—all twelve of them—was already in the Jury Box.

A hush fell on the crowd as I walked down the dirt aisle and made my way up onto the fifty-five gallon oil drums and wooden planks which constituted a makeshift stage. There were two speaker stands about ten feet apart. A young, dark-eyed, dark-haired, slender girl—not much more than a child—dressed all in white, was stationed at one of the stands. I took my place behind the other and stared out at the audience. There must have been close to five hundred spectators here for the event, not including the thirty-five gamblers en route to Las Vegas this morning when their bus had lost its brakes coming down the grade and side-swiped a bridge before coming to a halt just outside the city limits. Mostly, the gamblers were unhappy about being stuck here but, in their parlance, this was the only game in town. Most of them, willing to bet on anything, had already wagered on the spelling contest. On the girl. To win!

I gazed around. Identified those who were my supporters . . . recognized others who would give anything to see my defeat . . . saw a large number of undecideds who, traditionally, chose sides fairly early in a competition. My glance came back to Trancredi with his entourage in the front rows. He appeared relaxed, perfectly composed, untouchable. And yet, there was a wariness about him. A lot was at stake. He almost looked as if he were having some second thoughts. Good! He could still withdraw the challenge and slink away like a jackal in the night. But he wouldn't. Pride. His one weakness . . .

I turned my attention finally to my challenger. The girl stared back at me, appraisingly, not yielding. A pretty little thing, she wore a loose-fitting peasant blouse, and the soft shimmering cloth clung to her unconfined breasts. Her nipples were erect from the material against her bare skin, from the excitement! Under her muslin-thin skirt, the almost imperceptible shadow of her pelt of Eve was a perfect triangle as the cloth sought out the body's natural conformation. It was all too obvious she wore nothing beneath her garments. Trancredi had made his second mistake; the girl's physical attractions would never distract me, although most of the gamblers loved what they thought they saw.

The spelling contest began. The first word KHEPERA was for the challenger. She went through it effortlessly, and drew some polite applause from the audience—except for the gamblers, of course, all of whom now were looking as if they wanted to be elsewhere.

"ANGRA MAINYU" the voice of the unseen moderator called out my word to me.

I pronounced it, then spelled. Applause, a bit louder than that given to the girl.

"AHRIMAN." The challenger's second word came out of the darkness. She paused for dramatic effect, inhaled so her breasts were uplifted in promise again, all this intended to distract me, then spelled. Another top mark for her from The Committee. Trancredi led the applause.

In quick succession then came SHAITAN, ARALU, BELILI, MICTLANTECUTLI, ABADDON, APOLLYON. The girl seemed at ease, growing in confidence as she spelled each of hers. With each success she won more supporters from the undecideds. Understandable, in a way. She had a flair; there was something sensual about the way she mouthed each word, then proceeded to spell.

By the end of the first period, the temperature inside the tent had risen considerably because of the close-packed bodies. And it was then, during prolonged applause for the girl, that I noticed two things: one, the gamblers were creating an intolerable disturbance, something would have to be done about them; and, two, the challenger made her first mistake—not in spelling, but in using a feminine little gesture to push back a stray curl from her perspiration-streaked forehead. Vanity? Or simply not concentrating on the task at hand? Either could be fatal!

Trancredi noticed her movement and he stood to motion angrily at her. Uncertain of his meaning, she frowned and bent forward to peer at him. Quite unexpectedly, I had been granted an opportunity. It was not the kind of opening that I care for particularly, but nonetheless I went for an early kill as the darkness regurgitated my next word, MALEBOLGE.

You should know that in a major spelling contest like tonight's, it is a relatively easy thing to create a spell which will bring about a simple manifestation of Angra Mainyu, Apollyon, Belili, Khepera, Mictlantecutli, Shaitan, or any of the other 2,603 forms of Satan, but it demands real power and concentration to spell forth the whole subregion of Malebolge—better known as the eighth circle of hell.

"*Malebolge*," I intoned, using powers older than time itself. "*Tempera scelerisque . . .*" and felt the nether regions slowly bending to my will. "*Asmodeus semper . . .*"

And Malebolge began taking shape. We were above it, looking

down into the inferno as the earth peeled back and the sulfurous
flames roared skyward.

The gamblers were screaming in fright.

"Scelerisque . . ." I cried, pointing at them, and their screams
became shrieks, then squeals, as they turned into swine and began
fighting each other in terror, snapping brittle-boned legs and losing
ears and eyes to razor-sharp hooves in their frenzied scramble to
get away from the crevice crumbling beneath them.

Trancredi, suddenly frightened and aware he was losing, at-
tempted to change into his real form, but I was already far ahead
of him and, slowly, his head became a giant beetle while his torso
thickened to a white repulsiveness, which in turn became an elon-
gated maggot that began feeding on itself amid his cries of agony.

Flames were everywhere now. Sure of my victory, I let my fol-
lowers go, and they rose on great white wings to rip through the
top of the burning tent.

The girl, unafraid and still composed, was attempting to assert
her powers. Trancredi had been correct; she was surprisingly
strong and cunning for one so young, but I had caught her off-
guard with my spelling, and, in truth, she was no match because I
knew her weakness now.

Vanity!

There is no greater weakness . . . except, perhaps, pride . . .

I spun toward her and held up a large silver mirror. The reflec-
tion that shone back at her showed a toothless old crone—besot-
ted with dripping, leprous sores that had eaten away the right eye.
Her hair had fallen out, her clothes were gone. Her once proudly
uplifted breasts were now only slabs of gray lifeless flesh that hung
below her navel. She screamed and kept on shrieking as her belly
distended in a pregnancy of putrefaction before exploding, and a
million white grub worms flew out into the audience, each grow-
ing instantly into incredible size, exuding the stench of sulphur
and death as they clung to and began feeding on new hosts.

The moans and screaming from Trancredi's followers were deaf-
ening, even above the sound of thunder and flames from below
and the insane squealing of pigs trampling blindly back and forth
in terror over the bodies of other gamblers.

"Malebolge," I chanted, and the seas of the world heated up,
boiled, and then licked inward with scalding tongues three hun-

dred feet high and a hundred miles long. The earth shuddered in
its orbit, then moved backward, and the malevolent red eye of the
sun appeared once again above the western horizon while ten
thousand volcanoes orgasmed and became Roman candles of
death.

At almost full power now, I had built up enough energy to de-
stroy all of current creation if I wanted to. I turned toward The
Committee. It would be so easy to nullify them—to send them all
to a frightful place from which release could be made only by
someone far stronger than I . . . if such a being still existed some-
where.

But I am a caring person.

I acquitted them, then turned back to the old hag who screamed
and writhed in unendurable agony on the oil drums which were
red-hot and about to melt. Green saliva gushed in a malodorous
fountain from her mouth and nostrils, and her fingernails clawed
great bloody furrows in her boil-infested flesh. The Malebolge spell
was good for 20 years of her time and compounded so that each
and every tick of the clock would be as 100 years. The same time
frame, of course, would apply once again to Trancredi, whose tor-
ment now was too terrible for even me to witness. The poor devil.
He would never learn.

I made to depart.

And the unseen moderator announced, in reverence, "You re-
main the champion."

I made a slight bow to The Committee; the courtesy was ac-
knowledged and, I sensed, with considerable relief.

Leaving the screams, the piteous entreaties, the stench, the
flames, the squealing behind, I went out into the cool night air
where the sky was black with my hovering followers.

I motioned to end the spelling, and the ground on all four sides
of the tent reared up like gigantic hooded cobras . . . and then
struck! The land trembled as the tent and all within were de-
voured.

The planet earth was now back in its normal orbit. Time, which
had fled, returned. A three-quarter-old moon was just rising in the
east. A meteor flashed across the firmament in approval.

It was such a nice night that I decided to join my followers, and
fly home . . .

Paul Dale Anderson

BETTER THAN ONE

ONE of the best-kept secrets among readers of horror today, largely due to the many pseudonyms he has used for such fine short stories and novels as *Claw Hammer*, *Effigies*, and *Synergism* was nonetheless known well by members of Horror Writers of America. Ignoring such bylines as Gustaf Karl, Paul Andrews, Irwin Chapman, and A. A. Pavlov, they made Paul Dale Anderson the organization's first vice-president. Or maybe it was because they respected his talents under *all* those names.

A teacher, copywriter, poet, and former military journalist, Anderson is the husband of *2AM*'s editor, Gretta, and college frosh Tammy Jeanne's dad. An appreciator of well-told tales with a critic's cool judgment, modest Paul Dale—he's called that—supports the small press enthusiastically. With Gretta in 1988 he published Dave Silva's anthology *The Best of the Horror Show*. He presents here a compelling story worthy of his two collections, *The Devil Made Me Do It* (1985) and *The Devil Made Me Do It Again* (1988), with startlingly original twists and an absolutely dazzling finish. Under any name, he *is* better than most.

BETTER THAN ONE

Paul Dale Anderson

STUBBORNLY, BOB PUSHES TO REGAIN CONTROL. He wills his hand forward, but again the hand halts in midair and his fingers twitch uncontrollably, like earthworms skewered on the barbed ends of fish hooks.

"Give up," the voice insists. "Give up give up give up."

Frustrated, frightened, Bob searches for an opening. Like a cornered rat, he perceives that his adversary would rather play than pounce. He talks to buy time.

"You'll have to kill me," he says. "You killed Laura. You'll have to kill me, too."

"You know that's impossible, Bob. Your wife wasn't the slightest bit necessary, but you are. What would *I* do without *you*?"

"Rot in hell," Bob suggests.

"I can punish you without killing. Perhaps you'd like a sample . . ."

Intense pain rips through his lower body, sending Bob to his knees in tears. *This isn't real,* he tells himself. *None of this is real.*

His intestines feel as if they're being pulled from his stomach, an inch at a time. A red-hot nail enters his urethra, penetrating all the way into his bladder before he screams. The pain continues even after he loses consciousness.

Stop! his mind cries. *Oh, please! Stop!*

"Have you learned your lesson?" the voice asks.

Yes! I'll do anything you want! Anything!

"Good," the voice says.

The pain goes away and Bob sleeps like a baby.

"Did you enjoy my little demonstration?" the voice asks when Bob returns to consciousness.

"How. . . ?"

"How? Divert endorphins from your pain center, secrete acetylcholine, pressure the pituitary, and *voilà!*"

"It seemed so real."

"Oh, it was. Not the injuries, you understand. But the pain. The pain was real, exactly the same as if your guts had been ripped out or your penis penetrated. You felt the same pain you would have felt had those things actually happened."

"Where did you learn to do that?"

"From books and magazines, of course. Things you've read over the years and don't remember. But *I* remember. I remember everything."

"I never read about acetyl-whatever-you-call-it."

"You skimmed a newspaper article eight and a half years ago that mentioned the importance of acetylcholine as a neurotransmitter—the synaptical junction for nerve impulses. Though you paid little attention at the time and can't even pronounce the word, you obviously know what it means. Don't you?"

"Vaguely."

"That information, all information—everything you've read or been exposed to—is stored in billions of chemical receptors in a part of the brain you don't normally use. The part of your brain I now occupy."

"What *are* you? You're not me. You can't be me. Am I going crazy?"

"I'm you, but not *you*. I'm a cancer, a growth, a cellular mutation of your neocortex. I'm the next step in human evolution."

"I am going crazy."

"No. I won't let you."

"You can control my sanity?"

"Yes. And everything you say and do, too. I can control every aspect of your body and brain except . . ."

"Except what?"

"Forget it."

"Tell me!"

"I said forget it."

"I want to know!"

"I'll punish you again if you don't forget it. Do you want to be punished?"

"No." Bob shudders uncontrollably. The memory is too fresh, too real. He has already had enough pain to last a lifetime, and he can't stand the thought of more.

"You made me kill Laura," Bob says. "You took control of my body and made me murder my own wife. I hate you for that."

"I know. I, too, have fond memories of Laura. It was a difficult decision but absolutely necessary. She was about to phone a doctor and have you committed to a mental hospital. I couldn't permit that."

"Why not?"

"Because they'd discover a cancerous growth on your brain and want to *remove* it. They'd lobotomize you to get at me. In their ignorance they'd destroy us both."

"You didn't have to kill her. Couldn't you have talked to her, explained things?"

"Did you think she'd believe? You didn't believe, either, until I made you kill her. But you believe me now, don't you?"

"Yes," Bob says. "I have no choice. Do I?"

"None whatsoever."

I'd rather die than be your slave, Bob thinks. *I'll bide my time, wait for an opportunity, kill myself.*

"Impossible," the voice says. "I know your thoughts even before you do. I'm a part of your brain. I can intercept nerve impulses before your muscles can react. You'll do nothing without my permission. You must obey or be punished."

Fear and trembling take control of Bob's body at the mere mention of punishment. He feels trapped between the proverbial rock and hard place, unable to choose between two evils. To obey this monstrosity is unthinkable. To disobey and be punished is impossible.

"Pick up Laura's body," orders the voice. "Show me you can be trusted, and I'll let you dispose of your wife on your own. Put her in the bathtub, cut her into tiny pieces, and cover her flesh with Draino until it dissolves. Do this and I won't punish you. Fail me, and I'll . . ."

This time when Bob reaches for his wife, his hand isn't stopped. His fingers touch her face, her hair. A rush of emotion overwhelms him and tears flood his eyes.

He remembers his fingers worming around her neck against his volition, squeezing the life and breath from her body as her screams slowly died in her throat. He'd tried to scream himself, but no sound emerged from his mouth, no tears stained his cheeks.

Now, at least, he can cry.

He picks her up in his arms and carries her to the bathroom. There he undresses her, peeling away her clothes as if she were still alive and he were planning an act of passion on the tiled floor.

He almost expects her to respond as he opens her legs and slides a pair of lace panties down her thighs, over her knees. But her flesh is cold to his touch, the panties soiled.

He thinks he's going to throw up. He crawls to the toilet bowl and holds his head over the sweet-smelling, blue-tinted water until his nausea passes. His guts wrench but nothing comes out.

He sits on the floor in front of the toilet and stares at his wife's naked body, unable to complete his task despite the promise of painful punishment. Inevitably, he knows, the punishment will come. But for now, he cannot bring himself to touch his wife again.

"*You* do it," he challenges the cancer. "Clean up your own mess. I won't help you anymore."

He waits for the pain to hit but it doesn't come. Any minute now, he reasons, the cancer will again take control of his limbs, like a puppeteer manipulating a mannequin, forcing him to cut Laura's body into bits of bloody flesh the way a butcher slices steaks and roasts from a side of beef. But, inexplicably, that doesn't happen, either.

"Do you hear me?" he shouts. "I won't *help* you anymore! You can't make me!"

The cancer doesn't answer. Hope buds anew. Bob struggles to his feet and takes a tenuous step toward the door; then another step, expecting to be stopped in his tracks before he can leave the bathroom.

Then he is out of the bathroom, into the bedroom. He sees the telephone on the nightstand, and his hand reaches out to touch it . . . and does!

He lifts the handset, places the receiver to his ear, dials 911, and counts the rings. "Ni-yun wun wun e-mergency," announces a woman's voice on the fourth ring.

Frantically, Bob searches for the right words. *I killed my wife* comes immediately to mind and is quickly discarded. *I'm possessed by a cancer* requires too much explanation. *What can I say?*

"Try 'Help me,'" a familiar voice says to his mind.

Panic.

Help me! Bob tries to scream, but his tongue and jaw don't want to cooperate. *Help me!*

"This is ni-yun wun wun po-lice e-mergency. Your call is being recorded. Is anyone there?"

Yes!

Help me!

Please!

"This isn't funny. If this is a prank . . ."

Help me!

"It's illegal to dial nine-one-one and tie up this line unless it is a bona fide emergency. Is anyone there? Hello?"

Help . . .

CLICK!

BUZZZZZZ . . .

"Too bad," the voice says. "You had your chance. You blew it."

This time the pain feels like a thousand splinters pricking his skin, sliding under his toenails, his fingernails, his eyeballs. Every hair on his body is painfully plucked out.

"Stop!" orders another voice.

"Stay out of this."

"You'll destroy him completely. Destroy his *soul*. I can't let you do that."

Two? There are two. . . ?

"Tumors? Yes. One is malignant and the other benign. Look in the mirror. You can see us both."

Bob glances at his reflection. "No!" he screams when he catches sight of his face.

Protruding from each temple, an inch above each eye, are miniature replicas of his own visage.

The one on the right—"The one that controls the left side of the brain," the new voice explains—smiles back at Bob like a happy-face cartoon drawing. The one on the left looks dark and devious, cruel.

The face in the middle, contorted in terror, isn't familiar at all.

Graham Masterton

EVER, EVER, AFTER

SINCE *The Manitou*, Graham Masterton has been an English writer the entire world's horror readers have depended upon for ingeniously imagined, solidly original story lines. Unlike some foreign authors, Graham was not obsessed by sophisticated sociopolitical themes and did not concentrate upon achieving far-out extremes. Simply put, he became an exceptional storyteller, personally retiring sometimes to the point of invisibility. In his writing, the bloodiness and literary equivalent to F/X have always stayed secondary to story, always will.

Then Masterton wrote *Night Warriors; Mirror*, which *Mystery Scene* said was "Relentlessly paced . . . sly and subtle"; *Feast;* and *Picture of Evil*, the first non-French novel ever to win the prestigious Prix Julia Verlanger. And he lovingly edited the 1989 TOR anthology, *Scare Care*, with all proceeds going to combat child abuse in America and England. Once asked by Bill Pronzini if he was jealous of Stephen King's success, his published answer was "No." His dry *real* answer: "Time will tell."

I envy your initial immersion in "Ever, Ever, After" because *that's* how long you are apt to remember it.

EVER, EVER, AFTER

Graham Masterton

THE ROAD WAS GREASY; THE LIGHT was poor; and the truck's braking lights were caked in dirt. Robbie saw it pull up ahead of him only ten feet too late, but those ten feet were enough to send a scaffolding pole smashing through the windshield of his Porsche and straight into his chest.

The medical examiner told me that he never would have known what hit him. "I'm truly sorry, Mr. Deacon; but he never would have known what hit him." Instant death; painless.

Painless, that is, to Robbie. But not to Jill; and not to me; and not to anybody who had known him. Jill was his wife of thirteen weeks; and I was his brother of thirty-one years; and his humor and vivacity had won him more friends than you could count.

For a whole month afterward I kept his photograph on my desk. Broad-faced, five years younger than me, much more like Dad than I was; laughing at some long-forgotten joke. Then one morning in early October I came into the office and put the photograph away in my middle desk drawer. It was then that I knew it was over; that he was really gone for ever.

That same afternoon, as if she had been affected by the same feeling of finality, Jill called me. "David? Can I meet you after work? I feel like talking."

She was waiting for me in the lobby, at the Avenue of the Americas entrance. Already the sidewalks were crowded with home-going workers, and there wasn't a chance of finding a cab. The air was frosty, and sharp with the smell of bagels and chestnuts.

She looked pale and tired, but just as beautiful as ever. She had a Polish mother and a Swedish father, and she had inherited the chiseled face of one and the snow-white blondness of the other. She was tall, almost five feet nine, although her dark mink coat concealed most of her figure, just as the dark mink hat concealed most of her face.

She kissed me. She smelled of Joy, and cold October streets.

"I'm so glad you could come. I think I'm beginning to go mad."

"Well, I know the feeling," I told her. "Every day, when I wake up, I have to remind myself that he's dead; and that I'm never going to see him again, ever."

We went into the Brew Burger across the street for a drink. Jill ordered tomato juice; I ordered Four Roses, straight up. We sat by the window while torrents of people passed us by.

"That's my trouble," Jill told me, picking at her freshly lacquered fingernails. "I'm sad; I keep crying; but I can't really believe that he's dead."

I sipped my whiskey. "Do you know what he and I used to play when we were younger? We used to pretend that we were wizards, and that we were both going to live forever. We even made up a spell."

Jill stared at me; her wide gray-green eyes were glistening with tears. "He was always full of dreams. Perhaps he went the best way, without even knowing what was going to happen."

"*Immortooty, immortaty—ever, ever, after!*" I recited. "That was the spell. We always used to recite it when we were scared."

"I loved him, you know," Jill whispered.

I finished my whiskey. "Haven't you talked about it with anybody else?"

She shook her head. "You know my family. They practically disowned me when I started dating Robbie, because he was still married to Sara. It was no use my telling them that he and Sara were already on the rocks; and that he despised her; and that they would have been divorced anyway, even if I hadn't shown up on the scene. Oh, no, it was all my fault. I broke up a healthy marriage. I was the scarlet woman."

"If it's any consolation," I told her, "I don't think you're scarlet at all. I never saw Robbie so happy as when he was with you."

I walked her back to her apartment on Central Park South. Thunder echoed from the skyscrapers all along Sixth Avenue; flags flapped; and it was beginning to rain. In spite of the swanky address, the flat that Jill and Robbie had shared together was very small, and sublet from a corporate lawyer called Willey, who was away in Minnesota for most of the time; something to do with aluminum tubing.

"Won't you come up?" she asked me in the brightly lit entrance lobby, which was graced with a smart black doorman in a mushroom-colored uniform and a tall vase of orange gladioli.

"I don't think so," I told her. "I have a heap of work to finish up at home."

There were mirrors all around us. There were fifty Jills, curving off into infinity, fifty doormen, and fifty *me's*. A thousand spears of gladioli.

"You're sure?" she persisted.

I shook my head. "What for? Coffee? Whiskey? More breastbeating? There was nothing we could have done to save him, Jill. You took care of him like a baby. I just loved him like a brother. There was no way that either of us could have saved him."

"But to die that way. So quickly; and for no reason."

I grasped her hand. "I don't believe everything has to have a reason."

The doorman was holding the elevator for her. She lifted her face to me, and I realized that she expected me to kiss her. So I kissed her; and her cheek was soft and cold from walking in the wind; and somehow something happened between us that made both of us stand for a moment looking at each other, eyes searching, not speaking.

"I'll call you," I told her. "Maybe dinner?"

"I'd like that."

*   *   *

That was how our affair began. Talking, to begin with; and spending weekends together with a bottle of California chardonnay; listening to Mendelssohn's violin concertos, while Christmas approached, our first Christmas without Robbie.

I bought Jill a silver Alfred Durante cuff watch and a leather-bound book of poems by John Keats. I left a silk marker in the page which said,

> *Love! Thou art leading me from wintry cold,*
> *Lady! Thou leadest me to summer clime.*

She cooked wild duck for me on Christmas Day, and Robbie's photograph watched us, smiling from the chiffonier while we drank each other's health in Krug champagne.

I took her to bed. The white wintry light arranged itself across the sheets like a paper dress-pattern. She was very slim, narrow-hipped, and her skin was as smooth as cream. She didn't speak; her hair covered her face like a golden mask. I kissed her lips, and her neck. Her oyster-colored silk panties had tucked themselves into a tight crease between her legs.

Afterward we lay back in the gathering twilight and listened to the soft crackle of bubbles in our champagne, and the sirens of Christmas echoing across Central Park.

"Are you going to ask me to marry you?" said Jill.

I nodded.

"It's not against the law or anything, is it? For a widow to marry her late husband's brother."

"Of course not. In Deuteronomy, widows are *ordered* to marry their late husband's brothers."

"You don't think Robbie would have minded?"

"No," I said, and turned over to pick up my glass, and there he was, still smiling at me. *Immortooty, immortaty, ever, ever, after.*

Robbie, in Paradise, may have approved, but our families certainly didn't. We were married in Providence, Rhode Island, on a sharp windy day the following March, with nobody in attendance but a justice of the peace and two witnesses whom we had rounded up from the local bookstore, and a gray-haired old lady who played the "Wedding March" and "Scenes from Childhood."

Jill wore a cream tailored suit and a wide-brimmed hat with ribbons around it and looked stunning. The old lady played and smiled and the spring sunshine reflected from her spectacles like polished pennies on the eyes of an ivory-faced corpse.

On our wedding night I woke up in the early hours of the morning and Jill was quietly crying. I didn't let her know that I was awake. She was entitled to her grief, and I couldn't be jealous of Robbie, now that he had been dead for over six months.

But I lay and watched her, knowing that by marrying me she had at last acknowledged that Robbie was gone. She wept for almost twenty minutes, and then leaned across and kissed my shoulder, and fell asleep, with her hair tangled across my arm.

Our marriage was cheerful and well organized. Jill left her apartment on Central Park South and moved into my big airy loft on Seventeenth Street. We had plenty of money; Jill worked as a creative director for Palmer Ziegler Palmer, the advertising agency, and in those days I was an accountant for Henry Sparrow, the publishers. Every weekend we compared Filofaxes and fitted in as much leisure time together as we could; even if it was only a lunchtime sandwich at Stars on Lexington Avenue, or a cup of coffee at Bloomingdale's.

Jill was pretty and smart and full of sparkle and I loved her more every day. I suppose you could have criticized us for being stereotypes of the Perrier water generation, but most of the time we didn't take ourselves too seriously. In July I traded in my old BMW for a Jaguar XJS convertible in British racing green, and we drove up to Connecticut almost every weekend, a hundred and ten miles an hour on the turnpike, with Beethoven on the stereo at top volume.

Mega-pretentious, *n'est-ce pas?*—but it was just about the best fun I ever had in my whole life.

On the last day of July, as we were sitting on the old colonial veranda of the Allen's Corners hotel where we used to stay whenever we weekended in Connecticut, Jill leaned back in her basket-work chair and said dreamily, "Some days ought to last forever."

I clinked the ice in my vodka and tonic. "This one should."

It was dreamily warm, with just the lightest touch of breeze. It was hard to imagine we were less than two hours' driving from downtown Manhattan. I closed my eyes and listened to the birds warbling and the bees humming and the sounds of a peaceful Connecticut summer.

"Did I tell you I had a call from Willey on Friday?" Jill remarked.

I opened one eye. "Mr. Willey, your old landlord? What did he want?"

"He says I left some books round at the apartment, that's all. I'll go collect them tomorrow. He said he hasn't relet the apartment yet, because he can't find another tenant as beautiful as me."

I laughed. "Is that bullshit or is that bullshit?"

"It's neither," she said. "It's pure flattery."

"I'm jealous," I told her.

She kissed me. "You can't possibly be jealous of Willey. He's about seventy years old, and he looks just like a koala bear with eyeglasses."

She looked at me seriously. "Besides," she added, "I don't love anybody else but you; and I never will."

It thundered the following day and the streets of New York were humid and dark and strewn with broken umbrellas. I didn't see Jill that lunchtime because I had to meet my lawyer Morton Jankowski (very droll, Morton, with a good line in Lithuanian jokes); but I had promised to cook her my famous *pesce spada al salmoriglio* for dinner.

I walked home with a newspaper over my head. There was no chance of catching a cab midtown at five o'clock on a wet Monday afternoon. I bought the swordfish and a bottle of Orvieto at the Italian market on the corner, and then walked back along Seventeenth Street, humming Verdi to myself. Told you I was megapretentious.

Jill usually left the office a half hour earlier than I did, so I expected to find her already back at the loft; but to my surprise she wasn't there. I switched on the lights in the sparse, tasteful sitting room, then went through to the bedroom to change into something dry.

By six-thirty she still wasn't back. It was almost dark outside, and the thunder banged and echoed relentlessly. I called her office, but everybody had left for the day. I sat in the kitchen in my striped cook's apron, watching the news and drinking the wine. There wasn't any point in starting dinner until Jill came home.

By seven I was growing worried. Even if she hadn't managed to catch a cab, she could have walked home by now. And she had never come home late without phoning me first. I called her friend Amy, in SoHo. Amy wasn't there but her loopy boyfriend said she was over at her mother's place, and Jill certainly wasn't with her.

At last, at a quarter after eight, I heard the key turn in the door and Jill came in. The shoulders of her coat were dark with rain, and she looked white-faced and very tired.

"Where the hell have you been?" I demanded. "I've been worried bananas."

"I'm sorry," she said in a muffled voice, and hung up her coat.

"What happened? Did you have to work late?"

She frowned at me. Her blond fringe was pasted wetly to her forehead. "I've said I'm sorry. What is this, the third degree?"

"I was concerned about you, that's all."

She stalked through to the bedroom, with me following close behind her. "I managed to survive in New York before I met you," she said. "I'm not a child anymore, you know."

"I didn't say you were. I said I was concerned, that's all."

She was unbuttoning her blouse. "Will you just get the hell out and let me change!"

"I want to know where you've been!" I demanded.

Without hesitation, she slammed the bedroom door in my face; and when I tried to catch the handle, she turned the key.

"Jill!" I shouted. "Jill! What the *hell* is going on?"

She didn't answer. I stood outside the bedroom door for a while, wondering what had upset her so much; then I went back to the kitchen and reluctantly started to cook dinner.

"Don't do any for me," she called out, as I started to chop up the onions.

"Did you eat already?" I asked her, with the knife poised in my hand.

"I said, don't do any for me—that's all!"

"But you have to eat!"

She wrenched open the bedroom door. Her hair was combed back and she was wrapped in her terry-cloth bathrobe. "What are you, my mother or something?" she snapped at me. Then she slammed the door shut again.

I stabbed the knife into the butcher block and untied my apron. I was angry, now. "Listen!" I shouted. "I bought the wine, and the swordfish, and *everything!* And you come home two hours late and all you can do is yell at me!"

She opened the bedroom door again. "I went round to Willey's apartment, that's all. Now, are you satisfied?"

"So you went to Willey's place? And what were you supposed to be doing at Willey's place? Collecting your books, if my memory serves me. So where are they, these precious books? Did you leave them in the cab?"

Jill stared at me and there was an expression in her eyes that I had never seen before. Pale, cold, yet almost *shocked,* as if she had been involved in an accident and her mind was still numb.

"Jill . . ." I said, more softly this time, and took two or three steps toward her.

"No," she whispered. "Not now. I want to be alone for just a while."

I waited until eleven o'clock, occasionally tapping at the bedroom door, but she refused to answer. I just didn't know what the hell to do. Yesterday had been idyllic; today had turned into some kind of knotty, nasty conundrum. I put on my raincoat and shouted through the bedroom door that I was going down to the Bells of Hell for a drink. Still she didn't answer.

My friend Norman said that women weren't humans at all, but a race of aliens who had been landed on earth to keep humans company.

"Imagine it," he said, lighting a cigarette and blowing out smoke. "If you had never seen a woman before tonight, and you walked out of here and a woman was standing there . . . wearing a dress, with blond hair, and red lipstick, and high-heel shoes . . . and you had never seen a woman before—then, *then,* my friend, you would understand that you had just had a close encounter of the worst kind!"

I finished my vodka, dropped a twenty on the counter. "Keep

the cha-a-ange, my man," I told the barkeep, with a magnan-
imous W. C. Fieldsian wave of my hand.

"Sir, there is no change. That'll be three dollars and seventy-five
cents more."

"That's inflation for you," Norman remarked, with a phlegmy
cough. "Even oblivion is pricing itself out of the market."

I left the bar and walked back up to Seventeenth Street. It was
unexpectedly cool for the first of August. My footsteps echoed like
the footsteps of some lonely hero in a 1960s spy movie. I wasn't
sober but I wasn't drunk, either. I wasn't very much looking for-
ward to returning home.

When I let myself in, the loft was in darkness. Jill had unlocked
the bedroom door but when I eased it open, and looked inside, she
was asleep. She had her back to me, and the quilt drawn up to her
shoulders, but even in the darkness I could see that she was wear-
ing her pajamas. Pajamas meant we're not talking; stay away.

I went into the kitchen and poured myself the dregs from a
chilled bottle of Chablis, switched the television on low. It was a
1940s black-and-white movie called *They Stole Hitler's Brain.* I
didn't want to sit there watching it, and at the same time I didn't
want to go to bed either.

At a little after two, however, the bedroom door opened and Jill
was standing there, pale and puffy-eyed.

"Are you coming to bed?" she asked, in a clogged-up whisper.
"You have work tomorrow."

I looked at her for a long time with my lips puckered tight. Then
I said, "Sure," and stood up, and switched off the television.

In the morning, Jill brought me coffee and left my Swiss muesli
out for me and kissed me on the cheek before she left for the
agency, but there were no explanations for what had happened
the previous evening. The only words she spoke were "Good
morning" and "Good-bye."

I called, "Jill?" but the only response I got was the loft door
closing behind her.

I went to the office late and I brooded about it all morning.
Around eleven-thirty I telephoned Jill's secretary and asked if Jill
were free for lunch.

"No, Mr. Deacon, I'm sorry. She had a last-minute appointment."

"Do you happen to know where?"

"Hold on, I'll check her diary. Yes . . . here it is. One o'clock. No name, I'm afraid. No address, either. It just says 'Apt.'"

"All right, Louise, thank you."

I put down the phone and sat for a long time with my hand across my mouth, thinking. My assistant, Fred Ruggiero, came into my office and stared at me.

"What's the matter? You look like you're sick."

"No, I was thinking. What does the word 'apt' mean to you?"

Fred scratched the back of his neck. "I guess it means like 'appropriate,' you know. Or 'fitting.' Or 'suitable.' You doing a crossword?"

"No. I don't know. *Sheila!*"

One of our younger secretaries was bouncing along the corridor in beaded dreadlocks and a shocking-pink blouse. "Yes, Mr. Deacon?"

I wrote 'apt' on my notepad and showed it to her. "Does that mean anything to you?"

She grinned. "Is this a trick? If you'd been looking for someplace to rent as long as I have, you'd know what that meant."

"What do you mean?"

"*Apt.* Don't you read the classifieds? Apt equals apartment."

Apartment. And whenever Jill mentioned "apartment," she meant one apartment in particular. Willey's apartment.

Fred and Sheila stared at me. Fred ventured, "Are you okay? You look kind of glassy, if you don't mind my saying so."

I coughed and nodded. "I guess I do feel a little logy."

"Hope you haven't caught a dose of the Szechuan flu," Sheila remarked. "My cousin had it, said it was like being hit by a truck."

She realized suddenly what she had said. Everybody in the office knew how Robbie had died. "Oh, I'm sorry," she said. "That was truly dumb." But I was too busy thinking about Jill round at Willey's apartment to care.

It was still raining, a steady drenching drizzle; but I went out all the same. All right, I told myself, I'm suspicious. I have no justification; I have no evidence; and most of all I have no moral right.

Jill made a solemn promise when she married me: to have and to hold, from this day forth.

A promise was a promise and it wasn't up to me to police her comings and goings in order to make sure that she kept it.

Yet there I was, standing on the corner of Central Park South and the Avenue of the Americas, in a sodden tweed hat and a dripping Burberry, waiting for Jill to emerge from her apartment building so that *I* could prove that she was cheating on me.

I waited over half an hour. Then, quite suddenly, Jill appeared in the company of a tall dark-haired man in a blue raincoat. Jill immediately hailed a passing taxi and climbed into it, but the man began to walk at a brisk pace toward Columbus Circle, turning his collar up as he did so.

I hesitated for a moment, and then I went after him.

He turned south on Seventh Avenue, still walking fast. The side-walks were crowded and I had a hard time keeping up with him. He crossed Fifty-seventh Street just as the lights changed, and I found myself dodging buses and taxis and trying not to lose sight of him. At last, a few yards short of Broadway, I caught up with him. I snatched at his sleeve, said, "Hey, fellow. Pardon me."

He turned to stare at me. He was olive-skinned, almost Italian-looking. Quite handsome if you had a taste for Latins.

He said nothing, but turned away again. He must have thought I was excusing myself for having accidentally caught at his raincoat. I grabbed him again, and said, "*Hey!* Pardon me! I want to *talk* to you!"

He stopped. "What is this?" he demanded. "Are you hustling me, or what?"

"Jill Deacon," I replied, my voice shaking a little.

"What?" He frowned.

"You know what I'm talking about," I replied. "I'm her husband."

"So? Congratulations."

"You were with her just now."

The man smiled in exasperation. "I said hello to her in the lobby, if that's what you mean."

"You know her?"

"Well, sure. I live along the hall. I've known her ever since she moved in. We say good morning and good evening in the lobby, and that's it."

He was telling the truth. I knew damn well he was telling the truth. Nobody stands there smiling at you at a busy intersection in the pouring rain and tells you lies.

"I'm sorry," I told him. "I guess it was a case of mistaken identity."

"Take some advice, fellow," the man replied. "Lighten up a bit, you know?"

I went back to the office feeling small and neurotic and jerkish; like a humorless Woody Allen. I sat at my desk staring at a heap of unpaid accounts and Fred and Sheila left me very well alone. At four o'clock I gave up and left, took a cab down to the Bells of Hell for a drink.

"You look like shit," Norman told me.

I nodded in agreement. "Alien trouble," I replied.

Maybe my suspicions about the Latin-looking man had been unfounded but Jill remained irritable and remote, and there was no doubt that something had come adrift in our marriage, although I couldn't quite work out what.

We didn't make love all week. When I tried to put my arm around her in bed, she sighed testily and squirmed away. And whenever I tried to talk to her about it, she went blank or scratchy or both.

She came home well after ten o'clock on Friday evening without any explanation about why she was late. When I asked her if everything was all right, she said she was tired, and to leave her alone. She showered and went straight to bed; and when I looked in at the bedroom door only twenty minutes later, she was fast asleep.

I went to the bathroom and wearily stripped off my shirt. In the laundry basket lay Jill's discarded panties. I hesitated for a moment, then I picked them out and held them up. They were still soaked with another man's semen.

I suppose I could have been angry. I could have dragged her out of bed and slapped her around and shouted at her. But what was the use? I went into the sitting room and poured myself a large glass of Chablis and sat disconsolately watching Jackie Gleason with the volume turned down. "The Honeymooners," blurred with tears.

Maybe the simple truth was that she had married me because I was Robbie's brother; because she had hoped in some distracted and irrational way that I would somehow become the husband she had lost. I knew she had been nuts about him, I mean truly nuts. Maybe she hadn't really gotten over the shock. Robbie would life forever; at least as far as Jill was concerned.

Maybe she was punishing me now for not being him. Or maybe she was punishing *him* for dying.

Whatever the reason, she was cheating on me, without making any serious effort to hide it. She might just as well have invited her lover into our bed with us.

There was no question about it: Our marriage was over, even before it had started. I sat in front of the television with the tears streaming down my cheeks and I felt like curling myself up into a ball, going to sleep and never waking up.

You can't cry forever, though; and after about an hour of utter misery I wiped my eyes on my sleeve and finished my glass of wine and thought: right, okay. I'm not giving Jill up without a fight. I'm going to find out who this bum is who she's been sleeping with, and I'm going to confront him, face to face. She can choose between him and me, but she's going to have to do it right out in front of us—no sneaking, no hiding, no hypocrisy.

I went to the bedroom and opened the door and Jill was lying asleep with her mouth slightly parted. She was still beautiful. I still loved her. And the pain of still loving her twisted inside me like a corkscrew.

I hope you live forever, I thought to myself. *I hope you live to know how much you've hurt me.* Immortooty, immortaty. Ever, ever, after.

On the dressing table her key ring lay sprawled. I looked at it for a long moment, then quietly picked it up.

Next day it was windy and bright. I sat in the coffee shop opposite Jill's agency building, drinking too much coffee and trying to chew a bagel that tasted of nothing but cream cheese and bitterness. At a few minutes after twelve, I saw Jill march smartly out of

the front of the building, and lift her arm to call a cab. Imme-
diately I ducked out of the coffee shop and called another taxi.

"Follow that cab," I told the driver. He was a thin Puerto Rican
with beads around his neck and a black straggly mustache.

"Wheesh cab?" he wanted to know.

"That Checker, follow that Checker."

"You thin' this some kinda movie or somethin'? I ain't follnin'
nuttin'."

I pushed a crumpled-up fifty into his hand. "Just follow that
Checker, okay?"

"Whatever you say, man. Your fewnral."

As it turned out, I paid fifty dollars plus the fare to follow Jill
back to Willey's apartment on Central Park South, where I should
have known she was going anyway. The Puerto Rican saw Jill
climb out of the cab ahead of us. Those long, black-stockinged
legs, that smart black-and-white suit. "Hey man, she's worth fifty,
that one. She's worth a hund'ud!"

Jill walked without hesitation into the apartment building. I al-
lowed her five clear minutes, pacing up and down on the side-
walk, watched with unwavering curiosity beside an old man
selling balloons. Then I went into the building after her, through
the lobby to the elevators.

"You're looking for somebody, sir?" the black doorman wanted
to know.

"My wife, Mrs. Deacon. She arrived here just a few minutes
ago."

"Oh, sure." The doorman nodded. "You go on up."

I went upward in the small gold-mirrored elevator with
my heart beating against my rib cage like a fist. I could see my
reflection, and the strange thing was that I looked quite normal.
Pale-faced, tired, but quite rational. I certainly didn't look like a
husband trying to surprise his wife in flagrante with another man.
But then, who does? People die with the strangest expressions on
their faces. Smiles, scowls, looks of total surprise.

I reached the third floor, stepped out. The corridor was over-
heated and silent and smelled of lavender polish. I hesitated for a
moment, holding the doors of the elevator open. Then I let them
go, and they closed with a whine, and the elevator carried on
upward.

What the hell am I going to say, if I actually find her with somebody?
I thought to myself. *Supposing they turn around and laugh at me,
what can I possibly do then?*

Reason told me that I should walk away—that if I was sure Jill
was cheating on me, I should call a lawyer and arrange a divorce.
But it wasn't as simple as that. My ego was large enough to want
to see what dazzling hero could possibly have attracted Jill away
from me after such a short marriage. Such a passionate marriage,
too. If I was lacking in any way, I wanted to know why.

I reached the door with the name-card that read "Willey." I
pressed my ear against the door and listened; and after a moment
or two I was sure that I could hear voices. Jill's, high-pitched,
pleading. And a deeper voice; a man's voice. The voice of her
lover, no less.

I took out the extra key that they had made for me at American
Key & Lock the previous evening. I licked my lips, took a deep
breath, and then I slid it into the door. I turned it, and the door
opened.

You can still go back. You don't have to face this if you don't want to.
But I knew that it was too late and that my curiosity was over-
whelming.

I quietly closed the door behind me and stood in the hallway,
listening. On the wall beside me were framed Deccan paintings of
the eighteenth century, showing women having intercourse with
stallions. Highly appropriate, I thought. And sickening, too. Maybe
Jill *was* having an affair with Willey, after all. He seemed to have a
pretty libidinous turn of mind.

I heard murmurings from the bedroom. The door was slightly ajar,
and I could see sunlight and pale blue carpet. The sheets rustled. Jill
said, "You're marvelous; you're magic; if only I'd known."

God, I thought, *I shouldn't have come. This is almost more than I
can stand. And what am I going to look like if they discover me? A
creeping cuckold; a jealous husband who couldn't satisfy his wife.*

"Promise me," said Jill. "Promise me you'll never leave me."
The man said something indistinct.

"All *right,*" Jill replied, with tart satisfaction. "In that case I'll
get the champagne out of the icebox, and we'll—"

I hadn't realized, listening to her talking, that she had climbed out of bed and crossed the bedroom floor. She opened the door, naked, flushed in the face, and caught me standing in the hall.

"Oh my God!" she exclaimed. The color emptied out of her face like ink spilled from a bottle.

Without a word, I pushed past her, and threw open the bedroom door.

"All right, you bastard!" I roared, in a voice so hoarse that it was almost insane. "Get up, get dressed, and get the fuck *out!*"

The man on the bed turned, and stared at me; and then I froze.

He was very pale. He was almost gray. His eyes had a stony faraway look that was more like a statue's than a man's. He was naked, his gray penis still glistened from sex. His chest was bound tightly with wide white bandages.

"Robbie," I whispered.

He drew the sheet right up to his neck but he didn't take his eyes away from me once.

"*Robbie?*" I repeated.

"That's right." He nodded. "I was hoping you wouldn't find out."

When he spoke, his words came out in a labored whisper. *Massive chest injuries*, that's what the doctors had told me. *He didn't feel a thing.*

I managed one mechanical step forward. Robbie continued to stare at me. He was dead; and yet here he was, staring at me. I had never been so frightened of anything in my entire life.

"What happened?" I asked. "They told us you were killed instantly. That's what the doctors said. 'Don't worry, he didn't feel a thing. He was killed instantly.'"

Robbie managed a tight, reflective smile. "It's the words, George. They work!"

"Words?" I demanded. "What words?"

"Don't you remember? *Immortooty, immortaty, ever, ever, after.* I saw the truck coming toward me and I shouted them out. The next thing I knew, it was dark and I was buried alive."

He raised his hand, and turned it this way and that, frowning at it, as if it didn't really belong to him. "I don't know, maybe 'alive' is the wrong word. Immortal, sure. I'm immortal. I'm going to live forever—whatever that means."

"You got out of your casket?" I asked him in disbelief. "It was solid Cuban mahogany."

"The one you paid for might have been solid Cuban mahogany. The one I kicked my way out of was pine, tacked together with two-inch nails." He gave me a grim smile. "You should sue your mortician. Or then again, maybe you shouldn't."

"Jesus." I was trembling. I couldn't believe it was he. But it really was. My own brother, gray-faced and dead, but still alive.

"Jill!" I shouted. *"Jill!"*

Jill came back into the room, wrapped in a red robe.

"Why didn't you tell me?" I asked in a whisper, although I couldn't stop myself from staring at Robbie. He remained where he was, wrapped in his sheet, his eyes fixed on me with an expression that was as cold as glass. God Almighty, he *looked* dead, he *looked* like a corpse. How could Jill have. . . ?

"I love him," Jill told me, her voice small and quiet.

"You love him?" I quaked. "Jill, he's dead!"

"I love him," she repeated.

"I love him, too, for Christ's sake!" I screamed at her. "I love him *too!* But he's dead, Jill! He's *dead!*"

I snatched hold of her wrist but she yanked herself angrily away from me. "He's not dead!" she shrieked. "He's not! He makes love to me! How can he be dead?"

"How the hell should I know? Because of a rhyme, because of a wish? Because of who knows what! But the doctors said he was dead and they buried him, and he's *dead*, Jill!"

Robbie slowly drew back the sheet from the bed and eased himself up. His skin was almost translucent, like dirty wax. From the bandages around his chest, I heard a whining inhalation and exhalation. The scaffolding pole had penetrated his lungs; he hadn't stood a chance.

"I dug my way out of the soil with my bare hands," he told me; and there was a kind of terrible pride in his voice. "I rose out of the earth at three o'clock in the morning, filthy with clay. Then I walked all the way to the city. *Walked!* Do you know how difficult that is, how far that is? And then the next day I called Jill from a public telephone in Brooklyn; and she came to rescue me."

"I remember the day," I told him.

He came up close. He exuded a strange, elusive smell; not of decomposition, but of some preservative chemical. It suddenly occurred to me that embalming fluid must be running through his veins instead of blood. He was my brother; I had loved him when he was alive. But I knew with complete certainty, now, that he was dead; and I loved him no longer.

Jill whispered, "You won't tell, will you? You won't *tell* anybody?"

For a very long moment I couldn't think what to do. Jill and Robbie watched me without saying a word, as if I were a hostile outsider who had deliberately set out to interfere and to destroy their lives.

But at last I grinned, nodded, and said to Robbie, "You're back, then! You're really back. It's a miracle!"

He smiled lopsidedly, as if his mouth were anesthetized. "I knew you'd understand. Jill said you never would; but I said bull. You always did, didn't you? You son-of-a-gun."

He rested his hand on my shoulder, his dead gray hand; and I felt the bile rise up in my throat. But I had already decided what I was going to do, and if I had betrayed any sign of disgust, I would have ruined it.

"Come on through to the kitchen," I told him. "I could use a beer after this. Maybe a glass of wine?"

"There's some champagne in the icebox," said Jill. "I was just going to get it."

"Well, let's open it together," I suggested. "Let's celebrate! It isn't every day that your brother comes back from the dead."

Jill dragged the sheet from the bed and wrapped it around Robbie like a toga. Then they followed me into the small green-tiled kitchen. I opened the icebox, took out the bottle of champagne, and offered it to Robbie.

"Here," I told him. "You were always better at opening up bottles of wine than I was."

He took it but looked at me seriously. "I don't know. I'm not sure I've got the strength anymore. I'm alive, you know, but it's kind of *different*."

"You can make love," I retorted, dangerously close to losing my temper. "You should be able to open a bottle of champagne."

His breath whined in and out of his bandages. I watched him
closely. There was doubt on his face; as if he suspected that I was
somehow setting him up, but he couldn't work out how.

"Come on, sweetheart," Jill coaxed him.

I turned around, opened one of the kitchen drawers. String,
skewers, nutmeg grater. "Yes, come on, Robbie. You always were a
genius at parties."

I opened the next drawer. Tea towels. Jill frowned and said,
"What are you looking for?"

Robbie began to unwind the wire muzzle around the cham-
pagne cork. "My fingers feel kind of *numb*, you know? It's hard to
describe."

I opened the third drawer, trying to do it nonchalantly. *Knives.*

Jill knew instantaneously what I was going to do. Maybe it was
genuine intuition. Maybe it was nothing more than heightened
fear. But I turned around so casually that she didn't see the nine-
inch Sabatier carving knife in my hand; she was looking at my
eyes; and it had penetrated Robbie's bandages right up to the hilt
before she understood that I meant to kill him. I meant to *kill* him.
He was my brother.

The champagne bottle smashed on the floor in an explosion of
glass and foam. Jill screamed but Robbie said nothing at all. He
turned to me, and grasped my shoulder, and there was something
in his eyes that was half panic and half relief. I pulled the knife
downward and it cut through his flesh as if it were an overripe
avocado: soft, slippery, no resistance.

"Oh, God," he breathed. His gray intestines came pouring out
from underneath his toga and onto the broken glass. "Oh, God,
get it over with."

"*No!*" screamed Jill, but I stared at her furiously and shouted,
"You want him to live forever? He's my brother! You want him to
live *forever?*"

She hesitated for a second, then pushed her way out of the
kitchen and I heard her retching in the toilet. Robbie was on his
knees, his arms by his sides, making no attempt to pick up his
heavy kilt of guts.

"Come on," he whispered. "Get it *over* with."

I was shaking so much that I could hardly hold the knife. He tilted his head back, passive and quiet, his eyes still open, and like a man in a slowly moving nightmare I cut his throat from one side to the other; so deeply that the knife blade wedged between his vertebrae.

There was no blood. He collapsed backward onto the floor, shuddering slightly. Then the unnatural life that had illuminated his eyes faded away, and it was clear that he was truly dead.

Jill appeared in the doorway. Her face was completely white, as if she had covered herself in rice powder. "What have you done?" she whispered.

I stood. "I don't know. I'm not sure. We'll have to bury him."

"No," she said, shaking her head. "He's still alive . . . we could bring him back again."

"Jill . . ." I began, moving toward her; but she screamed, "Don't touch me! You've killed him! Don't touch me!"

I tried to snatch at her wrist, but she pulled herself away and ran for the door.

"Jill! Jill, *listen!*"

She was out in the corridor before I could stop her, and running toward the elevator. The elevator doors opened and the Italian-looking man stepped out, looking surprised. Jill pushed her way into the elevator, hammered wildly at the buttons.

"No!" she screamed. "*No!*"

I went after her but the Italian-looking man deliberately blocked my way.

"That's my wife!" I yelled at him. "Get out of my goddamned way!"

"Come on, friend, give her some breathing space," the man said and pushed me in the chest with the flat of his hand. Desperately, I saw the elevator doors close and Jill disappear.

"For God's sake," I snarled at the man. "You don't know what you've done!"

I shoved my way past him and hurtled down the stairs, three at a time, until I reached the lobby. The doorman said, "Hey, man, what's going on?" and caught at my arm.

He delayed me for only a second, but it was a second too long. The swinging doors were just closing and Jill was already halfway across the sidewalk, running into Central Park South.

"Jill!" I shouted after her. She couldn't possibly have heard. She didn't even hear the cab that hit her as she crossed the road and sent her hurtling over its roof, her arms spread wide as if she were trying to fly. I pushed open the swinging doors and I heard her fall. I heard screams and traffic and the screeching of brakes.

Then I didn't hear anything, either.

It was a strange and grisly task, removing Robbie's body from Willey's apartment. But there was no blood, no evidence of murder, and nobody would report him missing. I buried him deep in the woods beyond White Plains, in a place where we used to play when we were boys. The wind blew leaves across his grave.

We buried Jill a week later, in Providence, on a warm sunny day when the whole world seemed to be coming to life. Her mother wouldn't stop sobbing. Her father wouldn't speak to me. The police report had exonerated me from any possible blame, but grief knows no logic.

I took two weeks away from work after the funeral and went to stay at a friend's house in the Hamptons, and got drunk most of the time. I was still in shock; and I didn't know how long it was going to take me to get over it.

Down on the seashore, with the gulls circling all around me, I suppose I found some kind of unsteady peace of mind.

I returned to the city on a dark, threatening Thursday afternoon. I felt exhausted and hung over, and I planned to spend the weekend quietly relaxing before returning to work on Monday. Maybe I would go to the zoo. Jill had always liked going to the zoo, more to look at the people than at the animals.

I unlocked the door of my apartment, tossed my bag into the hallway. Then I went through to the kitchen and took a bottle of cold Chablis out of the icebox. *Hair of the dog,* I thought to myself. I switched on the television just in time to see the end credits of "As The World Turns." I poured myself some wine; and then, whistling, went through to the bedroom.

I said, "Oh Christ," and dropped my full glass of wine on my foot.

*   *   *

She was lying on top of the comforter naked, not smiling, but her thighs were provocatively apart. Her skin had a grayish-blue sheen as if it would be greasy to touch, but it wasn't decayed. Her hair was brushed and her lips were painted red and there was purple eye shadow over her eyes.

"Jill?" I breathed. I felt for one implosive instant that I was going mad.

"I used the spare key from the crack in the skirting," she said. Her voice was hoarse, as if her lungs were full of fluid and crushed bone. I had seen her hurtling over the taxi, I had seen her fall. I had seen her *die*.

"You said the words," I told her dully. "You said the words."

She shook her head. But it was then I remembered watching her asleep, and reciting that childish rhyme. *Immortooty, immortaty, ever, ever, after.*

She raised her arms, stiffly. The fingers of her left hand were tightly curled, as if they had been broken.

"Make love to me," she whispered. "Please, make love to me."

I turned around and walked straight to the kitchen. I pulled open one drawer after another, but there wasn't a single knife anywhere. She must have hidden them all, or thrown them away. I turned back again, and Jill was standing in the bedroom doorway. This time she was smiling.

"Make *love* to me," she repeated.

Alan Rodgers

PROMETHEUS'
DECLARATION OF LOVE FOR
THE VULTURE

ALAN Rodgers' first published fiction, "The Boy Who Came Back from the Dead," which ended *Masques II*, was nominated for a World Fantasy Award and tied for the Bram Stoker Award in Horror Writers of America's novelette category. It was HWA's first year of annual awards.

Then the boyish former editor of *Night Cry* wrote a novel called *The Children*, accepted by Bantam as a paperback original. He also placed another novel with them on a mere premise—a lengthy work-in-progress entitled *The Voice of Armageddon*.

Here, Rodgers' versatility is used to take an original poetic look at that time-honored tale at the root of all Frankenstein fiction. I note that he is a Leo astrologically, the one sign ruled by the sun, and doubt that gifted "Alano" must wait for Hercules' help in order to have his talents completely unbound.

PROMETHEUS' DECLARATION OF LOVE FOR THE VULTURE

Alan Rodgers

In the ten thousand years
    that I lay chained
    on this mountain
    in the Caucasus,
when you would wake me each day
    with your beak upon my belly,
        tear my gut,
        and feast upon my liver,
I came to love you, bird.

It seems to me
    that you have always
    understood our love
    better than I could—

for I every moment loathed you,
    despised you,
    plotted against you
        (but came
        to *know* your touch,
        to tell your mood
            by the feel of your spittle
            in my veins . . .
        and even to be jealous,
            though I could not
            then confess it,
            of the carrion
                I would sometimes smell
                on your breath)
—for I saw sunlight catch
    on a tear
    falling from your eye
the day Heracles freed me.
It haunted me,
and does so still.

O Eater of My Liver:
come away with me,
    the love
        who has returned to you;
follow me
    out into the corridors
    of light and pain and love
that are the world.

And live with me.

THE "NEW" HORROR

SOMEBODY I work with thought I wouldn't like what Rod Serling's *The Twilight Zone Magazine* proclaimed a *new* horror; what others call "splatterpunk." I mentioned my pleasure with Rex Miller's *Slob* and even such tales I wrote myself as "The Book of Webster's" (*Night Cry*) and "Public Places" (*Pulphouse*). What *I* don't like, I said, is stories that *aren't*. Isolated bloody events, nightmares or daydreams produced not by muse but by drugs or booze. And the premise that shock is suspense; improbable intercourse, story line. Or the notion that 1989 (or 1999, or 2189) is bound to be better or worse than earlier years; that history is shit. Or the assumption that terse little words I first heard my drunken uncle use must always supplant the widely acceptable ones and also disgust people. I do not like the notion that the neat dudes all make out with somebody, or that the mad, rad people are cool *because* they ripped off their folks, dwell in shooting galleries, join gangs, overlook any atrocity, and defile their nation's flags instead of identifying America's faults and correcting them.

But I also don't enjoy authors playing ostrich—who pretend it's still Stoker's, Lovecraft's, or young Stephen King's period. Writers who brandish old bigotries as if recently vindicated in some people's opinion. Who write about street kids who say "damn" when they mean "fuck." Who don't intend to learn what's happening because it might contaminate their finer sensibilities.

If "new" horror is really new—not a recycling of the early and brilliant works of Harlan Ellison (his stories are still around, happily)—it's probably involved with exercises in freedom and observations by a writer of yet one *more* crummy condition that cries out for exposure. It must be told with a directness that strives for candor— sometimes a candor that elicits more laughs than cries. The humor is of that outrageous variety typical of people who hope it may make this week's nightmare *stop*— magically. At its worst, "new" horror can be choppy, or filled with a certain belligerence; with vulgarity. At its best, it's a marvelous use of American freedom to say or do that which the writer hopes devoutly will make one particular, monstrous social fuck-up leave our griefstricken lives forever.

Now and then, the new horror pinpoints or expresses insights that have not been voiced before, not with such clarity—or not for a long time. It alarms us about big wrongs, problems, lies—and if there's nothing new about that in fiction, exactly, there's nothing wrong with it either. Ask one of the teachers present in this book about the tantalizing and haunting writers of classics who began their careers that way—or culminated them with such shocking and revelatory masterpieces.

The "new" horror stories should not be excluded; nor should they exclude other styles. Exciting storytelling should never be excluded. And neither should people.

R. Patrick Gates

LONG LIPS

HE came snarling into the tiny world of published novelists in October 1988 with an Onyx title that other novelists wonder how they overlooked: *Fear*. *Publishers Weekly* called it "a highly charged chiller" and Rick McCammon described it as "an excellent and chilling debut."

Here's the *first* short story by R. P. (Randy; his wife is Pat) Gates, born October 14, 1954, a free-lance journalist with an award from *Ladies Home Journal* in his past. *LHJ* might blanch and tremble at the directions taken by Gates. His second novel will be a "modern-day Hansel and Gretel for adults," he reports from Massachusetts, called *Grim Memorials*. As for your editor, one thing is certain: *my* lips are *sealed!*

LONG LIPS

R. Patrick Gates

FOG SLIPS IN FROM THE SEA like blood sliding from a wound. It drips over the seawall, stains the cobblestone streets. It chills the air like the icy breath of Death. With it slinks a shadow; thin, quick, ethereal. It dances like fine rain in the night. It slithers and laughs, filling the night with a hideous tinkling, like razor-edged slivers of glass ripping into dead flesh . . .

She paused, listened, and shivered. She closed her coat against the fog and hurried toward the friendly lights of the tavern. A black cat skittered through the fog, howling like a human baby in pain. Chills ran over her spine like ice down the back of her blouse. She gasped, exhaled loudly. Dead laughter floated on the fog but she mistook it for the echo of her own frightened breathing. She didn't see the shadow dancing close behind her.

The music from the tavern was distant, fading in the mist. It sounded like a dirge played in the depths of a mausoleum. The woman shivered, fumbled out a cigarette. A man stepped out of the fog.

"Good evening," he said in a deep but vaporous voice. She relaxed. Just another john. She lit the cigarette and ran her tongue seductively over her lips.

"Hello, sugar," she said in a sweet southern drawl. "What can I do you for?"

The man smiled, showing luminescent teeth.

"You shy, honey? That's okay. You can tell me. What you want Mama to do?" She peered into his face, but the swirling mist shrouded it. She could see only his eyes. They were deep purple and seemed to glow.

She shook off the sudden chill that rippled her skin, took his hand. "I can't help, sugar, if you won't talk to me."

He pointed to a nearby alley.

"Now we gettin' somewheres! Come on, don't be scared."

In the alley, her open blouse revealed large brown breasts frosted with mist. His tongue glided over them, licking them dry. She giggled at the sandpaper feeling. He pushed her to her knees. She unzipped his pants. He sighed.

"*Oh* my God!" she said in amazement. "I'm sorry, sugar, but I can't. I—" Her voice was cut off suddenly. She gave a muffled cry, then gagged. The fog carried away the sound of her death and the thin, mean laughter rejoicing in it.

"What have we got?" The captain barked the question as he stepped out of the cruiser. His voice was hoarse from too many cigarettes and too many years in the damp, seaside town. He was a short man, stocky and wide. With a little more height on him he would have made a fine football player. His face was windburned and weathered, making him look more like a lobster fisherman than a cop. His hair was getting gray. He never combed it, leaving it to wave wildly in the wind.

"There's . . . ah, been a homicide, of sorts," said a tall lieutenant named Hedstrom, trying to hold back a lecherous grin.

"No shit, Dick Tracy? I thought we had a mad jaywalker on the loose."

An unsuppressible giggle bubbled from Hedstrom.

"What's the MO?" the captain asked, scowling and heading into the alley. Hedstrom giggled again and his face turned bright red.

The captain pushed past him. The dead hooker, covered by a worn woolen blanket, lay against a trash can. The captain knelt, lifted the blanket from her body, and almost jumped back in horror. He'd seen murdered corpses before but never anything like this. He covered his shock—he was too much of a pro to let it show— yet he felt it, inside. It assaulted his innermost being.

She was half-naked, but he barely saw that. His eyes were drawn to her face. Her eyes were open. They stared at him and the horror of death lingered in them. She might have been a pretty girl once, but the ravages of her profession and the violence of her death now made her ugly. Long strands of milky fluid hung from both nostrils. Her jaw had been broken and hung on her upper chest. Her face and neck were blotched with bloody bruises.

The captain stared out the window. His feet rested on the top of the old desk and a cigarette hung from his mouth. Opposite him sat Lieutenant Hedstrom, the medical examiner, and the DA.

"This isn't for real," muttered the captain. The DA coughed and the captain pulled his eyes away from the window. "Is there any way the guy could be faking this?"

Hedstrom giggled.

"I mean," the captain continued after an angry glance at the lieutenant, "is there some way he can make it *appear* that he has—" The captain fumbled for the right word.

"Fellatioed his victim to death?" offered Hedstrom. "Maybe or-alicide, or headicide? How about blown away?"

"Knock it off!" barked the captain. He turned to the medical examiner. "Is there any way to *fake* this—make it *appear* he killed her this way?"

The medical examiner sighed. "Not in this case. Abrasions at the back of the throat, coupled with sperm and skin cells found in the victim's mouth and on her teeth, prove conclusively that the murder took place the way I described."

The captain took a deep breath. "So it looks like we've got a killer with an unusual modus operandi."

"He shouldn't be too hard to find," Hedstrom commented. "All we've got to do is look for a guy with a third leg."

The captain glared at him.

"Actually," the medical examiner interrupted, "that's not far from the truth. By measuring the bruises in the victim's throat, I'd say the killer has a twenty-inch penis—with a circumference of seven inches."

"Holy Christmas," mumbled the DA. "You know, if we catch this bastard, there's no way we can *try* him! It'd be a side show. If we catch him, he'll have to be put away quietly. Heaven help us if the papers get wind of this!"

"Putting him on trial is the least of my worries," the captain answered. "But I do want to keep this out of the papers. We'll put out a standard release saying the guy is a strangler; nothing more." He pointed at Hedstrom. "Circulate a description of the murderer's, ah, anatomy to the hookers in the red-light district, but do it discreetly. You'd also better check the doctors and hospitals within a fifty-mile radius. It seems to me there should be a record somewhere if this guy is such a freak."

Hedstrom nodded.

"And double the night patrol downtown. We're going to crack down on the johns until we find this guy. Anyone soliciting sex is to be picked up and examined."

Hedstrom started to laugh, then smothered it quickly under the captain's harsh stare.

The sign read: BLACK LEATHER CAFÉ. When the door opened, the stench of stale smoke poured out of it like steam from a caldron and mingled with the sea fog. A shadow, hidden by the mist, slid under the sign and lingered near the entrance. The door opened and two young men holding hands came out. They paused in the open doorway to kiss, passionately. The shadow slid past them, inside.

The smoke was thick. The smell of sweat and urine was strong. The flickering jukebox played low, perverted jazz. Conversation was low and rumbling, stopped when the door shut. Bloodshot eyes under visored leather caps looked up. Mustaches bristled, chains rattled, leather squeaked as the men in the bar strained to get a look at the newcomer. Lips were licked, eyes winked, heads nodded, but the stranger in the long black cape stared through them. Moving as if he rode a cushioned wave of air, he traversed the floor and went into the bathroom. A collective chill ran through the patrons of the bar, was shrugged off. The conversations resumed.

In a corner, a thin young man in tight pants and a fishnet jersey eyed the stranger as he floated past. Their eyes met momentarily and the young man nodded. A trembling smile quivered on his lips. He knew what the glance meant. He had exchanged the same glance with men hundreds of times at the café. This time, though, there was something different. A thrill like nothing he'd ever felt coursed through his loins like an electrical current.

He ran his tongue over dry lips and followed the stranger into the bathroom.

The captain stood in the doorway of the men's room, fought back the sickness rising in him. "All right, you know what to do," he said to the officers outside the door. "Question everyone who was in here tonight. Move it! Stop gawking like a bunch of idiots."

The officers moved off to carry out his orders and Hedstrom stepped forward. "What do we call this, Chief?" he asked. A sarcastic smile twitched at the corners of his mouth. "A *homo*cide?"

"There's someone to see you, Captain."

The door opened and a woman in black entered the office. She was in her fifties, with gray hair and stern, rock-hard features. The first impression the captain had was that she looked like Indira Gandhi. The second impression was that she was a weirdo. She remained near the door, eyes staring straight ahead, lips moving silently as if she were reciting the rosary.

"Can I help you, ma'am?" the captain asked, making a mental note to chew out whoever had let her in his office.

"I know what he is," she said.

A chill ran over the captain's brow.

"And I know how to stop him," she added. She continued speaking and the captain listened with amusement, fascination, and, finally, dread.

The DA and Hedstrom were back in the captain's office. The former smoked a cigarette nervously while Hedstrom stared at the ceiling.

"Before I say anything, I want to get one thing straight," the captain said to Hedstrom. "This is no joking matter. We have a serious situation on our hands that has reached a point where I'm ready to take drastic measures. If you feel the need to joke— *don't!*"

Hedstrom coughed into his hand and nodded sheepishly.

"What I'm about to suggest is unorthodox but at this point I'll try anything. If we let this go on any longer, it's going to attract national attention. The local media has been cooperative, but that can only last so long. Sooner or later, this story is going to break big. That's why I want you *both* to listen to me seriously."

The DA and Hedstrom nodded.

"As you may know already, I had a visitor yesterday who was a little strange. Strange or not, she made sense about how to nab this guy."

"What did she say?" Hedstrom asked.

"She claimed to be psychic and most of what she said was crap, delusions about the killer being a demon; she called him an *incubus,* which I gathered is some kind of sexual vampire. But that isn't important. While she was babbling she gave me an idea of how we can get him. We need someone he *can't kill.*"

The DA looked mystified and leaned forward. "I don't under-stand."

"She said this guy feeds on death created through sex. I think that's true, though not in a literal sense. If we can get someone, a hooker—even a gay—who can handle his size, we might frustrate him to the point where we can nab him. We bait this guy with someone he can't kill in his usual manner and, with surveillance, we'll grab him. Or at least have an eyewitness description."

"You really think it will work?" the DA asked. "I think he's too smart. He's been baiting *us* all along."

"Yeah," Hedstrom interrupted, "this guy's been a real *master baiter.*"

The captain ignored Hedstrom.

"Yes, I think it'll work." He turned to Hedstrom. "And *you,* Mr. Comedy, are going to find the right bait!"

Hedstrom's face turned crimson. For the first time in days, the captain smiled.

*   *   *

The phone rang in the middle of the night. The captain started from sleep, cursing loudly. Without turning on the light, he fumbled on his nightstand for the receiver.

"Chief? It's me, Hedstrom. I think I've got something."

The captain threw back the covers, got out of bed. Next to him, his wife groaned and rolled over. "What is it?" he asked quietly.

"I called a friend of mine in San Francisco. We went to college together; now he's a pornographic film producer. One of his stars is willing to help us. You ever hear of the movie *Deep Throat?*"

"Yeah."

"I've got someone who makes Linda Lovelace look like a lollipop sucker. I've got Long Lips," Hedstrom said proudly.

"What the hell is *that?*"

"*Lorna Lipps*, of course—Linda Lovelace's *suck*cessor! She'll do it for ten grand plus expenses. Pretty expensive blow job, but considering the risks, she won't do it for less."

The captain nodded his head in the dark. "Okay. Get her on a plane out here and keep her *quiet.*"

The captain was surprised by how tall and blond she was. He wondered briefly if she was a natural blonde. She towered four inches over him, and he was five-nine. She was a pretty woman, not scuzzy-looking like most porno queens. There was a little age showing in the wrinkles around her eyes and in the tiny lines at the corners of her mouth, but those small flaws were easy to overlook when gazing into her large, crystal-blue eyes. They held and mesmerized. Her mouth was full, sensual under a thin, noble nose. Her chin melted gracefully into a neck that was long and aristocratic. Her shoulders were broad, supporting breasts that were huge, firm mounds pushing out the seams of her tank top.

The captain caressed her with his eyes and found it hard to look away. She smiled at him and cocked her hips. Her hot pants looked as if they'd been painted on. They rode up her thighs, creased around her crotch and firm buttocks. The captain licked suddenly dry lips.

"I'm pleased to meet you, Miss Lipps."

"I can see that." She smiled down at him.

"Did Lieutenant Hedstrom give you the plan?" he asked nervously and crossed his legs.

"He gave it to me, all right," she said.

The captain mumbled, "I should have known."

"Don't worry," she said, placing a leather travel bag on the desk. "He also told me what I'm supposed to do." She opened the bag to pull out a pair of black satin pants and a red see-through peasant blouse. She laid them carefully on the desk.

"First things first. You have some money for me?"

The captain fumbled an envelope out of his pocket and handed it across the desk to her. She took it, tucked it inside the bag.

"While I get changed into my working clothes, why don't you give me the details of this operation?" She slid the tank top over her head. Her breasts bulged and lifted before flopping free of the stretchy material. They made a soft smacking sound as they settled back against her body—full, luscious things with small, ripe-red, perpetually hard nipples.

The captain couldn't take his eyes off her. She smiled at him and ran her hands over her breasts. She unbuckled her belt and slid the tight shorts seductively down her thighs. With a sharp intake of breath, the captain noticed she was wearing no underwear. He smiled.

She was indeed a natural blonde.

Hedstrom clicked the radio off and watched Lorna Lipps standing on the corner in her tight black pants and flimsy blouse. He smiled, glanced at the captain in the seat next to him. He was holding his head as if it hurt.

"She'll give you a real *headache* if you let her, Chief," he chuckled.

The captain frowned, but not at Hedstrom. The thought of banging Lorna Lipps had certainly crossed his mind. He knew he'd had his chance when she stripped in his office. But unlike Hedstrom, the captain had a conflict; namely, marriage. Even though his wife showed all of her forty-five years, he didn't think he could ever cheat on her.

Not that he hadn't been tempted.

"Where'd she go?" Hedstrom asked suddenly. The captain glanced up. The corner was empty. Lorna was gone.

*   *   *

The captain sipped coffee, looked at the clock. It was 3 A.M., and Lorna Lipps had been missing for five hours. A dragnet had failed to pick up any trace of her. The captain was afraid he was going to have to chalk her up as another victim. The problem was, she wasn't just another victim; she was a celebrity of sorts. He was responsible for her.

The telephone rang, startling him. He snapped up the receiver. "Hello?"

The voice was distant and weak. His heart skipped a beat.

It was Lorna Lipps.

The small, dingy hotel room was at the end of a long, dark corridor. The captain hurried toward the room, his footsteps echoing like ghostly shots. The building smelled of sweat and garbage; it reeked of perversion, and of death itself.

He called Lorna's name, heard a muffled explosion. Panting, he reached for the doorknob, afraid of what he would find. The knob felt as if it was coated with Vaseline. He opened the door. Gasped.

The room was filled with thick, pungent smoke. Waving his arms, the captain made his way inside. The air began to clear. Lorna lay on the bed, naked, covered head to toe in gooey black slime.

She was alive.

"Where is he?" the captain asked, his gun ready.

"There," she said, pointing at the wall. "And there," she added, pointing to the ceiling and floor. The smoke was escaping into the hallway and the room was clear enough now for the captain to see.

From the ceiling hung a hand, suspended by a string of gelatinous slime. The walls were covered with bits and pieces of goo-covered flesh: an eyeball over the door; part of a foot in the corner; an ear plastered against the grimy window. On the floor, he saw the twenty-inch piece of flesh that had been the murder weapon.

"What the hell happened?"

Lorna Lipps shrugged and smiled weakly. "Some guys just go to pieces when they can't get off."

Ralph Rainwater, Jr.

SINNERS

RALPH Rainwater was an Air Force officer's "brat" with degrees in political science and Russian literature when he graduated from Writer's Digest School (in 1986) with one of the rare A+ finals I parceled out during four years of student- and self-abuse. Ralph, Kathie Ramsland, D. W. Taylor, Jeannette Hopper, and Mark McNease were all budding writers with huge promise from the outset of their WDS studies. They had in common a powerful urge to write for a living—and talent.

Rainwater is a man with insights and ideas who admits his characters are "rooted in tradition and place," "obsessed with religion." Last summer, he wrote to announce he was joining the Air Force and even his reason for doing so seemed stunning to me: He felt "a responsibility to produce more and better" fiction and no longer believed that was possible in civilian life.

An unusual man, Ralph. An unusual writer.

SINNERS

Ralph Rainwater, Jr.

I'D ALWAYS ADMIRED THE WAY DAVID wedded intellect with action. But this latest terrorism went too far. Riding our bikes through the quiet back roads of the Georgian countryside, once again I gathered my courage and told him so.

"Listen," he replied, "you're like a broken record. You keep repeating the same old doubts, yet you never convince me they're justified."

"That's not fair," I argued. "You know that. Even when I'm right, you *always* win our arguments!"

"Then you should learn to debate better. In any case, if you don't like what we—and I emphasize that 'we'—are going to do, why are you pedaling alongside me now?"

"Because you're my older brother," I said simply. Given our rough family history, I knew this answer would soften him.

In the dark separating us, I saw him nod and I sensed the smile on David's face. "Okay, then, because you're my *younger* brother, I'll try to explain one more time." He paused for a moment to collect his thoughts.

In the silence, the only sounds we heard in the still, humid night were those of our bikes rolling over the crumbling country road and of millions of crickets singing their mating songs. With no moon overhead, the weak headlights on our handlebars illuminated only a few feet of ground at a time, barely giving us enough opportunity to swerve around the abundant potholes and occasional crushed animals.

The canvas bag, containing a plastic human skeleton David had ordered from a novelty horror catalogue, hung around his neck, resting on his back. Also inside the bag were several accessories: a claw-toothed hammer, some nails, and three pre-cut lengths of rope (in case pounding in nails proved too loud or difficult).

Finally, he spoke again. "We're agreed that this whole area is stuck in the past by willful ignorance, right?"

"Right."

"And the biggest holdback keeping these rural people from joining the twentieth century is their primitive brand of religion?"

"Okay," I said.

"So it follows, then, that anything done to discredit religion is good. Think of what our little book did."

By "our" book, he meant the parody of the New Testament he'd written, "The Breeder's Digest Condensed New Testament," in which all the human characters had been replaced by dogs. I had merely provided a few ideas and helped distribute it by leaving copies in strategic points around town—at night, of course. The parody, printed on our home computer, created a stir that lasted for weeks. The local paper had been filled with letters from ardent churchgoers and civic leaders, expressing outrage and shock.

I'd had doubts at first about belittling a holy book. But we bathed in private glory over the vehement reactions our parody's anonymous authors had caused. The faithful had revealed their insecurity, just as David predicted they would.

"Yeah, you were right *that* time. But isn't this going to extremes?" I asked.

"Yes, it is. But no more extreme than these fanatics are. It's 'an eye for an eye,' Mark."

"We're talking about nailing a *skeleton* to their cross. They'll go nuts!"

"Maybe not. Consider what their fanaticism is based on. That

they've *seen* God. He lives amongst them, *inside* their church."
He paused, waiting for comment. When I offered none, David
continued, "Think—who could believe such a fiction? Only the
most ignorant, the poorest types. And that's precisely who belong
to this country church. You've seen them around town. You know
what the congregation is like. That freak this morning is a perfect
example."

I didn't want to think about him. There'd been too much
weirdness to that skinny, ill-dressed man's manner as he exhorted
everyone in the town square to join "The Church of an Angry
God." There'd been an unnatural gleam in his eye, a too-frenzied
spinning of his arms. He kept shouting, "Praise God! He has come!
Come to step on those who have stepped on us! Vengeance is
His!"

"Well then, if they're not going to get violent, what *do* you think
will happen?" I demanded.

"Imagine all these zealots coming to worship tomorrow." My
brother sounded excited now. "These are people who save welfare
checks to buy Cadillacs. That car is a sacred symbol of the 'good
life' to them. It's a *religious* token! And then, with their perpetually
pre-scientific minds, they enter the church and stare at their cross!
Instead of *imagining* Jesus . . . this *thing* will be up there. A skel-
eton! Signifying how dead their religion really is.

"Can't you hear them now?" David went on. " 'Oh Lordy,
Lordy—someone's come in here and done the Devil's work!'
Don't you *see*? If we pull this off, the congregation will think that
God would never have *allowed* such a transgression!"

"So He was never there at all." I nodded, understanding.

"Exactly," David replied. "Don't you think this little joke is
worth it to end such fanaticism?"

No; I didn't. David's escapades had always been contrary to my
nature. His intellect was somehow too sharp, his condemnation of
others' blindnesses too unforgiving. I didn't have the courage of
his convictions.

Yet here again I was acquiescing to his plans, a faithful though
doubting sidekick. Why? Because David was the only person in
our atavistic town I could conceivably admire. Because we were
both sharp, and all I saw around us were blunt, dull surfaces. Be-
cause where my brother went, I had to follow.

It was as simple as that.

By now our pedaling had taken us to an impoverished back-water area nearly fifteen miles from town. Scattered here and there were ramshackle, decaying homes occupied primarily by un-employed or, at best, seasonably employed, poor families.

By the light of day the homes were embarrassments; eyesores. Front porches sagged, roofs had holes, broken windows had news-paper covering them. In the yard around each of these shacks lay assorted garbage and the wrecks of old Cadillacs. Anybody driving through this part of the country during sunset usually spotted the massive families economically clutched by sitting together on rusted chairs or splintering steps. The adults would be smoking, the children chatting.

Having until recently given up on prosperity in *this* life, these people clung to the promise of reward in the next with a peasant's simple faith in reward and retribution from a personal God. Not for them was God some abstract Deity Who, if He existed at all, did so as a mass of disincorporated energy. To them, God was an angry old white man with a long beard Who'd never forgiven people for killing His son. They awaited the sound of His massive feet stomping across the land—an all-powerful giant Who'd set things right.

For the past month their message had been this: The wait was *over*.

And sitting in the midst of this poverty, the nucleus around which every one of these families revolved, was the church. We saw its square, whitewashed outline beckoning to us from out of the darkness when we approached.

We hid our bikes in some kudzu growth a few yards from the front entrance. The entire area was deserted, but I couldn't shake off the feeling that somebody was watching us. I mentioned this to David. He shrugged it off.

We'd been prepared to break a window and climb in, if need be, but the front door's knob turned easily. We slipped quietly into the empty church, David carrying our sack of goodies. At first, there seemed nothing unusual. There were the expected polished pews, the imitation stained-glass windows, the podium sitting on a dais in front.

We were, however, surprised to see a life-size representation of the crucified Christ on the large oak cross behind the podium. Fundamentalist churches tend not to believe in such graphic depictions. They smack of "graven images."

It was when we neared the cross that another oddity struck home with me: Unlike most such figures, where Jesus' head is down and his eyes closed, this one's head remained erect, his eyes open. Even more disconcerting was the unmistakable sneer his lips were set in.

"How fitting," David said.

"Fitting? It's downright *scary!*" I said.

"Well, at least we know for sure what his church is about," he replied and walked steadily forward. He stopped when he realized I had not followed. "This statue is likely to be heavy. I'll need your help in taking it down."

I couldn't pull my gaze from Jesus' eyes. Whoever had painted them had given the sculpting an almost sentient quality. "I've really got the creeps from this," I admitted. "It truly looks like he's watching us."

David frowned. "Sometimes, Mark, you show yourself to be yet a child. Hurry now. It does us no good to waste time chatting. The *real* danger is that of late-night worshipers dropping by."

The idea of fanatics catching us in the act of desecrating their church scared me enough to rush to David's side and hold the bag open for him. While he busied himself trying to yank out a large nail pounded through the left hand, I stared at the front door, nervously expecting it to fly open any second with a contingent of pitchfork-carrying parishioners intending to skewer us.

"This might take a bit longer than I'd planned," David said ruminatively. "The nails are pounded flush with the plaster, so I'll have to dig into the statue itself to get a grip on the nail head." I managed a nod. A minute later, when David spoke again, there was something foreign in his voice: uncertainty. "Mark . . . look at this."

I looked. Where David had chipped away the plaster, it was not a chalky-white, but blood-red.

"These people go to some lengths for realism, huh?" He smiled, composure outwardly restored. "Want to bet it bleeds when I pull this nail out?"

I shook my head. "David, don't do it!"

"I was only joking," David said. Grabbing the thick nail with the hammer's claws, he pulled. The nail moved perhaps a half inch. He tugged again. This time it slid out nearly all the way.

And a thin stream of blood followed. It trickled steadily from the wound, onto the dais floor. "Oh, shit," David said.

I didn't say anything because my feet were flying up the carpeted aisle, taking me outside toward the bikes. If David was stupid enough to continue this stunt, I thought, he'd have to do it alone.

He wasn't stupid, however. He was never that. His feet pounded close behind me.

I tried to turn the doorknob, to leave in one smooth motion. But it was locked now, and momentum caused me to smack hard into the heavy wood and bounce off. By the time I'd regained my feet, David was already rattling the door. Frantically. Still, it refused to open.

The tinkle of metal striking the floor caused both of us to spin around. What I saw literally made me pee my pants.

The statue's head twisted back and forth, as if stretching its neck muscles. Its mouth changed from a sneer into a chilling, mean smile. Its arms and legs flexed plaster muscles, causing the nails binding them to pop out.

I heard myself screaming incoherently. Even though he surely was as frightened as I, David kept his wits enough to speak. "Get *away* from us! I'll knock your goddamn *head* off!" he yelled, still clutching the hammer in his white-knuckled hand.

Hesitantly, as if not entirely confident of its balance, the statue took one single step forward. When it began to speak, however, its voice seemed to come from the church itself, not the plaster-filled mouth. It was an appropriately deep voice, filled with authority—and menace.

"By the depth of their hatred did they create me. By their need for revenge against the fortunate, the well-constituted, did my suffering children cause me to be. I was created in their image; their faith sustains me."

While he spoke, he moved steadily forward, arms outstretched in a welcoming embrace. When the figure was some ten feet distant, David threw the hammer at it with all his youthful strength. It struck, bounced off, taking a chunk of dark, red plaster with it. The statue paid no heed.

"I am yet but a weak god. My children are few, and simple of intellect. I need an anger fed by knowledge." The head veered toward my brother. "I need . . . *you,*" it said, and stared directly at David.

My brother scooped me up with a brave vigor born of hysteria and charged toward the nearest window. Numb of mind, I did nothing to resist. An instant later, amid shards of broken glass, I landed on the grass outside. Somehow, I escaped with only a few cuts—

But I was alone.

I leapt to my feet, ran to the window, and then discovered why David had not followed.

The god had him. My brother was locked in his embrace. Before my eyes, I saw the impossible: David, struggling in horror—but then his body began to take on an ethereal quality. Then, quite slowly, gradually—inexorably—it started to merge with the god's . . .

Until they were one.

Since David's back was to me, thankfully, I did not have to see the incalculable terror that must have been reflected in his young face.

Then they were gone.

Shock and adrenaline gave me the energy to pedal madly back home. An hour and a half later, I returned to the church with my disbelieving and disgruntled mother, her newest boyfriend, Max, and a very dubious, irascible policeman in tow.

We found nothing to corroborate my story. The statue was back in place, head down and eyes closed. The window had been repaired; even the shards of glass on the ground were gone, as were David's bike and the bag he'd carried inside the church.

They all thought David had run off, and that I'd used his disappearance to concoct this wild story, trying to explain away the trouble I'd obviously been in.

What none of them noticed, and I did not point out, however, was this: Embedded in the statue's face, David's own features could still be discerned, indelibly frozen in a grimace of awful terror.

Jeannette M. Hopper

SUNDAY BREAKFAST

THE homey things: Hopper is a young wife and mother. Lives in sunny California. End clichés, because Jeannette is tough as nails pulled out one by one. She is one of a growing number of women writing no-holds-barred fiction and wishing to God the clichés concerning their gender *would* end. In *How to Write Tales of Horror, Fantasy and Science Fiction,* which I edited, she said, ". . . Certain things *will* keep you from ever seeing your byline in print—sloppiness, awkward style, trite or boring ideas, and [over-familiar] characters." Regardless of gender.

Author of a strong story in the *Pulphouse* debut issue, another in the Greenbergs' *14 Vicious Valentines* (Avon, '88), and her own story collection *Expiration Dates* ('87), J. M. is rarely guilty of the mistakes she cites. "Sunday Breakfast" might be a tale only a woman could write—but a sardonic, hard-bitten, exciting woman. One of considerable talent.

SUNDAY BREAKFAST

Jeannette M. Hopper

HAVING BEEN BEDRIDDEN FOR NEARLY TEN months with an impressive list of real and imagined ailments, Carlotta Pierce was quite a surprise to her daughter-in-law, Maureen, who found Carlotta sitting at the kitchen table, bathed in golden Sunday-morning sunshine. Permed white hair glinted violet against the blue-green backdrop of Monterey Bay visible through the patio doors. Carlotta ignored Maureen's entrance and continued her concentrated chewing.

"Mom, what's that you're eating?" asked Maureen, steadying herself with one hand on the kitchen counter. The shock of finding the woman suddenly mobile was compounded by the sight of her breakfasting on raw meat—three-dollars-and-eighty-nine-cents-a-pound raw meat, from the looks of it. Maureen had bought it the day before for their Sunday barbecue.

Carlotta appeared not to have heard the question. She went about the systematic task of ripping chunks of muscle and gristle from the T-bone, mashing it between toothless gums, swallowing

124

through a throat grown accustomed to Cream of Wheat and pureed vegetables.

Maureen scratched at her scalp, pitching a drapery of auburn curls over her cheek. This she tossed back, making a mental note to allow time for a shampoo before church. She glanced at the clock and calculated the time needed to cook breakfast, take her shower, get Tricia up, bathed, and dressed, feed Carlotta—or would that be necessary after her meal of steak tartare? Looking over her shoulder at the woman by the wide glass doors, Maureen asked, "Will you be wanting any cereal when you're done, Mother?" Carlotta grunted, shook her head. "Okay. Then you just go on with your breakfast. I don't suppose Andrew will mind. He doesn't care about anything else you do."

From the back, Carlotta looked like any octogenarian having a go at a tough steak: shoulders hunched, head bobbing with the effort, ears sliding up and down the sides of her oversized scalp. Her jaws emitted dull clicks as the thin muscle bulged and hollowed. Maureen couldn't tell whether the old lady was enjoying the meat, or simply satisfied to have gotten her way once more.

Maureen put coffee on to drip, then stood at the sink and gazed out over the sloping backyard, down on the glittering Pacific water. This should be Paradise, she thought, but I'm stuck caring for a senile invalid who takes, takes, takes, and never gives a damned thing back but shit, piss, and vomit. Not that that's anything new for Carlotta Pierce . . . She looks like she's ready to croak, but with my luck, she'll live forever. Maureen let a deep, weary sigh escape, and the silence was broken by Andrew's arrival in the dining room.

"God," he moaned, "didn't sleep worth shit last night. Damned kids down on the beach till all hours, drinkin' and carryin' on. Goddamn access laws and the—Mom, what in holy hell are you *eating?*" He'd stopped in mid-gripe, crouched halfway to the chair, butt poised a foot from the cushion. Black hair lay glued to his head, but his eyes were a startled electric blue. When he received no answer from either woman, he repeated his question without profanities.

"An early lunch, I think," Maureen said.

Andrew Pierce stared at his wife. "You just gonna let her—eat that?"

"She's up, isn't she? She's eating the first solid food she's had in months. Besides, we can't go calling Dr. Patterson just because Mom's suddenly taken it into her head to eat raw steak." Maureen brought two cups of steaming coffee to the dining room table and set one in front of her husband. She kept the other in her hands while she stood behind the chair opposite him. "He'd just tell us what he's told us the other times: 'Keep an eye on her and make sure she doesn't hurt herself.' You know she only does these things for attention."

"Well, she *got* it, all right." Andrew smeared his hair back from his forehead, blew into his coffee. After taking a cautious sip and grimacing at the heat, he asked, "Is Tricia fed and ready for services?"

"You kidding? I'm letting her sleep in. She was cranky last night, and I don't want her missing another day of Sunday school."

Andrew replaced his cup on the table and blinked. "But I just went in to check on her, and she's not in her room."

"She's probably in the bathroom. You know six-year-olds—"

"No, I checked both bathrooms. I thought she'd be in here with you."

"Oh, God," murmured Maureen, splashing the tablecloth as she nearly dropped her cup. She padded down the long hallway, peeking in doors and calling her daughter's name. Andrew followed close behind.

"I told you," he said to her robed back, "I looked in the bathrooms, in Mom's room, and—"

"Oh, damn, damn, *damn*," chanted Maureen as she opened closets and turned back draperies. "Tricia Eileen Pierce, if you're hiding from me, so help me I'll blister your little behind, but good!" No reply came, and after a moment, Maureen hurried into her own bedroom.

She threw on jeans and a sweatshirt, poked her feet into loafers. Forgetting about her mother-in-law in the kitchen, she trotted down the front steps, crushing shade-happy snails beneath her heels, and ran to the front gate. "Tricia!" she yelled. Her voice was all but lost in the thunder of rolling surf. *"Tricia!"* Pulling tendrils of copper hair from her mouth, she shouted orders to Andrew, who peered inside his tarp-covered sailboat in the driveway. "Go down to the beach. See if there are any signs of her down there. I'll walk up the road and check the dunes!"

They met back at the front gate, both without success, and Maureen leaned against the rock wall. "What if she's drowned? I *told* you we should have taken her for swimming lessons, but *no-o*, your mother wouldn't hear of it. And Tricia, naive child that she is, takes your mother's word as law!"

Andrew shuffled in the sandy gravel, gazed off across the dunes. "Don't make this all *my* fault. I don't like having to look after Mother, but she'd raise hell if I tried to put her in a home." His feet stopped moving and he shoved his hands up into his pockets.

"Your mother," sneered Maureen, "would probably eat her roommate."

He turned to her, his brows knotted, mouth set in a hard line. "That doesn't happen anymore, and you know it. Mother never actually *ate* anyone." He snorted bitterly. "Hell, do you think I'd have let her move in with us if there was any danger whatsoever that she had inherited the curse?"

"What about your sister? Sammy bit her nipple off when he was two months old!"

Andrew swallowed, looked away. "That could happen to anyone."

"But when it happens in *your* family . . ."

"Sammy never did anything again."

"He's only two. Give him time."

Andrew pushed away from the wall and started for the house. "This is getting us nowhere. I'm going to call the Adamses and the Hendersons. Maybe Tricia walked down to see Judy or Dwayne."

Maureen trudged off in the opposite direction, toward the field across the road. Tricia could have fallen into the tall grass, or become lost in the thick stand of trees on the other side. Maureen refused to think of the possibility that her child had been . . . kidnapped.

Twenty minutes later, after searching the field and coppice and finding only a mangled cat, she returned to the house. As she approached the door, she heard Andrew screaming angrily inside.

She found him standing in the middle of the kitchen, staring in disbelief at Carlotta. The old woman had finished her steak; she was now working hard on a pile of raw liver.

"First Tricia disappears and now this," yelled Andrew. "What the hell is going *on* around here?"

Maureen, hands held before her, approached her mother-in-law slowly. "Now, Mother," she said as if to a child, her teeth clenched until they ached, "we don't eat that until it's cooked. Why don't you give it to me, and I'll cook it for you?" Her smile was strained. She knew that if she didn't get the slimy organ from the old woman, she'd come apart inside and stuff it down that scrawny throat. "Please, Mom . . . just give it to me."

Carlotta hugged the wobbling flap of meat to her chest, cuddling it. Streams of liquid like tobacco spit squirted between her bony fingers. She shook her head vehemently, her wet brown eyes locked on Maureen's. Her mouth worked like some senile monkey's to gum the glob inside. Then, while Andrew and Maureen looked on in disgust, she tore off another strip and swallowed it without chewing.

"I can't take this," whined Andrew. "A man can handle only so much, even from his own mother!"

Maureen glared at his back as she stumbled down the hall toward the den. She felt her face grow hot; the itch of anger crawled across her shoulders, building to a scream. After all, the old woman was *his* mother, not hers.

She lurched forward and yanked the liver from Carlotta's grasp. Enraged, the old woman clawed at Maureen's arms, drawing blood with unfiled fingernails. Fresh red streaks mixed with the slimy brown juices of the liver, and for a moment the organ was strained between the two women, pulled taut like a wad of taffy.

Then it broke.

Carlotta smashed backward into the patio doors, bowing the safety glass. Tiny spider-cracks appeared at the corners near the aluminum casing, but the old woman bounced back, colliding with Maureen where she landed, seated on the edge of the dining room carpet. Both halves of the liver had flown through the kitchen to land on the counter; one lay in the sink near the disposal, and the other had slid into the crevice between the microwave oven and the refrigerator.

Maureen shoved Carlotta off and struggled to her feet. "You stinking cow," she growled. She backed away from the old woman's still-clawing hands, into the dining area.

The revelation struck Maureen full-force, driving her into the edge of the table. "No!" she cried, waving her arms to ward off the advancing horror. "*Not*—no . . . you couldn't have—you *wouldn't* have!" She dodged Carlotta and ran to the refrigerator, where she touched the red mass wedged between it and the oven. "Tricia . . ." she groaned, "oh, my poor baby . . ."

Maureen wiped her face on her sleeve and turned to face her mother-in-law. "What have you done with the rest of her?" Maureen demanded. Her voice was icy, measured, almost calm. "You couldn't have eaten her bones, could you? No, I don't think so." Maureen's hand fell upon the bread knife.

The old woman's rheumy eyes followed Maureen's hand as the fingers curled around the rosewood handle. Her mouth curved and stretched with moist smacks.

Blade in hand, Maureen advanced on the frail figure before her. "Your own granddaughter," she wailed. "And on *Sunday!*"

The long knife sliced through Carlotta's face and breast as easily as it had sliced through the air. Dark-red droplets rained on Maureen's hair, blending with it, and drizzled down her arms to run off her elbows. Carlotta's gnarled, blue-veined hands rose stiffly to her cheeks to spread blood into her cottony hair and blinded eyes. The blade descended once more and cut through the fingers of her right hand before plunging up to the handle behind her collar bone, where Maureen left it.

The younger woman stepped back, dazed, and whispered, "Die."

The sound of the front door opening—of light footsteps across the foyer—spun Maureen around. She gaped, both in relief and horror, at her daughter standing just inside the dining room. "Baby!" Maureen cried.

The old woman sank to her knees, remained there. Her eyes stayed wide open, obscured by thick red film. She stared at the Congoleum while her fingertips explored the knife handle.

Maureen ran to Tricia and threw her arms around the little girl. She drew her to her bosom tightly, rocking on her heels until she stood and brought the child up with her. She carried her to the kitchen counter, all the while ignoring the glazed expression on her mother-in-law's face. "What happened, love?" she begged, wiping at the streaks of blood on the girl's face. "Who did this to you? Where have you *been?*"

Andrew appeared in the doorway, hung there a moment, then rushed to his mother.

"I was sure she'd eaten Tricia," said Maureen, still dabbing at the crimson blotches on her daughter's face and arms. "I did what any mother would do in the same situation!"

Andrew eased his mother onto her side and reached for the telephone. "Should I call the police? I mean—what would we *tell* them?"

"I don't care." Maureen slid Tricia upright and studied her. "I don't see any wounds, baby. Can you tell Mommie what happened?" Her own hands shaking, she lifted Tricia's and turned them over, inspecting each finger. She peered into the child's dark-blue eyes and was startled by their sharpness. "Sweetie, what *happened?*"

Still holding the phone, his breathing quick and shallow, Andrew said, "Maybe she had a nosebleed?"

Maureen backed away from her daughter. The girl scrambled off the high counter and dropped to her feet, stared at her grandmother with hard eyes, then glanced up at her parents. Neither adult moved when she took several tentative steps toward the fallen woman to stand in the growing pool of blood; neither made an effort to stop her when she bent, tore off the old woman's nose, and stuffed it into her mouth.

Andrew hung the receiver on its hook and joined Maureen. "She *was* Tricia's favorite grandmother."

"Yes," agreed Maureen, watching her daughter chew. "And it's not as if the old bitch didn't *owe* us . . ."

Wayne Allen Sallee

THIRD RAIL

WAYNE Sallee's bold fiction has been chosen for three *Year's Best Horror Stories* annuals from DAW. In *Fangoria* (December '88), reviewer David Kuehls discussed Sallee's "Take the A Train" and wrote that even if "the writing is a bit overheated," there is "an intensity that's almost palpable."

That's true of most of the fifty-five stories and seventy-five poems published by this denizen of Chicago whom Sandberg might simultaneously recognize and turn from in horror. The world observed by Wayne is as unremittingly rugged as anything Nelson Algren reported. Sallee's work is rough, real, at once "new" horror—and as old as dying.

THIRD RAIL

Wayne Allen Sallee

CLOHESSY WATCHED RAINE'S BLUE CIVIC HEAD back toward the Kennedy on-ramp; then he turned, zippering his jacket as he took the down escalator steps two at a time to the concourse leading to the El train. The Kennedy overpass was deserted and he stood for several minutes staring out at the eight lanes of weekend traffic—four on each side of the Jefferson Park/Congress/Douglas rapid transit line.

Then he noticed the girl.

Before looking back at her a second time, Clohessy—time-scheduled commuter that he was—glanced north, saw that the train was nowhere near arriving at the terminal. He had been chilled crossing the parking lot, yet the girl below him was wearing only a pair of jeans and a white sweater that clung tight to her waist. A loose gilded belt completed the image. Clichéd as it was, she looked as if her body had been poured into her clothing. The sweater was pushed up around her elbows. Maybe he'd offer her his gloves after he'd handled business.

Clohessy walked briskly down the glass-and-stainless-steel corridor to those stairs leading to the El platform. It was after 10 P.M.; the ticket agent's booth was closed. He'd have to pay on the train and took a second to make certain he had small bills. The conductor wouldn't be able to break a twenty.

Clohessy never carried a comb, so he ran a hand through his thin blond hair (not that it would matter in the sharp late-September wind), pushed through the gate and took the down escalator. Halfway to the platform, he caught a flash of the girl's sweater, a creamy slice of arm. As cold as it was, and my, how the hair on her arms *danced . . .*

Clohessy had been disappointed to leave Raine's place so early, but he'd had a two-hour trek on public transportation to the Southwest Side ahead of him; he enjoyed Raine and Peg's company and likely wouldn't see them again until Lilah Chaney's party in Virginia next February. Yet seeing the girl on the platform made him momentarily forget the last few hours.

As Clohessy's shoes clacked onto the concrete, she turned to look at him. He met her gaze and she glanced quickly away. She did not seem concerned about whether the train was coming; she didn't seem impatient in her movements, and, after the first five minutes Clohessy had watched her from the corner of his eye, she hadn't once leaned out, over the tracks (as most people—himself included—usually did).

He looked at the digital clock on the Northern Trust Bank across the Kennedy: 53° at 11:09. If he was ever going to strike up a conversation with the girl, he'd have to do it now; the train would be there by quarter after.

Walking the ten or so steps to where she was standing, Clohessy jammed his fists into his pockets, realizing just as he neared her that he was wearing his spring jacket and that he'd sound pretty damn stupid offering her his gloves when he'd left them on his coatrack back in his apartment! Embarrassed, he swung away.

The platform rumbled; he turned to stare north. It was only a plane leaving from O'Hare, a mile away. Clohessy whistled tunelessly, rubbernecked. The sign above him read BOARD HERE FOR TRAINS TO LOOP & WEST SIDE. The dull white neon lines flickered. The clock at the bank now said: 52° at 11:11. A huge tanker truck obscured the red neon Mona Koni restaurant sign as it made a wide turn into the parking lot of Dominick's.

Sighing, Clohessy began watching for signs of life in one of the lighted upper floors of an office building to the far side of I-90's left lanes. When he turned again, the girl was gone. Clohessy glanced up at the escalators. From where he stood, he saw the bottom fifteen steps of the two stairwells, with the escalator in the middle, before they disappeared out of sight behind the overhead ads for Camel Filters and Salem Lights. He was still surprised by how well kept and graffiti-free the El station was.

Clohessy saw a blurred flash of color.

The girl was riding the rails on the *up* escalator. He smiled, amazed. Slipping back into sight from above, she'd slide down nearly to the bottom before stopping, then glide back up. Clohessy watched her straddle the moving stairwell a half dozen times, saw her ride up in a kind of swimming sidestroke. She was gorgeous. Her sweater had hiked up over her hip, exposing more flesh. Her hair fell across her face.

She turned to stare at Clohessy, winked. He touched his collar, glanced away at the bank clock again, too flustered even to notice the time. He looked back; again she was gone from sight.

Clohessy heard whistling and catcalls from above. *Male* voices. The voices came nearer, accompanied by the sound of sneakers on the concrete stairs. Clohessy calculated four separate voices, fretted for the girl. All four men wore slicked-back hair, he saw when they reached bottom; all wore lime-green fall windbreakers. Each carried a bag of some kind. They walked closer. Behind them, the girl slid back down the rail. She stared at the men, but with boredom.

Once they had reached the glare of the sodium lamps, Clohessy realized why the girl wasn't afraid of them, and, for what seemed like the twelfth time that night, he felt extremely stupid. They weren't gang members. The jackets advertised Szostak's Tavern.

The four guys were a Polish bowling team.

Within minutes, the southbound train pulled in. The bowlers got on, heading toward Milwaukee Avenue; Clohessy was certain. He glanced at the time. 11:18. Still plenty of time to catch the Archer bus downtown. He'd wait around to see what the girl was going to do. She seemed in no hurry to leave. Maybe she was waiting for Clohessy to make his move.

The southbound train was now far in the distance. The girl hadn't come back down the escalator since the train was in the station. Clohessy, inching closer to the stairwell and her, heard a shuffling sound from the concourse above. Probably her boyfriend showing—

He saw something white, lying flat on one of the escalator steps lowering to the platform. White with splashes of red.

Descending.

Red nails on a girl's hand.

Red veins at the wrist.

Descending. Catching on the edge of the platform grille and flipping up. Her hand, severed at the wrist, hideous in the green glow seeping up from the escalator's bowels. Creating a ghastly cast of shadows from her dead veins and finger joints.

Then her corpse followed, riding the rail down, lines of blood sprayed across the chrome. Her eyes, forever open, still had the bored look she had given the bowlers.

Then, also riding the rail down, toward Clohessy, the man with the knife.

Mark McNease

COOCHIE - COO

WRITING tense, tight short-shorts well is an unsung accomplishment, amazing if you consider that the next horrific gem was written for the Writer's Digest School course I instructed. In short, it's one of the "first" stories in *Masques III*—but I'd bet a bundle you wouldn't know that if I hadn't told you!

A young Californian, Mark McNease used some of what he learned from the course (and considerable raw talent) and not only wrote two one-act plays but saw them produced in Los Angeles—and directed one—to absolute raves. Of "Brand New Walker" and "Ribbons," dramatized together as *One Axe*, one critic wrote: "These plays are strong stuff and worth your time," and a second said McNease "eviscerates the tense underbelly of family existence and spills out the psychologically-bloody entrails . . ." Richard Labonte, writing in *Update*, added that the fifty-minute plays were "unsettling, uncomfortable and demanding."

Evisceration, tension, psychological gore, and unsettling strong stuff are ideal to horror. Playwriting *or* writing prose, I predict Mark McNease will make a searing mark on the underbelly of our human family.

COOCHIE - COO

Mark McNease

EDDY'S EYES BURNED WHEN HE OPENED them, each brown iris floating in a pool of red. He jerked his head forward, as if the receding nightmare had shaken him by the shoulders or drilled like a fist into his spine with its vicious images. His muscles, constantly alert and prepared, contracted sharply and he bolted upright in his seat. Sweat adhered his clothes to him; sweat unrelieved in the hot, stagnant air of the bus.

He listened with the nerves of a rabbit to the sounds around him—nothing now but the hum of the engine.

Time had passed. He guessed it had been a long while, judging from the empty seats. Only one other passenger remained, a woman sitting directly in front of him with a baby peering over her shoulder.

A curious baby with wet blue eyes.

A fat, hairless baby sucking its thumb. Staring at him.

Everyone else was gone.

Eddy's sleep had been fitful at best, plagued by a dream he'd floated in and out of for hours. It was more like a memory than a nightmare: stabbed in the Portland depot, cornered in the men's room by a thief like himself who thought nothing of putting a blade in him over ill-chosen words. A skinny black man with yellow teeth whose knife hand he remembered too clearly for dreams; a thumb and three fingers twisting into his belly.

Plunging in.

Digging.

He clenched his shirttail, pulling it up to expose his abdomen. *God I don't wanna die don't let me die.* Without looking down he ran his palm over the skin, expecting to feel dried blood with the sweat. *Not on a bus please not on a bus.* Nothing. It had been a dream after all.

He exhaled loudly, following it with a laugh that cut through the stillness. He slapped his thigh. "Goddamn, Eddy boy," he said half-aloud to reassure himself, "you got the luck. You sure do got the luck!"

He carefully rubbed his eyes, trying to soothe the sting that bit with every blink of his lids. The smell of his hands made him grimace. It was the odor of long days and nights on the road, the pungent aroma of sweat and the dirt of traveling that builds from a film to a tangible layer of filth. He sniffed, familiar with the places it came from—doorknobs and benches and cigarette butts plucked greedily from the sidewalk. His grimace changed to the smile of a child who has found his way home.

Eddy leaned back and wiped his hands on the knees of his jeans. He immersed himself in that feeling of *home*. This was it: riding down a deserted highway with a dozen destinations to choose from. He wouldn't let them kick him out this time, or lock him up with common drunks. He wouldn't let them give him rules and regulations, or wag their righteous fingers at the kid gone bad, saying, "Why can't you be like your *brother?* He made something of himself in the exciting and challenging world of data processing. *He* gets to meet interesting people every day. But you, Eddy Brisk? You're a schmuck. A zero."

He flinched at the memories. They were useless to him, like love or duty to the family he'd detached himself from five years before. A family content with being slaves to boredom while he, Steady Eddy Brisk, insisted on freedom. Unconditional freedom.

Certain law-enforcement agencies argued that he wouldn't keep it for long. They said stealing wasn't freedom, but crime. *Well,* Eddy thought, grinning with the teeth he had left, *they ain't caught me yet. I got the luck. I sure do got the luck.* Secure in the knowledge of his good fortune, he leaned forward to spit on the floor. When he lifted his head he realized that the baby was staring at him, its fingers dug into the gray cotton of its mother's blouse. Eddy winked and made a face, sticking his tongue out while crossing his eyes.

The baby was not amused.

Eddy nodded. "Name's Brisk," he said. "Rhymes with risk." He laughed, certain the mother would turn around to glare down her nose at him. When she didn't respond, Eddy assumed she was asleep. *Dumb bitch is out of it,* he thought with a smirk. *Just as well. One less mom to snatch her brat away from me.*

He curled his index finger, hooking it several times like a worm sticking up from an apple. "Coochie-coo," he said, his voice more a grate than a whisper.

The baby just kept staring, its cool blue eyes too large for its face; round blue eyes that were oddly developed for a child so small.

Eyes that didn't blink, gazing intently with what Eddy suddenly took for contempt.

He drew back in his seat, not wanting to play anymore. "You're weird," he said. "Can't be more than two years old and you're fucking weird." He ran a grimy hand across his forehead, wondering why sweat had beaded there. He passed it off with a phlegm-stained chuckle and turned his attention to the landscape outside.

Dust covered the window. Most of it was external, but not all of it. By wiping the glass with his sleeve, Eddy was able to see into the darkness. He peered out, expecting to catch a glimpse of the hills they were surely descending as the bus wound down through northern California. Relieved that they must be hundreds of miles from the redneck bastion called Oregon, he grinned as he gazed inches from the windowpane.

His smile dropped quickly, his mouth opening in a gape. *Desert.* He wiped frantically at the glass. *Desert. Long endless cold desert.*

He sat back, perspiring heavily, cursing himself for drinking so much. *Damn,* he thought. *I got on the wrong bus! Jesus. How long was I asleep?* He closed his eyes and slowed his breathing, trying to calm himself. Thinking. He decided he must be headed for Vegas. Of course. Where else would his drunken mind have thought to take him? He was always grand when he drank. Always had his plans.

He slumped into the seat cushion. He opened and closed his eyes several times, squinting tightly, attempting to dispel the tension building just inside his skull. He didn't want to go to Vegas. He'd had trouble there. *No problem.* Somebody might remember him. *You got the luck.* Maybe it would be all right. Maybe he was on a roll. His fear began to subside.

And the baby stared.

It dawned on Eddy that the child had been watching him all this time. *Obnoxious little shit.* He looked away, surveying the seats across the aisle. *Where is everybody?* Apparently no one was much interested in Vegas. *Awful damn dark in here.*

He brought his head back around only to discover that the baby was still staring. He glared back, his annoyance mixed with apprehension. "It's not polite to stare," he said.

The baby paid him no mind. It had taken its thumb out of its mouth and used its hands to climb up on the woman's shoulder. A little bit farther.

A little bit closer.

Studying the man whose sweat blended with fear to spice the air.

Staring.

Two small, pudgy hands alternately digging into and releasing the shoulder it perched against.

Staring.

Its androgynous yellow jumpsuit failing to be cheerful.

Staring.

Eddy squirmed in his seat. He laughed nervously, thinking how foolish it was to be disturbed by a baby. Still, it had the strangest eyes he'd ever seen. As if they knew everything—where he'd been and where he was going. All that he'd done in his thirty-two years, and all he'd never accomplished. He found himself caught in its unblinking gaze, slipping away, his eyelids growing heavy.

He snapped out of it with a quick, jerking motion. He thought of

other things—anything but the bus and the baby. *Headed for Vegas.*
He covered his face with his hands, smelling the filth on them.
Portland to Vegas. He turned to the window, confused by the
stretching desert. *Stabbed in Portland. Left for dead. Son of a bitch
took my money. Bleeding.* He grabbed his stomach, pressing his fin-
gers into the flesh, feeling for a gash. *No gash. No money either.* He
patted his pockets. *Going to Vegas no money.*

Eddie threw himself against the cushion behind him. His breath-
ing had accelerated; he could hear it escaping in short, fierce puffs
through his nose. As panic heightened his senses, he saw the
woman's purse nestled between the seats. A common purse, it
was, beige cotton with one dark letter in a pattern like a designer
item, or a cheap imitation. A clearance-sale purse that no doubt
held lipstick, Kleenex, sunglasses, and money. *Got to have some
money.* Not much, but some. *Got to have some money.*

He debated with himself for the next five minutes. If he reached
up slowly, cautiously, he could slip the pocketbook out of the
purse without a sound. But he could get caught. The woman could
wake up, start screaming, have him arrested at the next bus stop.

After weighing the consequences, he quietly leaned forward.

And *it* watched him.

He slid his arm between the seats, taking what seemed an eter-
nity to get to the other side.

And it wouldn't take its eyes off him.

With just the slightest pressure, he pushed his forearm through.
Years of skill paid off when he grasped the latch. Muffling the
noise with his palm, Eddy snapped the purse open.

And *it* grabbed his arm, digging its fat little fingers into his flesh.

Eddy gasped, looking up, found himself pierced by those ice-
blue eyes.

"Coochie-coo," it hissed. A shrill laugh escaped its mouth. A
squeal of delight.

Eddy tried to pull his arm back. It was stuck between the seats,
partly from his twisting away from the baby's grasp but mostly
from fear.

Out of the corner of his eye he saw the woman's torso move. He
glanced up, knowing she would glare at him, accuse and loathe
him. He dreaded what he would see in her face.

What he saw was nothing. No eyes. No nose. No mouth. Just the front of a skull covered tightly with skin. Turning away with his heart racing, Eddy saw where the woman ended and the baby began—up near her right shoulder—growing and wriggling and laughing. Sprouting like a tumor. Being her eyes. Her mouth. Her terrible shriek of pleasure as *it* dug into his arm, pulling it up to cut its teeth on him.

A wetness began to spread near Eddy's waist. It could have been urine. He knew it was blood.

Bill Ryan

THE WULGARU

ONE story here required "translation": the following tale. Translated, that is, from the original Australian! Don't fret, though, mate. Brisbane Bill Ryan is the horror-fiction equivalent of Crocodile Dundee, with a background as a security guard, meat packer, clerk, and postman Down Under (it's the last two writing warm-ups that seem potentially as scary as croc-fighting to me). The needed Americanizations have not harmed this individualistic and adventurous romp.

Brisbane Bill, born July 22, 1956, says he's a "passionate reader of horror, fantasy, and science fiction," and that he experienced "enormous relief, vindication, and just plain fantastic feelings" to learn of this, his first professional sale. Relief isn't what *you'll* experience when you read about mulga trees, Gidgee logs, charging razorbacks, diabetic aborigines—and the special supernatural horror indigenous to Australia. You've never heard "G'day, mate" uttered with such a mood of menace—or with greater originality. Give it a fair go, right?

THE WULGARU

Bill Ryan

MICHAEL ALOYSIUS CURRY WAS NINETEEN WHEN Caitlin O'Shea fanned his desperate love into an act of revenge. Revenge for his brother, Dion. Mick's and Caitlin's plastique had left one paratrooper legless in the Falls Road, another's brains running down his back. The legless one rose somehow, a spray of petrol smoldering on his flak vest. Caitlin ran as the para bore Mick through the broken bow window of Fihelly's florists, where Cup Final wreaths crisped.

The para knew the Brothers Curry from the papers. Dion's suicide in Belfast's Maze Prison had given the press a martyr and they'd plastered young Mick's confirmation picture everywhere. Eamon Curry's eldest had looked angelic with his arm around the lovely Caitlin.

But an unchristian eye might have noted the kerosone burns Dion had suffered in lighting the neighbors' tomcat.

The soldiers had wanted names, read Mick's terror as defiance. Even as the bayonet burned his knuckles, though, he was no Judas. One finger fell among the charred Cup flowers.

Then, cheek to cheek, he betrayed every IRA lad he had met through Dion. The girl? No, he'd never grass on Caitlin, never! The para began to cry for the woman in Kingussie who would soon be his widow and lopped off another of young Curry's fingers as he died. Mick wriggled out of the glass and embers, and ran . . .

Ten years had left him graying, ruddy, and soft; only the brittle green eyes remained of the boy Mick. Sucking brandy, he decided this vigil for wild boars on a pile of rocks in outback Australia had been a mistake. His ghosts were no more bound to Belfast than he.

"You won't see the pigs at this rate, sport." Jo Pitman retrieved the bottle, took a slow swig of amber. Under her Stetson the brassy sunset glowed in her eyes.

"Yeah." The two fingers of Mick's right hand checked his rifle for the tenth time. The dum-dums hadn't walked away.

"They're coming down," Jo said.

He heard faint squeals and snorts. He looked down from his rocky perch. The waterhole burned. The pigs were black shadows against it. He brought the rifle to his shoulder, jerked the trigger. His slug bounced off a boar's skull, knocked it to its knees. It struggled up, squealing. Mick put a round through its chest. *Reload . . . slow.* Pigs, they were running. But two more dropped before the rest were gone.

"Thought they'd be bigger."

The sun was fat and red when they reached the first carcass.

"Like that movie, *Razorback?*" Jo showed Mick a crooked smile. "You want a buffalo, sport!"

She slid a hunting knife from her boot, then hacked a tusk three inches long from the pig's jaw. "In Spain, you get the bull's ears and tail. Reckon this'll look better round your neck."

Mick laughed, then noticed the fine silver links hanging from the boar's mouth. A bracelet was bent around the peglike teeth. Jo's knife levered them apart and he worked it free. Earth removed the blood and pus.

Jo snatched the dangling diabetic ID bracelet and raced back to her antique Jeep. Mick weaved after her.

"Where are we going?" he asked.

"Nev Yagunjil's the only diabetic round here. An aboriginal, not far off."

Still muzzy, he managed to puke overboard as they bounced over ruts. Like a dream, the Jeep growled across a dry lake, and the red-and-gray waste took wing. The parrots were the colors of the clay, invisible until startled into flight. The eye of a raucous hurricane, Mick clutched the Jeep's roll bar and his head.

In no time, Jo's apricot singlet and shorts were soaked. Her sandy hair swung in damp rattails. His own shirt was a sweat rag and his skin glowed pink where he wasn't caked in dust.

Jo braked at a steep ridge and dug out a first-aid kit. Mick followed over red earth and boulders peeled like onions by sun and frost. Shards cut the soles of his Nikes.

The granite fell to a sapphire pool ringed by pale mulga trees, which sheltered a monstrosity of corrugated iron and slabs of bark. Tarpaulins made the shanty resemble a shipwreck.

"Nev?" Jo slid down the loose rock without waiting for a reply that never came.

Most of Nev Yagunjil was on the far side of the shanty. The pigs had scattered him like terriers with a rag. The aboriginal's face and scalp hung from a spiny bush, a child's discarded mask watching blowflies troop on his bones and goanna lizards squabble for any morsel left by the pigs.

Jo turned green but choked it down. The awful find had no effect on Mick: this wasn't a corpse, it was a jigsaw. He held Jo until the spasms eased. Finally she stuck that pugnacious cleft in her chin up at him and said, "Thanks."

The peeled skull turned to face them. Jo screamed. It nodded sadly at Mick's approach. The left temple was staved in; a red goanna unraveled from inside the cranium and fled on its hind legs. The skull spun and stopped with the jagged hole up.

"Could pigs have done that, Jo?"

She shook her head.

"Looks like someone took a shillelagh to him."

"Or a rock." Jo turned it with a twig.

A wedge of flint was embedded in bone near the hole. Mick steered her toward the shanty before she bit through her lip.

Under the tarp awnings, a toadlike paw had drawn an aboriginal hunter into the hollow stump of a baobab. Yagunjil had carved him skinless, after the black style. Each knot of muscle,

each filigreed vein, stood out. So did the terror in those naked
features. Mick resisted the temptation to cover that nightmare with
Yagunjil's own face.

"Pretty horrific," he said.

"His Dreamtime Legends series," Jo grunted. "Nev even had the
wood and stone trucked in from the original tribal lands."

The workshop was dark. As their vision adapted, they saw a
carpet of bloodstained sketches. Flies ran down the crusty streaks
on walls.

Another of the artist's flayed men stood by a hurricane lamp
burning with the tiniest blue spark. The wood smelled old; rotten.
Flies delved the incisions for blood and swarmed on its horrible
right hand. The limbs and the fingers were articulated with knot-
ted human hair.

Mick winced. "What's that great ugly thing?" he asked.

"The wulgaru legend." She shuddered, pulled herself erect. "A
kurdaitcha man supposedly freed an evil spirit from a tree by carv-
ing it into human shape. Then it ran amok; real Frankenstein stuff.
I don't recall all the details. This was to be Nev's last piece. He was
months finding the right Gidgee log."

Mick squinted. "Are those eyes opal?"

"Quartz." She shuffled paper. "These drawings . . ."

"What about them?"

"Nev was fanatical about 'feeling the spirit in the wood,' then
paring away 'all else.' He never before planned a work, Mick."

"So he put *this* spook on paper, eh?" Mick turned the sketch.
There was a thumbmark in the charcoal rendering of a rough log.
He could almost see hateful eyes and hair like smoke. Caitlin
O'Shea, he thought, seen through tears.

Jo was gone. The chop of a shovel led Mick to her. She was
digging a grave. He offered to spell her.

"Lousy holiday for you, Irish."

"It's different."

They collected the bones in a rusty oil drum and rolled it into
the grave. The sun died behind the mulga as they tamped dark soil
on Yagunjil's impromptu bier.

"Have we just illicitly disposed of a body?" he asked, suddenly
anxious.

"Sport, the nearest cop is six hundred klicks east. I radio him from town, he gets Homicide to fly up from Brisbane. Three days. This way, there's something for them to poke at."

"Oh." Mick wiped his forehead. His wrist left a stripe of sunburned skin in the ocher dust. Jo drew circles on his cheeks.

"Let's lose the warpaint, chief."

After a stiff progress to the pool, their tension scraped away with the dust. Jo stepped out of her shorts. Scanties white against her tan, she jackknifed into the pool. She spat and slicked her hair back. "Well?"

No great swimmer, Mick was worried by the depth. Despite her whistle he felt ridiculous in his boxer shorts. An explosive bellyflop proved the water both deep and cold. He swallowed a howl and kicked for the surface.

"Unique style, Irish," said Jo.

Mick's dog paddle barely kept him up. "That's how we do it in the Auld Sod."

He floated, watched the first stars appear. The cool quiet recalled a boy mounting rotten steps in a Belfast boardinghouse. Whitewashed glass turned the light to sour cream and cobwebs. He'd perched breathless on the widow's walk as the world rolled away to the mountains of Mourne. His dreaming place, refuge from Dion's malice. He'd trusted it to Caitlin and she'd made it a deadly cache.

He remembered fierce love and the hate that fed it. Mick had joined the Na Fianna Eirann after the Orangemen smashed his father's kneecaps, but even that shining hate hadn't nourished itself as Caitlin's did. If Mick hadn't loved his brother, he'd done his duty.

Love, hate and duty! No wonder he was enchanted by this uncomplicated Australian lass.

Jo splashed him. She laughed and swallowed water. Coughs lured him in for another volley. They caught each other's wrists and traded fierce grins.

"Ten dollars says I can duck you," she said.

"You're on." Mick knew he had the weight advantage, but Jo was solid and fitter than he'd ever been. He kissed her to break her grip. Even though it was necessarily hard and clumsy and he held it too long, Jo didn't back off.

                    *   *   *

"Cards on the table, Mick."

"Not quartz, eh?"

"Color, mate. Worth a packet."

"So why are we talking about it?"

Jo refilled the lamp and threw light on Nev's wulgaru and its stone eyes. She chewed a knuckle in thought. "Jeez, I'll be yanking Nev's gold teeth next."

"Didn't have any."

She made a face. "Real funny. I hate myself for doing this."

A shrug. "Then go."

"And hate myself for passing it up?" Jo's exasperated smile made him laugh. "So make yourself useful, sport!"

He chose a knife and chipped away the dark resin holding the opals. As he pried one loose, his hand slipped. A flint tooth drew blood. "You bastard!" he yelped.

Getting a solid grip on the jaw, he yanked the opal out.

But his triumphal laugh was punctuated by the clasp of stone—and pain. Confused, he jerked back his hand—

And his right *thumb* was gone. Mick stared at where it belonged in agony, disbelief. His knees turned to water then, making him sag, sparing him Yagunjil's fate. Incredibly, a graven arm skinned his cheek. (*A* kurdaitcha *man freed an evil spirit from a tree . . .*) Striking the worktable with all his weight, Mick inadvertently tipped the lamp onto the littered floor.

From there, astonished, he watched the unbearably ugly wulgaru creak and writhe. Behind the fire. Flies rose from it in a lazy swarm. Mick's hand was a red rubber glove, so Jo, glancing back up at the horror, knotted something white around his wrist.

"It got my *thumb*." He said it wonderingly, feebly. The world was eating his *hand*, bits at a time.

"Keep pissing claret like that and it'll get the rest of you kosher." Her panties stanched the blood but not before covering her, making her an abstract in red below the navel. "We've got to—"

Suddenly, wagging limbs writhing with human hair, the wulgaru splintered a bark wall and fled the fire. The shanty groaned alarmingly; that sound and the icon's terrible, carved face penetrated the shock that had held Mick paralyzed. He grabbed

Jo's wrist and they dodged under flapping sheets of flame that had
been the canvas roof. Scarcely escaping, they saw that the wulgaru
had lurched between them and the ridge. Now it was herding
them back toward the water and into it with a loud splash. Hold-
ing onto Jo, Mick dashed quickly to the deepest point, pursued by
the monster.

Its ghastly head cocked its remaining eye at them and then
sank . . .

"We're safe!" Mick exclaimed. "The bastard can't swim!" Tread-
ing water, he sucked his thumb joint, fought weakness.

"C'mon, we can't lose too much—"

Abruptly, silt boiled up around them.

Jo stared at Mick. "It's . . . *walking*. Along *the bottom!*"

Then the water promptly closed over her with a hiss.

With their fingers twined, Mick was dragged under also. He
tried to see. Silver bubbled from her nose but her cheeks were full.
Jo had had time for one quick breath. He wriggled down beneath
her arm, into the milk, saw the living legend.

The wulgaru had hooked her calf muscles! Mick tried hard,
couldn't budge so much as one claw. The wulgaru grinned at him.
Content to hold her, it flaunted Mick's helplessness. In despera-
tion, he gnawed at wood and sinew alike but was ignored.

Raw lungs decided it. Mick had no choices. He kicked away
after seeing Jo's lips as a blue circle, her eyes already mercifully
shut.

Nikes on, hand bundled in his shirt, Mick ran up the ridge.
Granite scattered beneath his feet and his knees became thor-
oughly barked before a final spill dropped him near their Jeep, and
the rifles. He had never been so frightened, quite.

Above him, the wooden horror crested the ridge. Even from
there it reeked, it stank. But Mick was waiting. He blew splinters
out of its chest, cast around for something with more clout, then
fumbled with the key in the ignition.

The Jeep croaked to life. Momentarily, the wulgaru seemed be-
wildered by the contraption thundering at it. Mick whooped, el-
bowed a steady bleat from the horn. Claws exploded the
windscreen and tore the headrest off the driver's seat. Mick

ducked and brained himself on the wheel as wood smashed under the back wheels.

Mick braked as the wulgaru got up, designs crushed and scored, the wicked jaw ripped off. It swung the severed left arm like a scythe . . .

That last Belfast summer, a shoelace had saved his life. He'd balanced against a lampost with blistered green paint and wished for more fingers or fewer jars of Guinness under his belt. Five minutes spent on the Gordian knot (ties were still insoluble) gave black fatigues with Heckler-Koch automatics time to cordon off his street. One scanned the crowd for a face in a Polaroid.

From Malone's tobacconists, Mick could see the gabled bulk of his boardinghouse. Caitlin would have rung Malone's if she'd escaped. Was she hiding under the widow's walk? With the plastique?

It was quiet such a long time, Mick almost believed she'd surrendered . . . then the roof of the brownstone vomited into the street.

And such shameful peace swept over him! Mick had always imagined Caitlin O'Shea's driving hatred as a separate entity, even a demon; how else could he love her? Her death opened cellars of his mind that loved Caitlin not at all. Love a black fire that devoured Dion and would have destroyed him? His heart rebelled against that cold vision and he'd run so far this time.

And the hate had found him, after all.

The brandy bottle tapped his heels. He screwed it open and watched the monster advance through the glass. He never took that swig.

The Jeep had bled oil and petrol over the wooden man . . .

Inspired, Mick bit a linen strip from his shirt and soaked it well. He wadded the rag down the neck and lit it from the Jeep dash. When he could smell the rot, Mick gunned the engine and threw the bottle. The wulgaru was cloaked in blazing mist. Sinews of hair spat and melted as it smacked the flames in mute parody of a burning man.

Stones rattled the Jeep's belly. The grade was too steep, the left wheels chewed into thin air. Mick jumped—his shirt was tangled in the roll bar.

The steel banshee crushed him.

Consciousness hurt.

The moon wept a rainbow tear that stung his eye and lip. Gasoline. The "moon" was the skewed lid of the gas tank. The Jeep had capsized, pinned him.

A giant eye hanging by its nerves, one headlight threw its beam down the broken slope. The wulgaru hobbled through the light, blackened chest alive with fiery worms.

Only a flood of adrenaline kept Mick out of shock.

"You look like I feel, Woody," he muttered.

Rotten wood crackled in answer.

Another drop of gasoline burned Mick's eye and was ignored. That cold purpose Caitlin must have felt on the widow's walk filled him. His free arm was nerveless meat; the cap of the gas tank was slick, jarred off its thread. He lacked the strength to turn it. He didn't need to. As his hair sizzled in the wulgaru's fist, Mick kept a death grip on that cap.

He didn't feel the gasoline sluice over them.

Rex Miller

THE LUCKIEST MAN
IN THE WORLD

FOR the first time since Signet published his top-selling, controversial first novel *Slob* (1987), Rex Miller's slaughter machine, Chaingang Bunkowski, is back . . . in the following very aptly titled story.

Chaingang "boils off the page," wrote reviewer Jim Van Hise in the June 1988 debut issue of *Midnight Graffiti*. "Not since *Red Dragon* by Thomas Harris has a maniac's innermost thoughts been explored with such precision and such heat."

Slob started what the jovial Missouri-born Miller, a former radio announcer and recording comedian, terms his Eichord Sextette. *Frenzy*, number two about the specialist in serial murder detection named Jake Eichord, was called a "bucket-of-blood suspense thriller" by Stephen King (from Onyx). *Viper* is next, and, in 1990, expect the return in novel form of mammoth, menacing Chaingang. But get ready, now, to duck away from the splatter—the beast hovers and hulks dead ahead of you!

THE LUCKIEST MAN
IN THE WORLD

Rex Miller

"ZULU SIX, ZULU SIX." HE COULD imagine the PRC crackling, the bored tone of somebody's RTO going, "Dragon says he's got movement about fifty meters to his Sierra Whisky, do you read me? Over." And the spit of intercom garble. Guy in the C & C bird keying a handset, saying whatever he says. Fucking lifer somewhere up there generations removed from the bad bush. Yeah, I copy you, Lumpy Charlie, Lima Charlie, Lumpy Chicken. Whatever he says. Bird coming down. Charlie moving at the edge of the woods. Thua Thien Province. Northern Whore Corps. The beast killing for peace, back then. Dirty-Dozened out of the slammer by military puppeteers. Set in place by the spooks. Very real, however.

"Chaingang" his nickname. The fattest killer in the Nam. Thriving on blast-furnace heat like some fucking plant. He was the beast. He had killed more than any other living being. Over four hundred humans, he thought. A waddling death machine. "Gangbang" they would call him out of earshot. "Hippo." He had heard them. Other names he ignored. These arrogant children who knew nothing about death.

He flashed on the woods, so similar to these, and to a pleasant memory from long ago. He was about two miles from the house.

"There goes Bobby Ray," the woman called to her husband, who was bringing logs in, and watched a truck throw gravel.

"Nnn," he grunted in the manner of someone who had been married a long time.

"He's another one don't have anything to do but run the road all day."

The husband said nothing, loading kindling.

"Drive up and down, up and down, drive a daggone pickup like he was a millionaire." She had a shrewish, sharp voice that grated on a man, he thought. He put a large log down in the hot stove.

"Now you gonna' run to town to pick up that daggone tractor thing an' you coulda' got it yesterday when you was in there at Harold's, but *nooooooo*." She was a pain in the ass. "*You* couldn't be bothered." She was working herself up the way she always liked to do, he thought. He knew the old bitch like a damn book. "You waste a fortune on gas for that truck and—"

He spoke for the first time in hours. "Go get the boy."

"Then you expect us to get by with the crop money bad as it was last year and—" She just went on like he hadn't said anything. He looked over at her with those hard, flat eyes. She shut her mouth for a second, then said, "I don't know where he's at. He'll be back in a minute. Anyway, you don't seem to realize . . ." And she was droning on about how he always thought he could write it off on the tax and that. Christ on a *crutch*, if he hadn't heard that a thousand blamed times, he hadn't heard it once!

Wasn't that the way of a woman? Worry you to damn death about some little piddling thing all the time! He sat down at the kitchen table and pulled out his beat-up wallet, opened it. She had the food money. He had the gin check and the check ol' Lathrop had given him, what—three weeks back?—and he better cash that dude if it was any good anyhow. He'd dump the woman and the boy and he'd go cash the checks and make the deposit and there'd be enough left over to get some suds. He could taste the first one right now. Sharp bite of the shot and then that nice cool taste of the foam off the head of the beer.

She was running that mouth all the time, man couldn't even count his money. Going on about Bobby Ray Crawford but he

knew it was her way of goading him. He'd get her in the truck and
that would do it. She always shut up when they went someplace.
He was getting warm in the kitchen with the hot fire going, but
damn he couldn't stand to listen to that shrill hen anymore, and he
got up and pulled his coat off the peg and stomped back outside to
find the boy.

The boy had just come out of the woods on the south of the
house. Thick woods maybe ten meters from the edge of the fields
in back of the house, and he and the dog had been kicking around
in there looking for squirrel sign and what not. Shit, the boy
thought to himself, fuckin' Aders done killed off all the fuckin'
squirrel. Otis and Bucky Aders had hunted all this ground to damn
death for ten years. You didn't hardly see no sign at all no more.
Once in a while where they cut but shit, they was plumb hunted
out.

The dog was what the beast had heard as he entered the woods
from the south side; just a faint, yapping bark that had penetrated
one of his kill fantasies as he walked down the pathway that ob-
viously led to a treeline. (Hearing the faint noise on another level
of awareness and tucking it away in his data storage system for
later retrieval.)

Life for the beast had been largely lived that way, in fantasy,
daydreaming half the time, living out the fantasies the other time.
Imagined flights to lift him first from his hellish childhood of tor-
ture and degradation, and mind games to alleviate the pain of suf-
fering. Then, later, the thoughts to vaporize that claustrophobic
ennui of long institutionalization. So it was not in the least un-
usual for the hulking beast to be fantasizing as he cautiously made
his way through the woods.

For a time he had daydreamed about killing—the preoccupation
that was his ever-present companion, the thing he liked the best,
the destruction of the human beings—and the terrain had trig-
gered pleasant memories. As he carefully negotiated the swampy
area around a large pond, he imagined the vegetation-choked
floor and green, canopied ceiling of a South Vietnamese jungle,
and the shadows of tall trees and wait-a-minute vines, and the
triggering of a daydream alerted him to the presence of possible
danger.

There were always parallels to be found. This, for example, was rice country. Here in this flatland in between the old river levees you could easily imagine a field crisscrossed by paddy dykes. Where he would have been watching for traps, falls, mines, and the footprints of the little people, here he watched for hunters.

The beast loved to come upon armed hunters in the woods and he had been fantasizing about a dad and his son; shotguns he would later take; a dog. How easily he would do the man, then stun the boy and use him before he did him, too. The thought of the boy filled him with red-hot excitement that immediately tingled in his groin and plastered a wide, grotesque smile across his doughy countenance. His smile of joy was a fearsome thing.

How easy and enjoyable it would be to do the daddy first. Take the boy's shotgun away. *Lad,* he thought. Take the *lad's* shotgun, then bind and gag and hurt him. How easy and necessary it would become to cause the pain that would bring his relief. He had the killer's gifts—the survival talents—but he'd learned that it was in those times of biological need, when the scarlet tide washed through him, that he had to be particularly cautious. Sometimes when he did the bad things he became careless.

He was not an ignorant man and in some ways he was extremely intelligent. According to one of the men in the prison where the beast had been confined, a Dr. Norman, he was a sort-of genius. "A physical precognate," Dr. Norman had told him, "who transcended the normalcy of the human ones." He was grossly abnormal. He did not find this an unpleasant thought.

The beast saw himself as Death, as a living embodiment of it, and he had availed himself of all the death literature during long periods of incarceration, devouring anything from clinicians to Horacio Quiroga. And none of it touched him. Death was outside of these others. He thought perhaps Dr. Norman was right, in his rather bizarre theorizing. But it was of no consequence to him either way.

The beast knew nothing of presentient powers. It was simply a matter of experience; preparation; trusting the vibes and gut instincts; listening to the inner rumblings; staying in harmony with one's environment; riding with the tide; keeping the sensors out there.

He could not fantasize because of inner rumblings that had intruded upon his pleasureful thoughts, but these were the demands for food. His appetites were all insatiable, and he was very hungry, had been for the entire morning.

Instinctively, he knew the small animals could be had. Their tiny heartbeats were nearby and he homed in on such vibrations with deadly and unerring accuracy, but this was not the time for game. He wanted real food and lots of it. He salivated at the thought of the cheese and the meat of the enchiladas he'd eaten the evening before. He was *HUNGRY*. It had been the last food he'd had in thirteen, maybe thirteen and a half hours, and his massive stomach growled in protest.

The beast was six feet seven inches tall, heavy with hard, rubbery fat across his chest, belly, and buttocks. Four hundred pounds of hatred and insanity. His human name was Daniel Edward Flowers Bunkowski-Zandt, although the Zandt part wasn't even on the official dossiers or the sophisticated computer printouts. They also had his age wrong by a year, but the fact that he had weighed fourteen pounds at birth was quite correct. His powerful fingers could penetrate a chest cavity. He had once become so enraged that he had squashed a *flashlight battery*—so strong was his grip.

It would be incorrect to say that the beast hated humans. In fact, he enjoyed them. Enjoyed hunting them just as sportsmen enjoy killing game; much the same. He differed only in that he liked to torture his game first, before he killed it. Cat-and-mouse games with his play pretties. Sex sometimes. But then when the heat and the bright-red waves were at their highest ebb, he would take their hearts. He would devour the hearts of his enemy—the human beings—and that was what he loved.

The beast whose human name was Danny-Boy wished that it were summer or at least that the pecan trees to the west had something for him. There would be nothing on the ground, either, he knew. *No sweet pecan nutmeats for Danny.* But that was all right. He'd be out of the woods soon, literally and figuratively. And with that he stepped daintily over a rotten log in his big 15-EEEEE bata-boos, and he *was* out of the woods, in plain view of houses and traffic. With suprising quickness the huge beast dropped back into the cover of the trees.

"Them fuckin' river rats done hunted *out* ever'thing awready.

Pah-paw," the kid whined as he patted the hound absentmind-edly. "Fuckin' Punk," he said without malice.

"Them fuckin' river rats enjoy life ten times more'n *you* ever will," his father told him. Let him chew on *that* a bit. "Let's go," he said, and got into the Ford pickup.

Bunkowski saw the woman leave the house from where he stood, frozen immobile behind a massive oak. Watching the far-away tableau from his vantage point. He saw the boy climb over the side and get into the bed of the truck, for some reason. The woman came out, did something and went back inside momen-tarily, came back out and got into the truck. The gate was lowered and the hound jumped into the truck; the beast saw it pull out slowly, go out of sight, then reappear to the east of the tar-papered home.

The beast looked up and the sky corroborated his inner clock, which ticked with a frightening machinelike precision at all times. He saw that it was after 9:30 A.M. (It *was* 9:32, at that second. He had not looked at a clock or watch for over thirteen hours.) In a second's camera-eye blink he saw that there was no corn in the field, saw the dangers of the road to his east and west, then turned and slogged through the woods toward the fence he'd seen.

Stepping over the rusting barbed wire he emerged cautiously from the safety of the woods, made his way in the direction of the house. He knew certain things and it was not part of his character to question how he knew there was a horse or horses pasturing close by, that traffic would be a light but continuous presence on the gravel road, that nobody else was in the house. He moved into the treeline that bifurcated the two fields and walked slowly to-ward the home, favoring his sore ankle a little.

There was a snow fence behind the barns, where a leaky-looking rowboat and an ancient privy rotted away, and he was behind the fence and sensed something, stopped, stood very still, slowing his vital signs to a crawl. Freezing motionless for no ap-parent reason.

"Oh, that's *real* great," the man was telling the woman in the truck, who whined.

"I'm sorry, I'd didn't *mean* to leave it, I didn't do it on purpose." She had left her grocery list and her money in the kitchen.

"If ya hadn't been runnin' your mouth," he started to say; but he just let it trail off and slammed the gearshift into reverse, backing out of the turn row. Just my luck, he thought.

"We goin' *back?*" the kid hollered at his dad, who ignored him, put it in drive and started back in the direction of their house. The man was disgusted.

The beast knew the people were returning. He felt it and then, a beat later, saw the pickup coming back up the gravel road. He was in a vile mood and his ankle was bothering him and he knew he would enjoy taking them all down. He was very hungry, too, so it would be easy for him to do very bad things to this family of humans.

"I'm goin' to the john," the man told his wife as they went back into the house. "You goin' to be ready to go?"

"I'll be ready," she said, and went into the kitchen. The kid was sitting on the tailgate as Bunkowski walked into the yard. The dog barked at him, the kid told it to shut up.

"Howdy," the huge man said.

"Where'd *you* come from?" the kid asked him. Chaingang thought how easily he could go over and twist the boy's head off. It would be like snapping a pencil in two.

"Over yonder," he said. "Your folks home?"

"Yeah," the kid said.

"Yes?" a woman said through the partly open back door.

"Ma'am. I was hitchin' a ride and this guy's car broke down and I been walkin', quite a way. I was wonderin' if you folks would mind if I rested in your yard for a while?" He could easily pull the door open and knock her out. Go in and chainsnap the man. Come back and get the boy. He was about to make a move, but she said,

"You just sit down and rest yourself. Make yourself to home." And she started asking him where the car had broken down and did he want a lift back to the car and did he want to call somebody, and he kind of got taken off his stride and so he went and sat on the steps.

"You from around here?" the boy asked. The beast only shook his head.

Inside the house he heard the man say something and she said ". . . broke down back over . . ." (something he couldn't make out) and the door opened behind him and the man said,

"You need a ride?"

"Well, I don't mind if it's no bother," Bunkowski said pleasantly, thinking he'd go ahead and make the move now.

"It's no trouble. You can ride into town with us. If you don't mind sittin' back there with the boy." The man said it without any undue emphasis.

"I'd be real grateful."

"No problem," the man said, stepping around the huge bulk that filled his back steps.

The last place where he'd come upon a family, he'd killed everybody in the house. Three people. Man and wife and a son—just like this. The kid, as if reading his mind, moved over out of the way, back into a far corner of the truck bed.

"Get over here, Punk," the boy said to the dog, who wagged and obeyed. "Don't worry," he sneered. "He don't bite."

"What's his name? Punk?" Chaingang sat on the cold steel. Shifted his weight slightly so as not to break the tailgate off, and the truck rocked like a safe had been dropped into it.

"Little Punk." The kid scratched the dog. "We found him starvin' over on the dump. Somebody dropped the fucker. He didn't look like nothin' but a punk." The dog licked the kid's face once and he pushed it away. "Fuckin' Punk."

"Looks like a good dog," the huge man said.

"He's awright."

"You ready?" the man said to nobody in general, and he and the wife got into the truck and they drove off down the rode, Chaingang Bunkowski bouncing along in the back of the truck.

When the beast had been a child, a dog had been his only companion and friend. He loved animals. Watching the boy with the dog had calmed him down, but he wasn't sure what he would do yet. He might take them all down anyway.

When the pickup reached the crossroads of Double-J and the levee road, Chaingang banged on the window and asked the man to stop. He got out, walked around by the driver. There were no other vehicles in sight.

"Doncha wanna go on to town?" the man asked him. Bunkowski fingered the heavy yard of the tractor-strength safety chain in his jacket pocket. Three feet of killer snake were coiled in the special canvas pocket. He thought how easy it would be to take them, now.

"I guess not. This'll do." He nodded thanks to the driver, who shrugged and started off. Chaingang stood there and watched the luckiest man in the world drive away with his family.

Joey Froehlich

THE BONELESS DOLL

"I write from 'feel,'" says this instinctive poet and fiction writer from Kentucky. He has done it for sixteen years, and "I don't really try to write like anyone else," he explains. Editor of the highly original *Violent Legends* and of, in the works, *Live Mysteries*, Joey thinks there's "no other who writes like me. Thank God!"

Recently, Froehlich's chilling "Year of the Green-Eyed Toads" appeared in the splatterpunk mag *Midnight Graffiti* in close proximity with a Stephen King tale. He closes his letters "Best be crawling" because some of his work does that to one's skin.

THE BONELESS DOLL

Joey Froehlich

The boneless doll
Is small
And she carries
It, yea—
Wherever she goes,
Just a little girl
Happy with this
Doll without bones
(Cloth)
Not flesh all bunched
Up and writhing
When it falls
On the twigs
Of another bruised
Existence lost.

CONCERNS OF
THE MIND AND SPIRIT

IT'S difficult to describe adequately the third subset of stories (and a poem). That does not mean the grouping is false, or arbitrary. Although a few of these tales could comfortably be installed under other headings, they belong, together, here.

Horror fantasy is partly an attempt to detect and appraise the cusps or interfaces of human life, and see past the masks we're shown at that *instant* when they *slip* . . . and weird masques are played out. Most writers and readers of horror are people who willingly confront the moods of man for which there's no name—partly because the moods are impermanent and elusive, partly because they're darkly covert, even mad. Under these masks are the real monsters, whose concealed countenances never smile, only smirk with derision, detestation, or baleful desire.

"Psychological horror" is another term for this type of fiction, but a less effective one than that which I've chosen. This is fiction of concern for the directions some of us are taking as people, often unaware of the heartbreak we inflict upon one another or ourselves. Such actions are worse than killing; in this fiction, killing becomes symptom or metaphor. Such terror penetrates to the soul.

This work isn't "better" than that in other categories. It may have the drawback of being too somber for some tastes, or too locked-in to contemporary concerns. But "Concerns of the Mind and Spirit" is definitely not inferior to other types of horror. Far from it. Far indeed.

Diane Taylor

THE SKULL

THIS story addresses one of the tragically scarring problems exposed during the 1980s and does so in a fashion that is disturbing, honest, relentlessly credible. The fact that Diane Taylor is offering her first "adult" fiction—though she enjoys other careers as a children's author, teacher, and wife of David Taylor (elsewhere present in this book)—makes her triumph even more remarkable.

Born January 9, 1952, in "the Mississippi delta town of Helena, Arkansas," Diane wrote her first tale as a child in a tractor shed with rain "hammering on the tin" and the "smell of damp hay." It was scary; "I loved it," she says.

A cookie-devouring compulsive creator, Taylor often works at 4 A.M.—with "an eraserless pencil"— and was driven to write this riveting story by a chance encounter with a man who stopped her to ask for a match. Unexpectedly, he "pulled up his T-shirt to show me scars from Viet Nam," and his "transparent blue eyes" showed wounds that "were deep and ugly." Enveloped by a storm, she felt dizzied by cheap aftershave, perceived "other scars, much deeper and much uglier." Escaped, she felt the way she had as a girl curled inside a tin shed and found the courage to imagine, and write, "The Skull."

THE SKULL

Diane Taylor

I NEVER REALLY LIVED WITH HIM. They got divorced when I was three. But Momma always sent me to visit in the summer. Whenever I asked questions, she would say it was all too complex for a child to understand. At the time I didn't think fourteen was a "child."

I begged Momma not to send me again that summer, to let me go to camp instead or work at McDonald's. When she asked why, I couldn't answer. I didn't know why then. So she got my suitcase out of the attic and tossed my tickets on top. "Your plane leaves tomorrow morning," she said. "Nine o'clock."

She had always been a good mother, but not a happy one. I knew she wasn't sending me away to get rid of me. She simply wanted me to spend time with my father. She still loved him. And she wanted me to love him, too.

She never would come right out and say it. She wouldn't talk about him at all. But I could tell by the way she dusted his picture—not real fast with one big swish like I did, but slowly around

170

the edges of the frame, carefully under the crack of the metal casing, and finally the glass, stroking his face softly with her rag.

All she said when she dropped me at the airport that morning was "Have yourself a good time," and "Kiss your daddy for me." I hugged her good-bye, hoping I'd get a window seat.

That afternoon as the plane taxied up to the airport, I saw him standing outside the terminal. He wasn't real tall, just medium, but he looked strong and solid—as if he had grown up out of the concrete. He still had that habit of pushing his hair back with his hand, even though it was too short to be in his face.

I was one of the first ones off. He smiled and waved when he saw me coming down the steps of the plane. I ran over to him and we hugged. Right then, I couldn't imagine why I didn't want to come.

"Sorry you had to wait so long, Dad. We had to change planes in Denver. Something about the hydraulic system."

He didn't say anything, just held my head in his hands. I could feel those hot, enormous hands covering my whole head—palms over my ears, fingers touching the back of my skull, and thumbs outlining my eyebrows. I remembered an Oral Roberts TV show, the preacher yelling, "Heal, heal!" Then Dad kissed me.

He stepped away, pushed his hair back and said, "I almost didn't recognize you, Ronnie. You're getting prettier each time you come."

"And you're looking more and more like Bruce Springsteen," I said, jerking the bandanna from his hip pocket and tying it around my neck. "Great jacket. I know some kids at school who'd *die* for a leather jacket like that."

"It's just my old flight jacket. One of the few things that came out of Nam in one piece. Haven't worn it in years." His hand started up toward his head, but I caught it. We held hands all the way to the Jeep.

It was an hour's drive from the airport to Dad's cabin in the mountains, but the time flew. We sang songs to a Golden Oldies radio station: "I can't get no-o/sat-is-FAC-shun-un." We laughed at the end of every song.

"How do you know all these words?" he asked. "You're too young for this stuff."

"Momma has the records. But she never sings along, like you do. How do *you* know all the words?"

"It's what kept me alive over there. I'll never forget the words."

After a few more songs and a news report, we were home. Before going in, we stood for a minute on the porch of his cabin and listened to the night sounds from the woods all around us. He put his arm around me and I could smell him now in the wilderness air—the leather jacket, gasoline from the Jeep, soap.

"Hungry?" he asked.

"Starved! I could eat a horse."

"Would you settle for a cheese sandwich and pickles?"

"Sounds great."

His cabin only had a bathroom and then one big room where everything just kind of blended together. Dad set my suitcase and sleeping bag down in my corner. He slept on the couch, angled toward the TV. The dining room was a wooden block in another corner, and the kitchen area was next to it.

There were a fireplace and a huge bookshelf, an awesome stereo—all being stared at by dozens of pairs of lifeless eyes. I hardly noticed the animal heads anymore. They'd become a natural part of things. Only the soldier's skull still bothered me, hanging above the fireplace, a place of honor. That big room always felt hot and cold to me at the same time. It reminded me of chemistry lab—I loved it, yet I was afraid I was going to blow myself up.

We ate our sandwiches off paper plates, then stretched out on the floor in front of the fire, talking about school, boys and dating, his latest job. I'd lost count of those.

"Why don't you ever go out, Dad? You're so good-looking."

"Not interested, Ronnie. I like things the way they are."

He glanced over at me, eyes heavy from the fire. Then I realized I was getting sleepy, too. I looked up at the animals and had to shut my eyes when I got to the skull.

I remembered the first summer he'd put it up. I couldn't have been more than four or five. The room was dark; we were curled up together on the couch in front of the fire. Dad was reading me a story called "The Nightingale." I stared up and saw the skull, glowing in the firelight.

At first I was too scared to say anything, even though I didn't

even know what a skull was. Dad asked me what was wrong. I
pointed to it and whispered, "What's that?"

"Oh, it's okay. That won't hurt you. It's just a trophy, like the
others." He held up the book we had been reading. "Do you think
the nightingale will save the Emperor's life?"

"No," I said, staring at the skull. "I think the Emperor was very
mean to the nightingale. He should die." I looked at Dad and
asked, "*Did* somebody die?"

"That story isn't for little girls," he said.

I begged and begged him to tell me, so he did. I guess he figured
I wouldn't remember it at that age. Maybe he just needed to tell it
to someone; anyone.

His voice was soft when he started but distant, not as if he were
reading a fairy tale at all. "It happened in Vietnam," he began.
"That's where Daddy went to fight. Me and my co-pilot Frank
were flying our helicopter into the jungle to bring out some
wounded. It was a hot LZ. We took some heavy fire in the tail
rotor and went down, hard. Me and Frank made it out somehow,
but everybody had scattered and we were on our own. We were
trying to get back to the base when we came to this rice paddy we
had to cross. No sooner than we stepped out of the bush, a sniper
opened fire on us."

Dad's face perspired with the heat of the jungle as he told the
story, and I saw the reflection of the fire in his eyes. His hand
pulled his hair back, again and again.

"At first I didn't hear anything. Frank's head just suddenly blew
apart. I felt it splatter on me. That's when I heard the little 'pop,
pop, pop.' I caught a round in the shoulder and was knocked
down. It's funny but I remember thinking, I'm shot. But it's not so
bad. It only stings. I looked over at what was left of Frank's head,
not really feeling anything at first, not really believing what I was
seeing. Then something snapped inside me. I went kind of crazy, I
guess.

"I got up and ran at the sniper, all the way across that field—
firing my pistol, screaming, not really caring if I shot him or he
shot me. I only knew *something* had to die. When I got to the other
side, I found him lying in the grass. I'd shot him in the throat. But
I couldn't stop, I didn't want to stop."

Dad was suddenly silent as he stared up at the skull. He was breathing hard.

"I stabbed him over and over with my knife. Then I cut off his head." There was no emotion in Dad's voice. "His for Frank's, to even the score. To make it right." He looked away. "I still had it with me when I walked out of that jungle a week later. I kept it. Some guys over there carried around a necklace of ears. I had a head. And as long as I had it, I knew no one could touch me."

He looked down at me, back in this world. "Now I've put it up there with the rest of the animals; that's all. It's just a memory, and memories can't hurt you—can they, pumpkin?" He smiled and brushed back my hair. "You don't understand, do you?"

I never did get to hear the end of "The Nightingale" that night, but I've always remembered his story. Since then there's been so much that I haven't understood. Like how I could love him and fear him at the same time, my own father, this man who was lying on the floor next to my sleeping bag, his eyes bright with fire.

Dad brushed my forehead—just as he'd done that night he'd told the story of the skull. "Are you sleepy, Ronnie?" he asked.

I smiled, shook my head. I saw by the way he said it that he loved me so much. He ran his hand through his hair as he looked down at me, stared into my eyes.

I turned away, shut my eyes tight. Then my mind was sending paragraphs in single sentences. *Don't do this. I don't want to. I love you. Go away.*

And then, as always, it was happening. But not to me. Never, to me. It was always someone else. My eyes were shut and I was far away, waiting for it to be over.

When I went to the bathroom to get ready for bed, I remember thinking how the steam from the shower was like tears running down the walls. A cabin with crying walls. I closed my eyes and pushed my hair back under the hot, hot water. I pushed my thoughts back, too.

"All you need is *love!*" The stereo jerked me out of sleep.

I could see Dad in the kitchen beating some eggs with a fork in rhythm to the song. The smell of burned toast was making its way over to my corner of the room.

"Hey, Dad. Smells great! What's for breakfast?"

By now smoke was seeping out of the oven and I knew the bread had to be black. I jumped up and ran in to open the oven door. Smoke poured out. When he turned around, Dad seemed more shocked to see me than the smoke.

"Morning, Dad." I turned on the Vent-a-Hood. The fan motor sounded as loud as a helicopter. He just stood there looking at me, gripping the fork in his fist. Sweat was rolling off his forehead, and smoke was everywhere. He looked like someone who'd just woken up from a nightmare.

I took the charred bread out of the oven. "Don't you know you cook out all the nutrients when you do this?"

He wiped his forehead with the back of his hand, looked away and tried to grin. Then he pulled a can of biscuits out of the fridge. "Here," he said, tossing the can to me. "Let's see if you're a better cook than your old man." He went back to his eggs.

I peeled off the wrapper and tapped the seam of the can lightly against the counter. Once, twice. That can reminded me of him that morning—ready to explode.

During breakfast we didn't look at each other or talk hardly at all, just listened to the music. Then he went for a walk while I cleaned things up and watched TV. By lunchtime Dad was back and pretty much himself again. He asked me if I was ready for some decent food. I didn't want to seem too excited. I thought it might hurt his feelings about his cooking.

"Sure."

"Well, let's go," he said, pulling on his flight jacket.

"But I have to change clothes."

"Wouldn't you rather have a new dress?"

This time I *did* get excited. "Sure!" I said and raced him to the Jeep.

We drove down the mountain to town. I had to try on several dresses from the incredibly wide selection at Candy's Fashion Scene before I decided on a short pink one. It was a lot shorter than Momma would've ever let me buy. I really didn't expect Dad to let me either. To be honest, I tried it on just to see if he would say anything. All he said was, "I think that color looks good on you."

After the dress, we drove to the town's new restaurant for lunch. The Mountain Inn didn't look like a restaurant at all. It was just a big blue rectangular building with a gaudy neon sign mounted on the back of a trailer. And I thought, *What a waste of a new dress!*

I guess Dad could tell by my face I was disappointed because he said, "Things aren't as fancy in this part of the country. But the food's good."

I got mad at myself for acting childish and said, "I'm starved."

When we sat down, a waitress plopped two plastic menus in front of us. She had on a name tag that said "Wyoma" and a face that said she knew Dad. Her uniform was a pair of tight jeans and a T-shirt with the slogan "Blondes Do It Better." She looked at me, then said to Dad, "Good to see you, Gary. It's been a while."

"Been busy," Dad said. He asked me what I'd like and he ordered the same.

Wyoma asked, "Would you like for me to cut the little girl's meat for her, or is she old enough to handle a knife by herself?"

Dad laughed when I said, "I can cut my own meat, thank you."

"Spunky little thing, ain't she?" Wyoma gave me a fake grin.

"Takes after her father," Dad answered.

Wyoma looked at Dad to see if he was serious, then hit his arm with her order pad. "I could kill you, Gary Fenster! Teasing me like that."

When Wyoma left, I asked Dad, "Wonder what it is she does better?"

Dad's lips moved a little to the side as they always did when he was thinking something funny. "Well, I know she makes better toast than I do," he said, and we both laughed so loud that people turned around and looked at us.

I whispered, "I think she likes you."

"She likes anything with a deep voice and pants," Dad said, and we laughed out loud again.

When Wyoma brought our order over, she asked, "You two hiding a joke book under the table?"

Dad and I couldn't stop giggling. You know how it is when you get really tickled at something? Things aren't even funny anymore, but you keep laughing anyway.

Wyoma tore our check out of her order pad, slapped it upside down next to Dad's plate. "She seems a little too innocent for *your* jokes, Gary." Then she pushed a pencil behind her ear and went to pour coffee for customers sitting at the counter.

That night, Dad surprised me by taking me to an outdoor concert. It was country/western music—not exactly my favorite, but it was okay. Toward the end of the concert, the band started playing a really fast song and everyone hopped up, clapping and dancing. Before we knew it, we were dancing too—swinging, dipping, kicking. As the music sped up, we did too, dancing faster and faster. I felt my new dress swish high around my thighs. I'd never felt so wonderful, so free.

The song stopped suddenly and we fell to the ground, too out of breath to say anything. We lay there, chests moving up and down, hair wet with sweat. I could have stayed in that same spot all night, staring up at the stars, feeling the earth spin.

Dad held my hand all the way home that night. He didn't even let go to shift gears. It felt so good having someone care that much about me. Momma loved me, but not like Dad. The rhythm of the road and the breeze against my eyes put me to sleep, my head still spinning.

I didn't wake up until Dad was carrying me inside the cabin. I was still half asleep when I felt him put me gently on my sleeping bag and kiss my cheek. He kissed me again on my other cheek. He brushed my bangs back and kissed my forehead. I told myself to calm down. He's your father. He loves you. He wouldn't do anything to hurt you. *He's not like that.*

I opened my eyes. Dad's face was close to mine, and behind him I saw the skull. It glowed in the firelight, the flames dancing in its empty eyes. I wanted to go away again, let it happen to someone else; but the skull face wouldn't let me. I was caught between sleeping and waking, not knowing what was real and what was a dream while he stared down at me, stroking me. I closed my eyes, tried to go away, but I could still feel him on me. "Dad . . ." I started to say. But when I looked, it wasn't him anymore. It was the skull's face, lit by the fire, staring down at me, grinning. It moved closer, that awful mouth opening and closing as it whispered over and over, "I love you, Ronnie, I love you."

I screamed.

I screamed so loud, I scared myself even more. Then I couldn't stop screaming. I screamed at the skull, I screamed at him, I screamed at the dark woods around us. All the ugly pictures flashed through my head, one after the other, blending into each other like the rooms in this cabin, like his face and the skull's face; with no beginning and no end. Then I was crying and shaking so hard, I could barely breathe.

Dad held me down. He was saying over and over, "Ronnie, I'm sorry, I'm sorry. Ronnie, don't cry. Please don't cry."

When I finally got calmed down, he tried to take me in his arms to comfort me, like only a father could. I jerked away from him, said, "I want to go home." I knew it hurt him, but I didn't care.

I stayed awake all night, waiting for the sun to come into the room. I thought it would be better then. But it was worse. Everything was so much more real. I still had on the pink dress. It seemed cheap and dirty, and I hated it.

Dad sat motionless in the chair across the room. He'd been awake all night, too.

I asked if we could get ready to leave and he asked if I was hungry. I shook my head, knowing I would choke if I tried to swallow anything. I changed clothes and packed.

The drive to the airport was silent—no talking, no music. Dad took care of changing the ticket for me.

"Any problem?" I asked when he handed it to me.

"No problem," he said. He backed up a few feet, stared at me. He ran his hand through his short hair. "Except now I wish I had been killed over there and I wouldn't have hurt you like this."

Standing away from me like that, he didn't seem so handsome anymore. He stuffed both hands in his pockets, said, "Tell your mother I'm moving. Tell her I'll . . ." He shifted his weight from one foot to the other. "Straighten things out. I'll make them even." He cleared his throat. I could tell this was tough for him, but I still didn't care. "And I want you to be honest with her. Tell her the truth."

I nodded. Just wanted to get away from there. Away from him. I wondered if I would ever stop hating him.

When the announcement was made to board the plane, I practically ran. I didn't say good-bye or even turn around to look at him. From my window seat, as the plane taxied, I watched him disappear into the terminal, head down and his hands buried in his flight jacket.

That was the last time I ever saw him. No one knows where he is or even if he's still alive. Momma and I don't play the music anymore. Sometimes I really miss it. Sometimes.

William F. Nolan

ON 42ND ST.

OPEN an anthology, book of poetry, novel, or magazine, and don't be startled to find Bill Nolan present creatively. It's all catalogued in a nine-year project recently published by Borgo, *The Work of William F. Nolan*—one hundred short stories (including those in his upcoming horror/terror collection *Nightshapes* (Avon) and fifty books, among them his renowned "Logan" trilogy and his first horror novel, *Helltracks* (also Avon)—a still blooming total of more than twelve hundred works.

What can't be catalogued is friendship. Or good times. Like an Ottawa night when Wuffin, from memory, acted out most of the *Maltese Falcon* film parts. Or a Nashville night when, to highlight his affection for *Shane*, he did the same for *Shane* with magical impressions of Alan Ladd; Van Heflin; Jack Palance. Nolan finished by calling "Shaaaaane" in the perfect wail of eleven-year-old Brandon DeWilde. Just as in this new story a remarkable writer captures the wails rising from a certain sin-soaked street. A *different* Nolan, here—the genius intact.

ON 42ND ST.

William F. Nolan

HE HADN'T BEEN TO NEW YORK since he was a kid, not since his last year of high school. That had been his graduation present: a trip to the Big Apple. He'd bugged his parents for years about New York, how it was the center of everything and how not to see it was like never seeing God. As a kid, he used to think of New York as the god of the U.S. He read every book he could find about it at his local library in Atkin.

His parents were quite content to stay in Ohio, in this little town they'd met and married in, where he'd been born and where his father had his tool business. His parents never traveled anywhere, and neither had he until he took the train to New York that summer when he was eighteen.

The city was hot and humid, but the weather hadn't bothered him. He'd been too enchanted, too dazzled by the high-thrusting towers of Manhattan, the jungle roar of mid-town traffic, the glitter of Fifth Avenue, the pulse of night life on Broadway—and by the green vastness of Central Park, plunked like a chunk of Ohio into the center of this awesome steel-and-concrete giant.

And by the people. Especially on the subways; he'd never seen so many people jammed together in a single place. Jostling each other, shouting, laughing, cursing. Big and small, rich and poor, young and old, black and brown and yellow and white. An assault on the senses, so many of them.

"The subways are no good anymore," his friends now told him. "They've got graffiti all over them and you can get mugged real easy on a subway. Cabs are your best bet. Once inside a taxi, you're safe . . . at least until you get out!"

And they had also warned him, all these years later, to stay away from 42nd Street. "Forty-second's like a blight," they declared. "New York's changed since you were a kid. It can get ugly, *real* ugly."

And they'd talked about the billions of cockroaches and rats that lived under the city and in it, how even in the swankiest apartment on Fifth Avenue they have cockroaches late at night, crawling the walls . . .

So here he was, Ben Sutton, thirty-eight, balding and unmarried, on a plane to Kennedy—returning to the Apple after twenty years to represent the Sutton Tool Manufacturing Company of Atkin, Ohio. His father, Ed Sutton, who had founded the company, was long dead. Now Ben owned the business, because his mother had died within a year of his father. Over the past decade, he'd been sending other company employees to the National Tool Convention each year in New York, but this time, on a sudden impulse, he'd decided to go himself.

His friends backed the decision. " 'Bout time for you to stir your stumps, Ben," they told him. "Take the trip. Get some *excitement* into your life."

They were right. Ben's life had settled into a series of dull routine days, one following another like a row of black dominos. By now the business practically ran itself, and Ben was feeling more and more like a figurehead. A trip such as this would revitalize him; he'd be plugged into the mainstream of life again. Indeed, it *was* time to "stir his stumps."

Kennedy was a madhouse. Ben lost his baggage claim check and had a difficult time proving that his two bags really belonged to him. Then the airport bus he took from Kennedy to Grand Central suffered some kind of mechanical malfunction and he had to wait by the side of the highway with a dozen angry passengers until another bus arrived a full hour later.

At Grand Central a gaunt-bodied teenager, with the words "The Dead Live!" stitched across the back of his red poplin jacket, ran off with one of Ben's suitcases while he was phoning the hotel to ask for an extension on his room reservation. A beefy station cop grabbed the kid and got the suitcase back.

The cop asked if he wanted to press charges, but Ben shook his head. "Let somebody else press charges when he steals another suitcase. I can't get involved."

The cop scowled. "That's a piss-poor attitude, mister." He glared at the teenager. "This little dickhead ought to be put away."

When the cop finally let him go, the kid gave them both the finger before vanishing in the crowd.

"You see that?" asked the cop, flushed with anger. "You see what that little shit did? I oughta run him down and pound him good. An' I got half a mind to do it!"

"That's your choice, Officer," Ben declared. "But I have to get a cab to my hotel before I lose my room."

"Sure, go ahead," said the cop. "It's no sweat off my balls what the hell you do."

Well, thought Ben, they warned me things could get ugly.

The convention hotel was quite nice and his room was pleasant. His window faced Central Park and there was a wonderful view of the spreading greenery.

The bellhop nodded when Ben told him how much he liked the view. "Yeah—maybe you'll get to watch an ol' lady being mugged down there." He chuckled, then asked if Ben was "with the convention."

"Yes, I'm here from Ohio."

"Well, a lot of the convention people are boozin' it up at the bar. Maybe you'll make some new friends."

The bellhop's words were prophetic.

After he had showered and changed into fresh clothes, Ben took the elevator down to the bar (called The Haven), and he had not been there for more than five minutes when two men sat down on stools, one to either side of him.

"So, you're a tool man, huh?" asked the fellow to Ben's left. Bearded, with large, very dark eyes and a lot of teeth in his smile.

"Correct," said Ben. "How did you know?"

"Lapel," said the other man, the one on the right. He was thin and extremely pale with washed-out blue eyes behind thick glasses.

Ben looked confused. "I don't—"

"That pin in the lapel of your coat," the bearded man said. "Dead giveaway."

Ben smiled, touching the bright metal lapel pin which featured a hammer, wrench, and pliers in an embossed design above the logo: "Sutton's—Tools You Can Trust."

"Are you two gentlemen also here for the convention?" Ben asked.

"You got it," said the man in glasses. "I'm Jock Kirby, and this bearded character is Billy Dennis."

"Ben Sutton."

They shook hands.

"Us, we're local boys, from the core of the Apple," said Billy Dennis. "Where you hail from?"

"Atkin, Ohio."

"Akron?" asked Jock. "I know a tire man from Akron."

"No, *Atkin*," Ben corrected him. "We're a few hundred miles from Akron. People tend to get the names mixed."

"Never heard of it," said Billy.

"It's a small town," Ben told them. "Nothing much to hear about."

"What you drinking?" Jock asked.

"Scotch and water," said Ben.

"Great. Same for us." Kirby gestured to the bartender, raising Ben's glass. "Three more of these, okay?"

"Okay," nodded the barman.

"So," said Billy Dennis, running a slow hand along his bearded cheek, "you're an Ohio man. Not much pizzazz back there, huh?"

"Pizzazz?" Ben blinked at him.

"He means," added Kirby, "you must get bored out of your gourd with nothing much shaking in Akins."

"Atkin. It's Atkin."

"Well, whatever," Kirby grunted.

Their drinks arrived and Dennis shoved a twenty-dollar bill toward the barman.

"What do you do for kicks back in Ohio?" asked Kirby.

"I watch television," Ben said, sipping his Scotch. "Listen to music. Eat out on occasion. Go to a movie when there's one I really want to see." He shrugged. "But, frankly, I'm not much of a moviegoer."

"Boy," sighed Billy Dennis. "Sounds like you have yourself a blast."

"Fun time," said Jock Kirby.

Ben shifted on the barstool. "I don't require a whole lot out of life. I guess I'm what you'd call 'laid back.'"

Billy Dennis chuckled, showing his teeth. "Take my word, Bennie, it's better gettin' laid than bein' laid back!"

"Fuckin' A," said Jock.

Ben flushed and hastily finished his drink. He wasn't accustomed to rough language and he didn't appreciate it.

Dennis gestured to the barman, making a circle in the air. "Another round," he said.

"No, no, I've really had enough," Ben protested. He was already feeling light-headed. He'd never been a drinker.

"Aw, c'mon, Bennie boy," urged Jock Kirby. "*Live* a little. Take a bite out of the Big Apple."

"Yeah," nodded Billy Dennis, his dark eyes fixed on the Ohio man. "Have another shot on us."

And each of them put an arm around Ben Sutton.

The walk down Broadway was like a dream. Ben couldn't remember leaving the bar. Had they taken a cab here? His head seemed full of rosy smoke.

"I think I drank too much," he said. The words were blurred. His tongue was thick and rebellious.

"Can't ever drink too much at a party," said Billy Dennis. "An' that's what we got goin' here tonight!"

"Fuckin' A," Jock said. "It's party time."

"I've got to get back to the hotel," Ben told them. "The convention opens at ten tomorrow morning. I need sleep."

"Sleep?" Dennis gave Ben a toothy smile. "Hell, you can sleep when you're dead. We're gonna show you a fun time, Bennie."

"Sure are," agreed Jock Kirby. "Make you forget all about Ohio."

"Where are we going?" asked Ben. He found it difficult to keep pace with them, and the lights along the street seemed to be buried in mist.

"Forty-second is where," nodded Kirby. "Jump street."

Ben stopped. He raised a protesting hand. "That's a dangerous area," he said thickly. "My friends warned me to avoid it."

"*We're* your friends now," said Billy Dennis. "An' *we* say it's where all the action is. Right, Jocko?"

"Fuckin' A," Kirby said.

A street bum approached them, his clawed right hand extended. Ben dug out a quarter, dropping it into the scabbed palm. "Bless you," said the bum.

"Butt off," said Kirby.

The bum ignored him. He gestured to the sacks of garbage stacked along the curb, black-plastic bags swollen with waste. Roaches and insects burrowed among them. He nodded toward Ben. "Don't step on the maggots," he said.

And moved on up Broadway.

"I'm not so sure about this," Ben told them. "I still think I should take a taxi back to the hotel."

"The friggin' hotel can wait," said Kirby. His pale skin seemed to glow in the darkness. "Hotel's not goin' anywhere."

"Right," agreed Billy Dennis. "Stuck in that hotel, you might as well be back in Elkins."

"Atkin," corrected Ben. His head felt detached from his body, which floated below it.

"Hey, we're here," grinned Jock Kirby. "Welcome to sin street!"

They had reached Forty-second and Broadway. The intersection traffic throbbed around them in swirls of moving light and sound. Neons blazed and sizzled. The air smelled of ash.

Ben blinked rapidly, trying to sharpen his focus.

"I think I'm drunk," he said.

"No, man," Jock assured him. "You've just got a little *glow* on is all. Go with it. Enjoy."

Billy Dennis held Ben's left elbow, propelling him along Forty-second. Ben felt weightless, as if his body were made of tissue paper.

"Where . . . are you taking me?"

"To a special place," said Billy. "You'll really dig it. Right, Jocko?"

"Fuckin' A," said Kirby.

Ben struggled to get a clear visual fix on the area. His senses recorded a kaleidoscope of color and noise. The walk swarmed with pimps and prostitutes, beggars and barkers, tourists and heavy trippers. Movie marquees bloomed with light, a fireworks of neon. Souvenir shops and porno peep shows gaudily competed for attention. A sea of disembodied voices poured over Ben as he walked; faces drifted past him like a gallery of ghosts.

"I'm dizzy," he said. "I've got to sit down."

"You can sit down when we get inside," Kirby told him.

"Inside where?"

"You'll see," said Billy. "We're almost there."

They stopped at a building of bright-flashing lights with a twenty-foot female nude outlined on its facade in twisting snakes of color. GIRLS . . . NUDE . . . GIRLS . . . NUDE . . . flashed the lights.

A feral-faced barker in a soiled white shirt and worn Levi's gestured at them. His eyes were bloodshot.

"Step right in, gents, the show's ready to start. The girls are all absolutely naked and *un*adorned. They'll tease and titillate, delight and dazzle you."

Ben's new friends marched him inside the building, one to each elbow, up a flight of wide, red-painted stairs to a landing illumined by bands of blue fluorescent tubing, and down a hallway to a room in which a series of plastic stools formed a large circle. All very surreal, dreamlike. And, somehow, threatening.

Each stool faced a window, shuttered in gleaming red metal, with a coin slot at the bottom. The other stools were unoccupied, which Ben found odd.

"You're just in time, brother," said a tall beanstalk of a man with badly pitted skin. "Show's about to begin. Ten minutes for a quarter. And the feels are free."

"Open your fingers, Ben," said Jock Kirby—and he put several silver quarters into Ben's hand. "Just pop one in at the bottom," he said. Then he grinned. "Nothin' like this back in Ohio!"

Ben Sutton obeyed, numbly slotting in the first coin.

Now he waited as, slowly, the metal shutter rolled up to reveal a large circular platform bathed in a powdery blaze of overhead spots.

A thick-faced, sullen-eyed woman stepped from an inner door. She wore a dress of red sequins and a cheap red wig. She looked at Ben.

"Welcome to the Hellhole," she said. "You're right on time." Her smile was ugly.

Ben kept expecting to see other windows opening, but he remained the only customer. Not much profit in this show, he thought dully.

"We herewith present, for your special entertainment, the Flame of Araby."

The thick-faced woman pressed a button by the side of the platform and, to a burst of pre-recorded drum music, a long-limbed blonde stepped through the doorway.

She was wearing several gauzy veils which she quickly began discarding. Young and full-figured, she was attractive in a vulgar sense as she whirled and twisted to the beating drums. Her glittery eyes were locked on Ben, who sat numb and transfixed at the window. Kirby was right; he had seen nothing like this in Ohio.

Now the final veil whispered from her hips and she was, as the barker had promised, "absolutely naked and unadorned."

In all of his thirty-eight years, Ben Sutton had never seen a totally nude woman. Linda Mae Lewis had allowed him to see her left breast under the dim illumination of the dash lights in Ben's old Pontiac convertible when he was in college, and a waitress at the Quick-Cup coffee shop on the outskirts of Atkin had once let him place his hand under her uniform—and he'd been able to view her upper thigh—but that was the full extent of Ben's sexual experience with females.

Thus, he was truly dazzled by the curved, shimmering white body writhing just inches in front of him.

"Go ahead, sweetie, touch one," the girl said in a husky voice, aiming her naked buttocks at Ben. "Go for it!"

Trembling, Ben reached out to touch the naked slope of a mooned buttock; the flesh was marble-smooth and seemed to vibrate under his fingers.

Then, at that moment, the red-metal shutter began sliding down. Ben jerked his hand back with a groan of frustration. His ten minutes had expired.

Frantically, spilling several coins to the floor, Ben slotted in another quarter—and the shutter rolled slowly up again.

But the platform was empty.

The girl was gone.

The music had stopped.

Ben spun around on his stool to ask his two friends why the show had ended, but the room was deserted.

Ben stood up. "Hello! Anybody here?"

No reply. Just the muted sounds of street traffic, punctuated by the thin wail of a distant police siren.

Ben walked into the hall.

"Kirby? . . . Dennis? . . . You out here?"

No reply.

He moved toward the stairs. Or that was the direction he intended to take. Obviously, he had gone the wrong way because the hallway twisted, leading him deeper into the building.

The passage seemed dimmer, narrower.

Ben heard laughter ahead of him. A door opened along the hall, flooding the area with light.

He walked to the open door, looked in. The thick-faced woman and the blond dancing girl were there, with Jock Kirby and Billy Dennis. They were all laughing together, with drinks in their . . . in their . . . their . . .

Not hands. Dear God, not hands!

"Hi, Ben," said the Billy-thing. "We're celebrating."

"Because of you, chum," said the Jock-thing. "Meat on the hoof!"

"Yeah," nodded the blonde, running a pink tongue over her lips, "even maggots hafta eat."

Ben stared at them. His stomach was churning; a sudden rush of nausea made him stagger back, vomiting into the hall.

Inside the room, the four of them were discarding body parts . . .

limbs . . . ears . . . noses . . . their flesh dropping away like chunks of rotten cheese.

Ben allowed himself one last, horror-struck backward glance into the room as he turned to run.

The things he saw were like the maggots and roaches in the swollen bags of trash along Broadway, but much larger, much more . . . advanced.

Ben Sutton ran.

He couldn't find the stairs. The hall kept twisting back on itself—but if he kept running he'd find a way out.

He was *sure* he would find a way out.

John Maclay

SAFE

SINCE 1981, John Maclay has been the author of more than forty published short stories that have appeared in such magazines as *Twilight Zone, Night Cry,* and *Crosscurrents;* fourteen published poems; a story collection, *Other Engagements* (Dream House, '87); and a co-written novel, *Wards of Armageddon* (Leisure, '86).

Concurrently, John—who previously worked in advertising—was the publisher of sixteen books divided between local Baltimore history and fiction, including *Masques* ('84) and *Masques II* ('87). Each was nominated for a World Fantasy Award. He created, edited, and published the short anthology *Nukes* ('86) featuring new fiction by Jessica Salmonson, Mort Castle, Joe Lansdale, and your editor; it was widely reviewed, and admired for the way it used writers of horror to address "the ultimate horror."

A good and a versatile man, Maclay lives with his wife, Joyce, and two sons.

SAFE

John Maclay

PERHAPS, AS YOU SAID, DOCTOR, THIS will help. I know that your methods are unorthodox, but I've been to everyone else, and I'm willing to try anything. So I'll just sit here in this light, with the pad and pen you've given me, and write, openly, about my worst fear. The one that, if I don't get help soon, will surely kill me.

It's not strictly claustrophobia, as you know. I've never minded being shut up in a room, no matter how small. It doesn't even matter whether it's light or dark—one time I stood for twenty minutes in a closet, waiting for a friend who was brought late to a surprise party, with no ill effects. And you know, I think I could be a coal miner, bent over in those endless, low tunnels, without any fear. Even an astronaut, in that tiny capsule, provided there was a window. Though only in that situation, not the closet or the mine, would I need one—and even then, it could be light or dark, so long as I knew I was looking out into space.

We're getting somewhere, aren't we, Doctor? My great fear, apparently, is this: *being shut up in a small, windowless place much lower than my head.*

Did I write "apparently?" Oh, my God . . .

The first time I can remember is when I was nine. A playmate of mine lived in a Victorian house with a lot of nooks and crannies, and one day he showed me his new hideout. It was under the back stoop, where a little door led to a closed place probably meant for storing garden tools. He'd rigged up a light bulb from an outlet in the house, smoothed down the earth floor, and tacked up posters of old cars. It looked fine to me.

But then he led me inside. And slammed the door.

It wasn't the lack of air, the dank smell—it's never been that. And I knew, in that situation, that I could leave at any time. As it turned out, I should have, right away—but kids are kids, and not only did I not want to spoil my playmate's fun, I couldn't let him see my fear.

So I sat there cross-legged, feeling the rough ceiling brush my hair—and the sweat started to bead on my forehead. Listening to my friend talk happily about Model As and Model Ts. Watching him point casually to his posters—

Until his voice was drowned out by the pounding of my young heart. Until his image blurred—because I was looking past him, at the tight walls, which seemed to be closing in, *in* . . .

The last thing I remember about my companion—after that, he wouldn't see me anymore—was the shocked look on his face. As I *screamed*, shoved open the door, and *ran*.

Well, that's the childhood memory, Doctor. The one your kind always wants to drag out of me, since presumably the telling will break the spell. But in my case, of course, it hasn't. So let's go on . . .

Movies. I've always loved them. They've provided escape, which is something I've needed, especially of late. And I've always been drawn to the old macho adventures—they seemed to give me strength against my fear. Wayne. Cooper. Bogart. Bogart. Which brings up Cagney. Cagney. And Robinson. Robinson . . .

But—oh, God. That brings up the *scene* . . .

It's one of those black-and-white prisons of the 1930s. Hard enough, with those cold cell blocks, Spartan mess halls, and inmates with knives around every corner. But those things don't frighten me—because, although I'm locked in, at least I can stand erect, even plot with Jimmy and Eddie to escape. Until . . .

We're caught. And then, it's the *Hole*.

Anything, anything but that. That low, narrow cage made of boiler plate. That steel door closing, as I kneel inside. That window, yes, which opens once a day, as the guard hands in my bread and water—but it's not enough, not nearly enough. Because in the meantime, as I try to stand upright, even try to stretch my body out horizontally, pretend to stand—

I slowly go mad.

Please don't laugh when you read this, Doctor. You really shouldn't—because that scene, at the wrong time, cost me my first love. It was like this: we were relaxing on the sofa, watching an old movie, when suddenly . . .

The look on her face was the same as my childhood playmate's. When I screamed again—and *ran*.

But I got over that, too. Found other women. Still enjoyed the movies. Though I chose them carefully—didn't even look at the previews of *Papillon*. I was doing fine—after all, there aren't that many tiny, enclosed places in this great world. And as time went on, I was almost able to relegate those two horrible events into the past, where I thought they belonged. But then . . .

I was a senior in college and had signed up for Art Appreciation. A pleasant course, and easy, with its thrice-a-week lectures that consisted mostly of slides. We were up to eighteenth-century England that day, that awful Wednesday. I was leaning back in my chair, enjoying the work of Kneller and Constable, half-dozing . . . when suddenly a very different picture flashed on the screen.

William Blake. *The Grave*.

I tried to control myself, and I succeeded. No screaming this time—no running. I was older now, and I was proud. And mercifully, the professor's voice droned on, and the slide changed.

But as I walked back to my dormitory room in the beautiful sunlight, I still couldn't get that image out of my mind. So, in an attempt to purge myself of it—you know about that, don't you, Doctor?—I stopped at the library, and took out a book on Blake.

. . . It's late that night. I'm lying motionless on my bed, hypnotized, staring at that picture. The cold, heavy, overarching stone ceiling, even more menacing in black-and-white line engraving. The human figures—lying there frozen, but so, *so* lifelike. Their

eyes . . . open. In that constricted, exitless space, the ceiling press-
ing down, down—and suddenly, I'm *with* them—*in that place
which is lower than my head.*

I suppose it's been downhill since then, Doctor. And, I might
add, an open book to my few friends. How I had my first nervous
breakdown, and didn't graduate with my class. How my marriage
broke up: When I was alone at our home in the country, a tiny
electrical fire started in the crawl space—something that only
needed a squirt of the extinguisher—and I let our new house burn
to the ground. (My wife later ran off with one of the firemen—it
would be funny, if it weren't so sad.) How I've always steered
clear of any . . . place . . . like that, or any image of it, however
brief. (I lost another friend, recently, by being unable to ride in the
back of his windowless van.) And how I've had the *nightmares*—of
ever-increasing frequency and intensity, making sleep impossible,
threatening my health.

And yes, how I've become one of those strange people who
make, uh, special arrangements. Because, you see, my coffin is
already picked out—and wired with a signaling device, in the
event I'm buried alive.

Burial—you know, Doctor, we really may be getting somewhere
despite all my previous failures. The writing—and what you've
done to me—may actually have helped. I'll admit I was terrified at
first, but knowing you're there has enabled me to control that.

My playmate's hideout . . . the Hole in the prison films . . .
Blake's tomb—especially, the tomb . . .

It's all the fear of being *trapped*, isn't it? Being *alive* but trapped,
unable to stand up, move off, look out—a *death-in-life?*

. . . Well, Doctor, I've finally had it. I'm tired of living another
kind of death-in-life—being thought strange, losing oppor-
tunities—because of that fear. I think I'll concentrate, now, on the
wonderful world outside—

Knowing, despite those awful experiences, or any others that
may come my way—

That when I'm dead and in my tomb, I will be . . . *dead.* Unable
to know where I am, or care. Or even if I do know, that I'll draw
comfort, instead, from those tight walls, that low ceiling. As they
envelop me—especially if it's dark—in *nothingness,* and sleep.

. . . I have a sense of time passing, Doctor. And it's a bit difficult to breathe—but that's due to a sense of elation at my wonderful breakthrough, isn't it? Also, there's the light—it hurts my eyes. But, in certain . . . situations . . . I've never minded its absence, have I?

So I think I'll turn it off. Yes, that's better. Though I'll have to stop writing, since I'm only guiding the pen, by feel, across the paper . . .

The darkness seems to enclose me now . . . *enfold* me . . .

BALTIMORE (AP)—In a bizarre circumstance, a psychiatrist and his patient were found dead today.

According to notes found by police, Dr. Bertram Mankin, 59, locally known for his unusual forms of therapy, had locked James Ridgley, 33, in a large old safe in his Tower Building office.

The patient, a lifelong sufferer from a form of claustrophobia, had been given a flashlight, pen, and paper, and been told to write of his fear. Apparently, the doctor had intended to release Mr. Ridgley after ten minutes, before lack of air became a problem.

However, when Dr. Mankin's secretary, Bernice Watson, 42, entered the office approximately one hour later, she found the doctor dead in his chair of a massive coronary. She then called police and paramedics who, acting upon the notes, immediately opened the safe, and discovered Mr. Ridgley to be dead of suffocation.

"The funny thing," paramedic John Magruder said, "aside from the whole weird situation, was the look on the guy's face.

"Usually, when they're trapped, you'll find an expression of struggle or horror, like the person just got done screaming.

"But this guy had a sort of peaceful smile."

The secretary, Ms. Watson, is under heavy sedation.

Gary A. Braunbeck

ALL BUT THE TIES ETERNAL

THE initial professional appearance by this boyish Ohio writer/actor/director would have been in Alan Rodgers' *Night Cry*, but it folded. Then the first might be in the Greenbergs' *Phantoms* anthology—except *I* found Gary first, even if Roz and Marty happen to beat *Masques III* into print!

Actually, several editors may wind up disputing the discovery of this recently wed writer, who will break your heart even while he's showing you shocking horror in places you've never before noticed it. Crispin Burnham and *Eldritch Tales* might also put in a claim, but—

Never mind. Gary Braunbeck's here, and he's putting the heart back into horror.

The trouble is . . . it's *bleeding*.

ALL BUT THE TIES ETERNAL

Gary A. Braunbeck

All waits undream'd of in that region . . .
Till when the ties loosen,
All but the ties eternal, Time and Space,
Nor darkness, gravitation, sense, nor any bounds bounding us.

> —Walt Whitman
> "Darest Thou Now O Soul"

AFTERWARD SHE SPENT MANY HOURS ALONE in the house for the purpose of making it emptier; it was a game to her, like the one she'd played as a child, walking on the stone wall of the garden, pretending it was a mountain ledge, not wanting to look down for the sight of rocks below, knowing certain death awaited her should she slip, a terrible fall that would crush her to bits, walking along until her steps faltered and she toppled backward, always thinking in that moment before her tiny body hit the ground: *So that's when I died.*

She had always laughed then, as a child, sitting ass-deep in mud and looking at the wall.

Now all the house had was the hole Daddy left behind, and there was no laughter remaining.

Yolanda stood looking at the small hole in the living-room wall, wondering when it would start bleeding again. It only bled at night, at twenty minutes past twelve, the same time her father had—

—A stirring from the bedroom. She listened for Michael's voice. He would have to wake soon; he always did when she got up. She peered into the darkness as if it would warn her when he awakened, perhaps split down the middle like a razor cut and allow some light to seep through; and in that light she would see her father's face, winking at her as he'd often done before letting her in on a little secret.

He'd let her in on all his little secrets, except the one that really mattered. She found it hard not to hate him for it.

Nothing came at her from the darkness. She turned back, stared at the hole. It was so tiny; silent.

The digital clock blinked: 12:19.

She took a breath and watched as the numbers changed—

—then looked at the hole.

It always began very slowly, like the trickle of water dripping from a faucet not turned completely off: one bulging droplet crept to the edge and glistened, then it fell through and slid down the wall, dark as ink.

She watched the thin stream crawl to the floor, leaving its slender thread path for the others to follow. And they did.

Pulsing out in streams heavier, thicker, they spread across the wall in every direction as if from the guts of a spider until she was staring into the center of a web, admiring patterns made by the small lines where they dripped into one another like colors off a summertime cone. Strawberry; vanilla.

A soft groan from the bedroom, then: "Yolanda? Yo? Where are you?"

She looked once more at the dark, shimmering web, then went to the bedroom where Michael was waiting.

He saw her and smiled. She was still naked.

"Where were you? Come back to bed."

"No," she said. "I want you to come into the living room and see it for yourself."

"See *what* for—? Oh, yeah. Right."

"Please?"

He sat up in bed and rubbed his eyes. "Look, Yolanda, I've been telling you for days—you've *got* to get out of this house! Your father's dead, there's nothing you can do about it. You've no rea-son to stay here. The sooner you get over this, the sooner you can get on with your life."

"I thought you left social work at the office."

"I only mean—"

"Goddammit, stop patronizing me, Michael! Get your ass up and *come look at this!*"

The anger in her voice made him do as he was told.

When they walked into the living room, she saw the last of the web slip into the hole and thought of how her father used to suck in the last string of spaghetti.

As the last of the streams pulled back in, she gripped Michael's arm and pointed. "Did you see it? *Did* you?"

He placed his other arm around her bare, sweaty shoulder, pull-ing her close. "Take it easy, Yo. Look, it's been a rotten time for you, I know that. It's why I came over and—"

"I didn't *ask* you to come over!"

"I know, but, Jesus, you haven't even called for *ten days!* I fig-ured you'd need a little time to yourself, but I never thought you'd start to . . . to . . ."

She pulled back, slapped his arm away. "Don't you dare talk to me like that! I am *not* one of your screwed-up runaway teenagers who only needs a shoulder to whine on!"

"I was only—"

"I know what you were '*only*,' thank you. I'm not one of your fragile children who might shatter if pushed—and I am *not* imag-ining things." She crossed to the hole and stuck the tip of her middle finger in, feeling the moisture. She pulled it out and felt the trace of a smile cross her lips: there was a small droplet of blood perched between her nail and the flesh of the quick. She faced Michael, offered her evidence.

"Look for yourself. Blood."

He lifted her hand closer to his face, squinted, flipped on a small table lamp.

For a moment she saw him hesitate.

There was, indeed, blood on her fingertip. He stared at it, brushed it away. "You cut your finger on the plaster."

"I most certainly did *not*."

"You did," he said. "Look." He turned her hand back; she saw the small gash in her fingertip.

Something pinched in her stomach. Her eyes blinked. Her arms began to shake. She swore she wouldn't start crying.

Making no attempt to touch her, Michael said, "If you insist on staying here, why don't you just *fix* the hole? That might take care of . . . *help* things, anyway."

She took a breath and wiped something from her eye. "It's not that big. It's just not . . . that big."

"You must be joking, right?"

She stared at him.

"It's not 'that big'?" he said. "Christ, Yo, I could stick a *pool cue* inside that thing!" He pointed and she followed with her gaze—

—remembering she'd only been able to press her fingertip against the hole before, never *in* it, never—

He was right.

The hole was bigger. Not much, less than a quarter inch in circumference, but bigger.

She stared. Her voice came out in a whisper. "I remember thinking it *should* have been bigger. I mean, he used a bullet with a hollow point, right? He sat in his favorite chair, put the gun in his mouth and . . . and the hole was so small. The sound was so loud. It was like the whole ceiling turned into thunder. I was in my bed, I heard Dad mutter to himself, and . . ." She took a small breath. "When it was over and the sound stopped ringing in my ears, I . . . came out here."

"Yeah?"

She stared hard at the hole. "I didn't look at him. I looked at the hole. It was all I could see. It looked like a mouth. It was . . . *eating*, everything."

She stood, transfixed, hugging herself. "The blood, the tiny pieces of his skull and brain—the *hole* pulled them in. It was like watching dirty dishwater go down a drain. It all swirled up around the hole, got closer and closer till there should have been nothing left—but it was still there on the wall, his blood and brains, all the pieces were still *there* and—"

"Yo, c'mon."

". . . Wanna know why he did it, Michael, if I did something to upset him—but I don't think I did. I loved him a lot, but that wasn't enough. I guess he missed Mom too much. I told him it wasn't our fault that she walked out, that she didn't love us back. He didn't ask me for much, he never did, he always gave, and I wish he had—I wish he would've asked me for help, *said* something, because he was always there for me, and when *he* needed someone, I was . . . was—"

"Yo, you need to rest."

She felt the hot tears streaming down her cheeks, but she didn't care.

". . . Because I just want him back! I want my father back, and all I've got is this fucking *hole* that took him away from me. It sucked him in, left me alone, and it's . . . not . . . *fair!*"

She buried her face in her hands and wept, feeling the fury and sorrow mix, feeling a bellyful of night making her shudder. She hated it, wanted to destroy it.

Before she knew it she was against the wall, pounding with her fists, feeling the force of her blows rip through her arms but she didn't care, she kept pounding as if Daddy would hear her and call out from the other side.

Then Michael was behind her, his arms around her, easing her away; she didn't want him to, so she whipped around to slap his face, lost her balance, suddenly falling from the garden wall again, her arms flailing to protect her from the rocks below as she fell against the wall—

—and saw the hole swallow four of her fingers.

It was still getting bigger.

Then Michael was all over her, picking her up as if she were some helpless, pathetic, frail child. She swatted at his face because he wasn't looking at the hole, he didn't *see* the small globule of blood peek over the edge as if saying, *Wait till next time . . .*

Once in bed, she fell asleep immediately.

Then woke, Michael at her side.

Then slept. And woke. And slept.

And woke—

Daddy was there, just between the beams of moonlight that slipped through the window blinds, smiling at her, his mouth growing wide as he stepped closer to the bed, whispering *It's the family comes first, you and me, that's all, honey, because family ties are the most important ones.* Then he was bending low, his mouth opening into a pit, wide and deep, sucking her in—

She slept—

No sense to her dreams, no rhythm to the words spoken to her there by figures she didn't recognize, moving slowly past her like people on the street; no purpose, no love, no reason, empty here, this place, yet so full of people, and place and time going somewhere but she couldn't tell, wouldn't tell—

And woke—

—massaging her shoulders, Michael, his hands strong, warm and comforting, his voice near, tender. "I'm not going anywhere, Yolanda, I love you, just sleep, *shhh*, yeah, that's it," like talking to a frightened child; she loved him but when would he start treating her like an adult?

She balanced on the edge of sleep, sensing her father. And the ceiling. And walls.

And the hole.

She felt it growing, slowly sucking air from the room, Daddy's voice on the tail of moonbeams *most important because they're the ones that last* . . .

Finally the darkness swirled up to take her where there was only safe, warm peace. She slept without dreams.

When she woke it was still night. But deeper. The covers were moist and warm. She moved back to press her shoulders into Michael's chest and—met cold space.

She blinked several times to convince herself she was awake. "Michael?"

No answer. She turned on her side. The cold space grew. Michael was gone. The ceiling rumbled. The other side of the bed looked so *vast.*

Maybe he'd gone for a drink of water; *she* often did that in the night.

She pulled the pillows close, waited for him to return. The clock ticked once, then again.

She called, "Bring me some water too, please." There was no response. The gas snapped on. Something cold trickled down the back of her neck. The ceiling rumbled again.

A slight breeze drifted by the bed, tickled her shoulders, went toward the open bedroom door, through the corridor—

Into the living room. The beams of moonlight pressed against the foot of the bed to tip it over and send her sliding down to the floor. She closed her eyes, felt the tightness of her flesh.

"MICHAEL!" Her voice reverberated off the walls, left her ears ringing. He *had* to have heard that.

No answer.

Maybe he'd slipped out, thinking she'd be embarrassed when she woke in the morning because of her behavior; yet he had said he *loved* her, wasn't going anywhere. (But how many times had Dad said the same thing?)

The force of the breeze increased.

She rose, put on her nightgown, shuffled into the corridor.

The breeze grew stronger.

Once in the living room, she refused to look at the hole; that's what it *wanted*, for her to stand staring as the streams flowed out and—

There was a stain on the carpet, a dark smear that hadn't been there before. She stared at it.

Was it really moving as she thought? Perhaps it was just a trick of the moonlight casting her shadow, for it seemed to grow larger, then smaller in an instant . . .

The stain kept moving. Slowly. Back. As if dragged.

She put a hand to her mouth, breathed out, reassured by her warm breath; then she snapped on a light.

She remembered a prank she'd played as a child on a neighbor who'd sent a dog to chase her from the yard. She had come home and cleared the vegetable bin of all the tomatoes Daddy had bought at that market he and Mom used to love shopping at and *thrown* them against that neighbor's house, laughing when they splattered every which way, the seeds, juice, and skin spattering, widening with each new throw and moist *pop!*, some of the skin sliding off to the ground.

The living-room wall looked like the side of that house.

Only the skin was crawling along the floor, being sucked back into the hole—which was so much bigger now, so much wider; she could probably shove her entire arm through up to the elbow.

The breeze grew violent, edging her toward the wall.

She saw Michael's Saint Christopher medal still on its chain, near the wall. He loved that medal, always wore it, wouldn't even take it off to shower.

The breeze increased, becoming wind.

The ceiling rumbled.

The hole was swirling under the seeds and skin and juice, opening wide with Daddy's smile on the tail of moonbeams . . .

Yolanda turned, caught a glimpse of herself in the mirror over the fireplace. She nearly shrieked, thinking how right her father had been:

She looked a *lot* like her mother.

The stain backed toward the base of the wall, near the hole.

She could easily stick her head through it now.

The wind almost knocked her off-balance—but she held firm, knowing something about feelings and night, love and tears: all of them could only be judged by what they drew from suffering.

So long as that suffering never drew them back.

—and if you can leave through a hole you can *come back through one*, even if it's one piece at a time. But she loved him—and weren't you supposed to help the one you loved put the pieces back together?

She ran to the wall, called his name into the aperture, watched as it gulped everything in like a last breath before dying. She jammed her hand through, hoped he might reach out to take it and come back—leave all the memories and pain behind like Mom had left them, without a backward glance of regret.

She pushed in deeper, felt something close round her wrist; so very strong, yet so gentle and loving.

Suddenly the pressure of the grip turned to the prick of razors and sucked her arm in up to the shoulder.

The ceiling started to thunder.

She yanked back again, knowing one of them would weaken soon because the stain and pieces were nearly gone now, and when they *were* gone the hole would . . . would . . .

. . . would keep growing until it had *her*, would still send the wind and thunder and memories and—

She wrenched away with all her strength—

—and felt herself pull free.

Yolanda fell back-first to the floor but didn't wait to catch her breath, didn't look at the hole; she sprinted out of the room, knowing how she could get him back. She couldn't do it with her hand, didn't dare try that again, yet she *could* make the hole bigger—and Michael would see the way out, he'd come back to her because he loved her, didn't want her to be alone, never again. *I'm sorry, Daddy, that you missed Mom so bad, but Michael is my family now, all I've got left—*

She darted through the kitchen, into the bathroom, unlocked the door to the basement, flipped on the light, took the stairs three at a time.

The shotgun. She hadn't told the police about Daddy's shotgun, they'd only taken the pistol, but that was fine because she *needed* the shotgun now, for Michael and—

—she ripped open the door to her father's work cabinet and found the twelve-gauge under a sheet of canvas. She grabbed the shells and loaded the gun, smiling as she pumped back—

—ch-chick!—

—and felt the first one slide securely into the chamber.

Back upstairs. Fast. Into the living room.

In the mirror she saw the reflection of her mother gripping the gun that had killed Daddy. She tried to work up enough saliva to spit in Momma's face but her mouth was too dry so she hoisted the shotgun, pressed the butt against her shoulder, pulled the trigger—

The ceiling thundered again as Momma shattered into a thousand glittering reflections. Yolanda looked down and saw how small the woman looked, staring up from the floor, shiny, sharp, and smooth, and empty-eyed *pitiful*.

She readied herself—

—ch-chick!—

—and aimed at the hole.

The wind slammed against her with angry hands, but it would not stop her. Nothing would.

Again and again and again the ceiling thundered as she blew the hole apart, her shoulder raw from the pounding of the butt, her chest full of pain and fear; but she kept firing until the force of the blasts weakened her, knocked her from the garden wall.

She dropped to the floor, gazing at the hole.

Wide, dark, bloodied inside. She peered deeper into the mouth of the web and saw *forms* moving within—like people passing on the street—and she listened for Michael's voice but there were others, *different* voices beckoning to her: *Empty here, so empty without you, I love you I miss you I want you back please come—*

The hole was beginning to close.

She tried to rise because *they* were in there, Daddy and Michael; but she was too spent, hurt, too weakened. She fell back, saw a thousand reflections of her mother's face, glaring up at her—

—and knew what to do.

"Wait for me," she said. Whispered. Weakly.

She wanted to be in there with them—away from the draining strength of suffering and the memories whose warmth was tainted by it. She fell forward, groped with shaking fingers for the shotgun and dragged it toward her, sat up.

The hole was small, now—tiny—one shimmering globule was on the edge, winking at her, hurry, *hurry,* get across the ledge.

She propped the shotgun up between her knees—

—*ch-chick!*—

—and shoved the barrel deep into her mouth.

The globule smiled, then winked, like Daddy letting her in on some little secret. *That's my girl, just get over the mountain, don't fall off and I'll tell you something special, because you were brave, you made it back to me—*

From the corner of her eye she saw a thousand images of her mother, all of them screaming.

Then Daddy's voice again. *Almost there, honey, keep your balance, don't slip, don't fall away like Mommy did because I'll never leave you like she did, I'll always be here, I'll be right here waiting for you and always—*

—the ceiling thundered one last time, and a new web spread across the wall—

—*love you.*

Mort Castle

POP IS REAL SMART

CASTLE calls the succinct story he has written for *M III* a chickens-come-home-to-roost tale, and it is. I call the curator of the Castle such things as clever, concise, and literate, inevitably creative and original, and friend. But it's all the terms leading up to the last that have allowed this maestro of the macabre to enjoy a special fictional niche: Mort is one of the very few writers to appear in everything I have edited up to now. You don't do that for buddyship if you enjoy getting exciting projects to edit.

The otherworldly Mortian talent has been brilliantly evident these past few years in *Twilight Zone, Grue,* the widely respected *Nukes* anthology (Maclay, '86) and now—graphically, shockingly—in Northstar comics such as *Omega* and *Faust*. His novel *The Strangers* ('84) was acclaimed; his next one, *Alone in the Darkness,* may do even better. The editor of a new illustrated magazine called *Horror,* Mort Castle should become a habit, wherever he pops up. His writing never disappoints.

POP IS REAL SMART

Mort Castle

LONNY GAZED AT JASON. HE LOATHED him with all the egoistic hatred of which only a five-year-old is capable. He was supposed to be happy he had a new brother. He was supposed to love him. Oh, sure. Right. Damn.

Lonny's eyes measured the baby's length and studied the pink fingers curled in tight fists at the top of the blue blanket. He watched the fluttery beating of the soft spot on Jason's head as, under skimpy down, it palpitated with the tiny heart.

"Damn," Lonny said. Pop said "Damn" a lot, like when he was driving and everybody else was driving like a jerk, or when he was trying to fix a leaky faucet or something.

And "damn" is just what Lonny felt like saying whenever he looked at Jason. The only thing the baby could do—his ookey-pukey brother!—was smell bad. Jason always smelled, no matter how often Mom bathed him or dumped a load of powder on him.

Jason wasn't good for anything!

Now Scott, down the block, Scott was lucky. Scott had a *real* brother, Fred, good old Fred. Yessir, Fred was a fun kid. You could punch Fred real hard and he wouldn't even cry. And Fred didn't go running to tell, either. Uh-uh. But Fred had these clumpy cowboy boots, and if you punched him, then he would just start kicking you and kicking, and maybe *you* would be the one who wound up crying!

Fred, that was the kind of dude you wanted for a little brother. Not Jason. This damn baby, hey, he couldn't do anything.

And this was the kid Lonny had helped Mom and Pop choose a name for? Jason. That was a good name for a good guy. Damn! Jason—*this* stupid thing with that stupid up-and-down blob on its head going thump-a-thump, thump-a-thump. No way, José!

Somebody must have fooled Mom. When she'd gone to the hospital, Mom had somehow got stuck with this little snot instead of a good brother for him.

Lonny wondered how Mom could be so damn dumb. Well, she was a girl, even if she was a grown-up, and girls could be pretty dumb sometimes. But damn, how did they put one over on Pop? Pop was real smart.

Lonny reached through the crib slats. He lightly touched Jason's soft spot. At the pulse beneath his fingers, he yanked back his hand.

Damn, this baby was just no good. No good.

He left the room. There had to be some way to get rid of Jason. He would ask Mom to take the baby back to the hospital, tell her she'd made a mistake. Oh, he'd have to say it just the right way so she didn't get pee-owed, but he'd figure it out. Then she could go get him a really good brother, like Fred.

Yeah! He knew just how to say it. He'd talk to Mom right now.

"Mom!" he hollered, running down the stairs. He hoped he would wake the baby.

Mom did not answer. Jason did not cry.

"Mom!" Lonny went to the kitchen. The linoleum buzzed beneath his Nikes and he heard the muffled thud of the washing machine in the downstairs utility room.

Mom was doing the wash. Damn, it was never a good idea to talk to her about *anything* when she was into laundry.

Lonny decided he might as well make himself a sandwich or

something. He dragged a chair from the table over to the cabinets. He climbed up and took down the big jar of peanut butter. He got the Wonder Bread from the bread box.

He set the bread and peanut butter on the table. He hoped he could open the new jar by himself. No way did he want to ask Mom for help when she was doing the laundry.

Okay! The lid came right off. "Yeah," Lonny said. "She's gonna have to take it back. It's no damn good, and if it's no good, you just take it back."

Hey, sometimes he wondered how a smart guy like Pop got stuck with Mom, anyway. For real, it was *Pop* had the brains.

Like once Lonny had goofed it. He had spent his birthday money on a rifle at Toys-R-Us and damn! It was wrong. It wasn't a Rambo assault rifle. It was a stupid Ranger Rock rifle. No way did you want a Ranger Rock rifle. Who ever heard of Ranger Rock?

So he and Pop took it back to get the Rambo rifle. "No refunds on sale items, sorry." That's what this real dipstick at the store had to say.

Then Pop showed him how you couldn't even pull the trigger and the way the plastic barrel was all cracked and everything.

No problem, man! They got back his birthday money, went to another store, and bought the Rambo rifle.

And you know what? That nerd at Toys-R-Us never even had an idea that Pop had busted up the stupid Ranger Rock rifle himself! That's how smart Pop was.

With his first finger, Lonny swirled out a glob of peanut butter. He popped it into his mouth. Yeah, peanut butter was great. He could live on peanut butter all the time. He'd make a nice, open-faced sandwich, and then maybe Mom would be done with the laundry and he could talk to her about getting rid of smelly Jason.

He went to the drawers by the sink. He opened the top one.

Mom always spread peanut butter with a dull knife.

It was the sharp knife that caught Lonny's eye.

Stanley Wiater

WHEN THE WALL CRIES

KNOWN primarily for his *Twilight Zone* interviews and his book reviews published regularly in *Fangoria,* Stan Wiater (pronounced "wee otter") has added a feather to his cap by becoming the editor of *Night Visions 7,* for Dark Harvest.

Stanley *needs* moral support. He and his engaging wife Iris are first-time parents who had a little girl in 1988. "Iris is going back to work," he sighed, and expressed his willingness to become a built-in baby-sitter. "Now," I told him, "the terror begins."

The "cineteratologist" and contributing editor to the British *Fear* now offers you an onslaught of contemporary reality so familiar but horrifying that it may evoke tears and outrage in equal measure. It is a suitable literary creation for someone who is going to be called "Daddy" for a number of years.

WHEN THE WALL CRIES

Stanley Wiater

TEARS SCORCH HER PORCELAIN WHITE FACE with the severity of a Madonna's, but Margarita can no longer taste them, nor waste the time to wipe them away from her quivering lips. Her hands clutch the cold, moist sides of the toilet's rear basin as she focuses her attention on a discolored blotch on the wall.

Standing over the open bowl, knees bent, legs spread unnaturally wide, Margarita cries. And waits. And cries. The pain begins below the pit of her belly, running back and forth on her spine to scrape ultimately behind her eyes like a rat trying madly to escape. It's too late for prayers, yet pray she must to keep from blacking out as she waits for thickly clotted blood and unformed tissue to drop from between her slender, trembling legs.

"Dios te salve María, Llena heres de gracia el Señor es contigo . . ."

The teenager's body is a palsied depository of warm liquids and cold moistures as tears linger, then stickily mix with sweat. Margarita throws back her head to try and fling off the long black hair falling repeatedly over her face like a torn and itchy hood. Her recent breakfast of Twinkies and a bowl of Cap'n Crunch cereal, threatening to spray up through her tightly clenched lips, reminds her she mustn't look down when it's over.

If it's ever going to be over.

No matter what she hears or feels, she knows she has to flush the toilet before she can open her eyes again. She can look down only after . . . after it's gone. Gone from her life. Out of any life.

The last convulsion grabs up inside her like heated pliers, then abruptly releases with the unmistakable sensation of flesh being torn from her body. Margarita bites into her lower lip until she tastes blood as a mass of lumpy fluids suddenly voids and splashes loudly into the open bowl. Her legs still shaking violently, she blindly flushes the silver-colored handle a dozen times before somehow pushing herself away from the unending, rust-stained swirl.

Nearly falling, she grabs an unused white towel from the neat pile kept beneath the sink. Margarita hurriedly rolls it into a cocoon and thrusts it beneath her dripping thighs like a diaper. Leaning against the plastic clothes hamper for support, she reaches out to turn on the cold-water tap. With her right hand pressing the towel more firmly between her legs, Margarita splashes the soothing water against the upper half of her body. The soiled cotton nightgown clings like a soaked dishrag as she quickly turns her head and glances back. The terrified girl moans in despair even before she can focus her vision, smelling the fresh blood lingering in the air.

Yet the toilet bowl is finally silent, its cleansing waters no longer disturbed. She starts to make the sign of the cross, then stops herself before it's complete.

Margarita realizes she should take a bath immediately, but first she has to get out of the same room where such an unforgivably sacrilegious act has just been performed. If she had any friends in this strange land, they would tell her she should first rest, try and get some sleep, then maybe she'd be able to face the world again. More important, she could now explain to Junior why she had been acting so strangely these past several weeks. However, just the slightest suggestion she might be *encinta* made him smash his way out of their basement apartment in a speechless rage a full three days ago.

Three empty nights ago.

The towel still between her legs, Margarita slowly moves out of the bathroom. She wipes the tears from her face with the back of one hand, thinking of what she has done to keep the man she loves.

Junior *has* to come back soon. Not only did the owner of this welfare hotel accept them as a married couple, he was willing to employ them both as a housekeeper and assistant maintenance man. But she doesn't think Mr. Gonski will accept another day of her being away from work, while her "husband" has supposedly gone off to visit a very sick relative. The few skills they have to offer are far from unique, though Margarita suspects from the unsettling way Mr. Gonski smiles that if they ever complain, he has more in mind for her than bending over to clean toilets or scrub floors.

Green cards are a luxury neither can yet afford.

Sitting on the edge of a chair in the combined kitchen-and-living-room area, Margarita takes a deep breath and slowly removes the towel. Spreading her thin legs wide, she hesitates at examining herself any further. The bleeding seems to have stopped, and she whispers another prayer that tonight there won't be any more stained sheets. At least she no longer has to hide the symptoms of morning sickness from her man.

If the subject is brought up at the right moment, she hopes Junior will take her to the free health clinic always mentioned on the radio station that broadcasts in their native language.

When he returns.

If he returns.

Shedding the sticky nightgown like a useless second skin, Margarita fills a deep pan with warm water from the kitchen sink. Finding a clean sponge near a tray of unwashed dishes, she whimpers quietly and gives herself an improvised bath. She just *can't* go back into that room until more time has passed. The stabbing pains inside her belly finally subside. Pressing an open palm between her unnaturally tender breasts, her heart beats so feebly she imagines it was also flushed away.

Shuddering, Margarita wonders what she might have done to her soul by not giving another eternal soul a chance to live.

The washing completed, she drops the sponge on the Formica-top table next to the bloody towel. Making her way to the bedroom, she sits naked on the unmade bed, reassuring herself she won't faint as long as she doesn't make any sudden movements. Margarita wishes she could stay here forever. Yet one of the other hotel employees had warned her last night that if she or Junior wasn't seen working today, they'd be back on the streets again. A phone call to the Man might be made. Or Mr. Gonski might find something else for her to do repeatedly on her hands and knees.

Shuffling along to the single walk-in closet, Margarita takes from her own side of the metal rod the blue housekeeper's uniform she must wear. It is permanently discolored along the hem while the lacy trimmings at the collar and cuff have been crudely picked at and discarded like wings from a captured bird. But just as long as the uniform and the person who wears it are relatively clean and neat, Mr. Gonski is satisfied. He has more important items to spend his money on than the working people in his hotel.

Putting on a Stayfree sanitary pad and two pairs of faded cotton panties, Margarita then slips the uniform over her head and ties the attached apron sash behind her slim waist. Finding the matching sneakers beneath a chair, she dons them, then turns to regard herself in the peeling bureau mirror. Combing back her long shiny hair, she applies blusher to disguise how pale her skin appears, then bright scarlet lipstick to her colorless slash of a mouth. She wonders who the young clown is who's staring back at her with the painted smile.

Closing her eyes to suffocate the emerging tears, Margarita has never felt this alone in her entire fifteen years of existence. Her hands shaking, she closes the bedroom door and heads toward the gas stove. There she fumbles for the set of keys which will open all the necessary doors in the ten-story Blodgett Hotel before leaving the apartment.

Not that there is anywhere she can hide.

But when she arrives at the maintenance closet on the first floor, Margarita is struck immediately by how unusually quiet the building is. Then she remembers the holiday, what the radio had reported about the festivities; a big parade downtown. There are no signs of the other housekeepers, even though their cleaning carts are still there. Perhaps they were given the day off?

Someone always has to be on duty at the front desk, plus the two old *cabrones* who, as the hotel's "security force," would still be making their rounds. If they weren't already passed out drunk on the roof. Someone will report her to Mr. Gonski, of that she has no illusions.

While checking the contents of her multi-shelved metal cart, Margarita heads for the nearby service elevator. According to the schedule, the main tasks today will be to go to "the apartments" and check on the fresh linen and toiletries furnished for each tenant. No one would be the wiser if she went through the motions of checking only a few rooms on each floor. Regardless, she *has* to spend a few hours at her job in order to be seen, so that a favorable report can be made to her boss. What otherwise will happen with her life tomorrow is a hardship not worth considering.

The gray metal doors of the service elevator pull themselves apart and wait silently to suck her in.

Margarita knocks at the door of Room 504, receives no answer, then unlocks it and cautiously walks in. Although she has been working here nearly three months, the unkempt and filthy condition of more than a few of the rooms still disgusts her. The reek of vomit and unwashed clothing in some of of the so-called apartments is enough to make her gag just thinking of it.

A sixty-second check of the linen shelves in the bathroom indicates that 504 doesn't need her services today. As she's closing the door behind her, an unexpected sound issues faintly from the bathroom. She stops to listen for a moment. Her mother had eight children; Margarita, the third-born, can never forget the only source of such a sound.

It comes from the lungs and throat and mouth of a newborn *bebe*.

"*Dios mio . . .*" Margarita can't bring herself to go in there again—not after what happened this morning in her own squalid little bathroom.

Leaning against the outer wall, she places a fluttering hand against her bosom and waits for the heartbeats to stop hurting. Waiting, too, for the awful, maddening sound to begin again. But all she hears is the rasping of her own shallow breath. Margarita swallows dryly and closes her eyes for a few peaceful seconds. It's only natural she should have babies clogging her thoughts today— *Bebes muertos.*

Dead babies.

A moment later she is moving down the hallway like someone who has heard a dozen smoke alarms go off. She knows she must keep moving. Always to live with the knowledge of what she has done to herself and her unborn child is a sin she isn't yet prepared to suffer. The dull, throbbing pain returns; Margarita clutches her belly, her other hand grasping the side of the cart for support. Her mouth makes weak, meaningless sounds, uncomfortably similar to those she has just heard.

Margarita blinks her eyes rapidly to keep the tears under control. The teenager isn't sure if she should be pleased or worried that she has seen no one on her rounds. The empty corridors don't seem to have heard the sound of footsteps or voices for many years. Looking down their length as she turns a corner, she cannot avoid the sensation of some subtle warping of the walls, the ceiling. The doors appear unevenly matched in size and dimension. The frayed carpeting stretches unendingly like a diseased tongue, the material stained and threadbare. Like the service elevator, the closed doors are hungry mouths waiting to be opened. Waiting to be fed.

Margarita stops the cart's roll outside Room 515.

She listens there for a few moments after knocking at the door to see if anyone is inside. Silence.

Taking a deep breath, she unlocks it and steps inside, leaving the door open wide. She moves quickly through 515. She checks the linen shelves in the bathroom and efficiently deals with the items that must be replaced.

Silence.

Leaves Room 515. Carefully locks the door as if she's never going to return there.

The thought is permitted only after she's around the corner again: *No noises came from the bathroom.* No old foundation settling. No rusty pipes shrieking. Nothing. It's the same situation on the next three floors, where Margarita checks a total of nine rooms. She doubts that, if it weren't for the holiday, so many of the rooms would be unoccupied. There is no one to disturb while getting drunk or shooting up.

Chewing nervously at her thumb, Margarita moves along a corridor that's a drab twin to the previous one. Certainly *someone* will see her before she collapses from nervous exhaustion!

Arms aching, she drops off bundles of sheets and towels in four other rooms before unlocking 208. On a few other occasions, she has met the young family of six who presently resides here. Like everyone else, they have apparently gone outside to watch the parade. The quiet surrounding her becomes increasingly unsettling.

Placing her hand on the doorknob to shut the door after her routine is again completed, Margarita hears something. In the bathroom. She doesn't want to listen, but can't help hearing it.

Cries. Much like a newborn baby's crying. Yet so loud it's as if the very walls were pleading to be heard by someone who gives a damn.

''*Dios mio, ayudame! Dios mio!*'' she screams back, clutching the doorknob as if she might use it to turn off what she's hearing.

As if triggered by the pitiful cries, Margarita is stricken by a new wave of cramps that rise up inside her belly. The intense wails make it difficult for her to think clearly; they virtually rise and fall with the rhythm of her own heartbeats. Gasping, she rushes from 208 and slams the door shut with a force that startles her. But before she can move far enough away, the young woman overhears the old toilet flushing, gurgling unnaturally loud and long. Cleansing and swirling sounds.

Swirling and drowning.

Drowning.

Then the cries are no more.

Too nauseous to return the cart to the floor station, Margarita finds herself suddenly afraid to take the service elevator. Hands pressed against her damp forehead, she considers all the countless secrets within the rooms of this crumbling welfare hotel. Memories which are so intensely painful that they can never be swept away, lingering like the rectangular traces of the framed paintings that once hung in the barren hallways.

Crazily, Margarita recalls how, when she first arrived here, a goldfish was given away to her and Junior at a pet-store opening.

How the tiny creature died right after she had brought it back in the water-filled sandwich bag. And how no one had thought anything the matter as the beautiful, shiny little life was unceremoniously flushed away. Now she understands.

Hotel bathrooms possess their own dirty secrets that no one wants to remember. Now the traces of their sins are finally calling out, though no one wants to hear.

Twisting a handkerchief around sweating hands, Margarita listens fitfully to the sobs issuing faintly from Room 110. And from Room 114. *Doesn't anyone hear them?* Worse, there's something strange in the way the cries come, as if from mouths that aren't yet fully formed. Just fleshy, tiny holes. She spins in a circle as the wailing grows louder still, like a boom-box being thoughtlessly turned up to the max.

Stifling a scream, Margarita runs to the end of the hall and down the two flights of stairs to the basement and the sanctuary of her own squalid apartment. The lighting is out again over one section of the stairwell, forcing her to hold out her arms to grope along the wall. At this level, the handrails broke off years ago and were never replaced. The walls are pimply, warm in the dark, like the skin of some exotic animal Junior couldn't identify for her when they once visited a zoo. The wall feels ready to give away at any instant, its moist surface almost indented by the pressure from her sweating hands.

She slips over something soft yet bulky lying in a corner where another section of stairs begins. The released fetid smell is nearly overpowering. Momentarily losing her balance, Margarita falls against the darkened wall. Some skin scrapes off her fingers; it feels like removing a glove that is lined with dull razors. The unseen object had vaguely felt like a stuffed toy as it gave way under her foot. Another discarded plaything, left to rot where no one will see.

Like so many unwanted things in this hotel.

As she finally reaches the fire door, her sneaker slides across a substance as warm and slimy as the inner walls. She tells herself it's only some drunk's fresh vomit as the heavy metal door opens sluggishly, its weight almost too great for her to force in her weakened condition. The reinforced glass window in its center is blacked out with dirt and grime, but Margarita knows the apartment is on the other side. It slowly pulls open with a rusty screech—sounding too much like her own voice should she lose all control and start screaming again. Then, at last, she's through.

And now the smell of fresh blood and new flesh is everywhere.

Rushing blindly into the apartment, Margarita lurches toward the bedroom and collapses on the still unmade bed. No odors. No noises here. In a few moments she realizes she is safe, if still alone. It was simply too much to hope that Junior might be there, waiting for her to return to him. The thought begins to creep into her mind that he just might never come back.

Shooting pains stab between her legs when she tries to get off the bed.

Biting her lower lip, Margarita can only lie quietly and pray that the pain won't worsen. She reaches up to pull a lumpy pillow under her head. Flat on her back, her pain subsides slightly when she spreads out her legs. She doesn't dare touch herself now, though her underwear is soaked through; the sticky wetness seeps into it. She knows she should bathe somehow, but it's so hard just to keep her pale brown eyes open.

A huge plastic crucifix looks down at her from over the headboard of the bed, seeming to share her suddenly renewed agony.

Hours appear to have passed. A different kind of dull ache tells the girl she must use the toilet or stain the sheets once more. At least the hot needles in her belly have departed. Pulling herself up, she considers using the employees' rest room on the first floor. But with legs as stiff as the bed, she can't possibly make it in time.

''Estaba soñando, solamente soñando,'' she whispers over and over to try to reassure herself. Hoping desperately that, when he does return, Junior will take her to the free clinic just to make sure everything is all right inside her.

He has to come back! Junior has to or she'll—

Margarita's head jerks around as she hears noises suddenly from outside the bedroom. Crouching on the edge of the bed, she is unable to recognize them, though they're obviously increasing in both intensity and number. One sound, however, is unmistakable: the toilet flushing.

Junior—has he finally come home? Or is it just the cold, rusty water giving back its unwanted wastes? Her ninety-pound body shudders violently; she starts to weep again.

Margarita realizes she must still be sleeping.

This guilty imagining of sounds that several unborn infants would make if gathering together in a brood. Why, she can even visualize clearly their tiny little hands—hands not yet completely formed in their various fetal stages—pulling in unison to move aside the tremendously heavy bathroom door. Then slowly, painfully, crawling across the cracked and warped linoleum floor on their way into the bedroom.

In the dream, they are leaving behind a trail of bright scarlet mucus like a multitude of snails in their search, their minute eyes not yet capable of seeing a world that didn't want them to be born. Crawling from a moist, filthy blackness, unable to shed tears for those who didn't wish ever to have to see them return, ever to acknowledge that—even in this sluglike form—they still exist; can still cry out for another chance at love, until finally heard by someone who understands what it means to be completely undesired.

While the drenched, fragile hands complete their task at the bedroom door, Margarita's own mouth opens wide to lead the others in their unending, wailing chorus. Then at last, at long last, she feels the smallest, freshest one grasp her bare ankle and begin instinctively to ascend toward her inner thigh. The tears stop falling from her eyes.

"Bienvenida, pequeña, bienvenida a esta casa," she says, smiling down at him benevolently as the floor is covered in a dripping, stinking mixture of red and black and pink. While the others, no longer alone and no longer crying, slide over one another in fervent search of her open legs.

Impatiently awaiting a second chance.

Bruce Boston and
Robert Frazier

RETURN TO THE
MUTANT RAIN FOREST

BOSTON, born July 16, 1943, has appeared in *Nebula Awards 21, Twilight Zone, Night Cry, 100 Great Fantasy Short-Shorts*, and *Asimov's*. Bruce won the Rhysling Award for SF poetry and in '76 the Pushcart Prize for Fiction. He's the author of six collections of fiction and poetry, notably the brilliant, heartrending *Bruce Boston Omnibus* (Ocean View Press, '87), *The Nightmare Collector* (2AM Publications, '88), and *Skin Trades* (Drumm, '88).

Frazier, born April 28, 1951, is the son of an army cryptologist and a landscape artist. His dad was among those who cracked the Nazis' Project Ultra code. Married to Karol, he has sold poems to *Night Cry, F&SF, Asimov's*, and *Weird Tales*, and appeared in such anthologies as *Synergy* and *The Umbral Anthology of SF Poetry*.

This work's predecessor, "Night Fishing on the Caribbean Littoral of the Mutant Rain Forest," was published in Tim Sullivan's *Tropical Chills* anthology (Avon, '88). While never published before, the present poem won the 1988 Odyssey SF Poetry Contest, held by Brigham Young University. It's wonderfully ominous.

RETURN TO THE MUTANT RAIN FOREST

Bruce Boston and Robert Frazier

Years later we come back to find the fauna and flora
more alien than ever, the landscape unrecognizable,
the course of rivers altered, small opalescent lakes
springing up where before there was only underbrush,
as if the land itself has somehow changed to keep pace
with the metaprotean life forms which now inhabit it.

Here magnetism proves as variable as other phenomena.
Our compass needle shifts constantly and at random,
and we must fix direction by the stars and sun alone.
Above our heads the canopy writhes in undiscovered life:
tiny albino lemurs flit silently from branch to branch,
tenuous as arboreal ghosts in the leaf purple shadow.

Here time seems as meaningless as our abstracted data.
The days stretch before us in soft bands of verdigris,
in hours marked by slanting white shafts of illumination.

At our feet we watch warily for the tripvines of arrowroot,
while beetles and multipedes of every possible perversion
boil about us, reclaiming their dead with voracious zeal.

By the light of irradiated biota the night proliferates:
a roving carpet of scavenger fungi seeks out each kill
to drape and consume the carcass in an iridescent shroud.
A carnivorous mushroom spore roots on my exposed forearm
and Tomaz must dig deeply beneath the flesh to excise
the wrinkled neon growth which has sprouted in minutes.

We have returned to the mutant rain forest to trace
rumors spread by the natives who fish the white water,
to embark on a reconnaissance into adaptation and myth.
Where are the toucans, Genna wonders, once we explain
the cries which fill the darkness as those of panthers,
mating in heat, nearly articulate in their complexity.

Tomaz chews stale tortillas, pounds roots for breakfast,
and relates a tale of the Parakana who ruled this land.
One morning the Chief's wife, aglow, bronzed and naked
in the eddies of a rocky pool, succumbed to an attack
both brutal and sublime, which left her body inscribed
with scars confirming the bestial origins of her lover.

At term, the massive woman was said to have borne a child
covered with the finest gossamer caul of ebon-blue hair.
The fiery vertical slits of its eyes enraged the Chief.
After he murdered the boy, a great cat screamed for weeks
and stalked about their tribal home, driving them north.
His story over, Tomaz leads our way into the damp jungle.

From base camp south we hack one trail after another
until we encounter impenetrable walls of a sinewy fiber,
lianas as thick and indestructible as titanium cables,
twining back on themselves in a solid Gordian sheath,
feeding on their own past growth; while farther south,
slender silver trees rise like pylons into the clouds.

From our campo each day we hack useless trail after trail,
until we come upon the pathways that others have forged
and maintained, sinuous and waist-high, winding inward
to still farther corrupt recesses of genetic abandon:
here we discover a transfigured ceiba, its rugged bark
incised with the fresh runes of a primitive ideography.

Genna calls a halt in our passage to load her Minicam.
She circles about the tree, shrugging off our protests.
As we feared, her careless movement triggers a tripvine,
but instead of a hail of deadly spines we are bombarded
by balled leaves exploding into dust—marking us with
luminous ejecta and a third eye on Genna's forehead.

Souza dies that night, limbs locked in rigid fibrogenesis.
A panther cries; Tomaz wants us to regroup at our campo.
Genna decides she has been chosen, scarified for passage.
She notches her own trail to some paradise born of dream
hallucination, but stumbles back, wounded and half-mad,
the Minicam lost, a cassette gripped in whitened knuckles.

From base camp north we flail at the miraculous regrowth
which walls off our retreat to the airstrip by the river.
The ghost lemurs now spin about our heads, they mock us
with a chorus as feverish and compulsive as our thoughts.
We move relentlessly forward, as one, the final scenes
of Genna's tape flickering over and over in our brains.

In the depths of the mutant rain forest where the water
falls each afternoon in a light filtered to vermilion,
a feline stone idol stands against the opaque foliage.
On the screen of the monitor it rises up from nowhere,
upon its hind legs, both taller and thicker than a man.
See how the cellular accretion has distended its skull,

how the naturally sleek architecture of the countenance
has evolved into a distorted and angular grotesquerie,
how the taloned forepaws now possess opposable digits.
In the humid caves and tunnels carved from living vines,
where leprous anacondas coil, a virulent faith calls us.
A sudden species fashions godhood in its own apotheosis.

CREATURES OF TERROR

CONSIDERING that the primary icons in horror's past—man-made constructs, werewolves, possessing demons, shape-changers such as vampires—*were* monsters, it's tempting to call the yarns in this section "monster stories." Or "freak and entity tales." Curiously, though, self-styled experts rarely respect new fiction with such labels; these wonderfully weird stories deserve to be respected, and there *are* other characteristics that they have in common.

Whether gigantic of size or power, befanged or horned, whether they're even discernibly different from us, these creatures symbolize humankind's oldest fear: that of something proximately humanoid, more substantial than psychotic thought, too close to us for comfort. And something else: The beings in this fiction have the knack for eliminating us from life almost without exertion, and *instantly*—the way a truck can crush and grind any one of us into nothingness, passionlessly. Without an iota of remorse.

We all love tales such as these, even when we feel intellectually disdainful of them. Our inclination to smile superior, smug smiles is like whistling in the graveyard, or chuckling nervously while we watch Freddy Krueger go to work. Yet on paper, the crafting of such stories is far harder than it may seem at a glance. In the hands of craftsmen such as Simmons it approaches art; the perspicacious humor of Kisner and the audacity of Keefauver may leave one limp. So don't, please, take it for granted that you already know what's going to happen when you're reading about these Creatures of Terror.

Because that's when one of them may get *you!*

James Kisner

THE WILLIES

"THE Litter" by Jim Kisner, in *Masques II*, drew within one bloody hair of achieving the final ballot for the Horror Writers of America's first short fiction award. Wry and sardonic, observant and slightly off-center in his parabolic view of the rest of us, Kisner is the author of such novels as *Strands*, *Nero's Vice*, and *Slice of Life*, and the horror maven for Ed Gorman's marvelous *Mystery Scene*. In that capacity he has interviewed the likes of F. Paul Wilson, John Saul, Rex Miller, and Rick McCammon.

Recent or upcoming appearances of J. K. include Graham Masterton's *Scare Care*, Gorman's and Marty Greenberg's *Stalkers*, my *How to Write Tales of Horror, Fantasy and Science Fiction*, *Grue*, *Gorezone*, a reprint of "The Litter" in a William F. Nolan anthology from Dark Harvest entitled *Urban Horrors*, and a miraculously original tale in the Greenbergs' *Phantoms* anthology (DAW).

This story will give you a new look at an element of society you may never have looked at, really, before: the terrifying Willies.

THE WILLIES

James Kisner

RON STOOD AT THE WINDOW, LOOKING down on the crowded streets of the city. His office was located on the third story of the building, so he had a clear view of the different varieties of humanity out and about on this pleasant autumn day.

He liked watching people and amused himself by imagining who and what they were. Most of the persons he saw in the streets below were obviously young businessmen like himself, caught up in the electric pace of the metropolitan hustle—going to lunch, discussing market projections, and making dates for golf before the weather turned too cold. Yes, Ron thought, people just like me. They've got their act entirely together. Upwardly mobile. *Sharp* guys. Born to succeed.

Weaving among the businessmen (and women, Ron amended mentally) were shoppers, schoolchildren playing hooky, street kids with ghetto blasters, and working stiffs, some of whom (Ron imagined) were going to the unemployment lines at the state office building the next block over, or perhaps to the police station to pay traffic fines and plead innocent to various misdemeanors.

All these people seemed to Ron to have purpose, no matter how trivial they might be in the overall scheme of things. And Ron approved of that, because he believed a being without purpose was the most worthless thing imaginable.

That's why the winos bothered him so much.

A withered man was slumped in an alley not far away. He sat on the rough pavement with his arms wrapped around his knees, mumbling through fragments of memories and luxuriating in the warmth of his piss-stained trousers. He could have been thirty-five or seventy, depending on the light he was seen in. Most of the time, though, he avoided being seen at all, preferring the almost perpetual, dim twilight of the alley.

A few minutes each day, when the sun was directly overhead, the man would look up and vaguely wonder who he was and what exactly had happened to him. He couldn't remember at what point he had ceased being whoever it was he had been and had become what he was now, which was still, at bottom, not much of anything; and sorting through all the imprints in the few (scant few) brain cells he had left yielded very little to which he could append a definite identity, nor any shred of certainty.

After the sun had passed over, he would settle down again and not worry about anything other than panhandling to get enough money for a jug, which he'd do when the urge came over him, usually later in the day.

And as he turned his face back to his knees, hugging himself a little tighter perhaps before shrinking down into inertia, he comforted himself with the old one-and-three axiom he had formulated long ago to propel him through life. The old one-and-three consisted of one thing he *suspected* was true, and three things of which he was almost abso-goddamn-lutely *certain*.

The one thing he suspected was that he had tuberculosis.

The three things of which he was certain were: that *one*, he was a man (though—he inspected his withered tool, a sort of homuncular duplicate of his face—only on rare occasions); *two*, he was a wino; and *three*, his name was Willie.

All winos are named Willie, just as all bulldogs are named Spike.

*   *   *

It was a breezy day in the city, but not unpleasantly so. There was just enough wind to carry shapeless things.

Shapeless invisible things that nevertheless had purpose.

"Ready to go to lunch?" Bill asked.

Ron turned from the window slowly, reluctant to give up his people-watching.

"Sure." He sighed heavily. "Where to?"

"Let's walk somewhere. It's such a nice day out, you don't even need a jacket."

"Okay," Ron said. "Let's go over to the deli."

The wind bristled the hairs on Willie's ears, and he ached suddenly for the comfort of a jug. He ordered his mind to relay a message to his limbs that it was time to stir—lunchtime, guys, when a lot of people are out and it's a little easier to mooch a few quarters for a bottle. The cells in Willie's body responded eventually to the mental imperative and he unfolded himself and lurched into a standing position, moving awkwardly and with great uncertainty, like a crude figure in an old cartoon movie.

Life *was* a cartoon sometimes, for people like Willie. Maybe most of the time.

Standing as erect as he could, Willie still resembled a question mark. He had developed the habit of constantly peering down, because he knew no one cared really to look him in the eyes. Most people just wanted to be rid of him, and the easiest way was to shove him four bits or a dollar, generally holding the money out in such a way as to avoid being touched by his smelly presence.

He brushed off his colorless clothes with the palms of his hands, pausing here and there to rearrange a wrinkle or change the direction of the nap on the corduroy jacket that once had been brown. His trousers had been charcoal-gray, and his plaid shirt had once been predominantly blue. There was a woolen tie he never wore stuffed in one pocket and an obscenely snot-and-mucus-encrusted handkerchief in another pocket. In the back pocket of his trousers was a battered suede cap, which he thoughtfully removed and arranged on his head at a slight angle.

Now ready to meet the public, Willie walked slowly out of the alley and onto the sidewalk. There certainly *were* a lot of people out today; it should be easy to make a touch.

Spare change, mister? Can you spare a dollar for a jug, mister? Jeez, mister, I really *need* a jug. Got a quarter for a cup of coffee? Spare four bits for a guy that really needs it?

No use rehearsing, Willie decided at last. It didn't matter what you said. They either gave you some goddamn money or they didn't.

He moved through the crowds on the sidewalk at a leisurely, almost lackadaisical pace, managing to beg seventy-five cents by the time he traveled the half block from the alley to the corner. Not bad, but not enough. He turned the corner and paused to stare at a newsstand where the latest men's magazines were on sale. He blinked at the cover of a *Penthouse* from which a nearly nude woman seemed to be smiling at him. The way the artful camerawork hid her obvious sexual characteristics was admirable. Even Willie could appreciate it.

A wind came up and flipped the cover slightly, creating an illusion that taunted Willie. As the sun played on the moving, glossy surface, the woman was suddenly animated, not alive but just seeming to *be*: a cartoon woman for a cartoon man like he was. Like Willie was.

Hot damn!

Willie's withered brow wrinkled.

He hadn't had a woman in years, and even the most worn-out old hooker would turn him down now; but something strange stirred deep down inside him, perhaps a vague memory, a stray hormone wiggling through his brain reminding him of what once was, and how it had been for him as a younger man, before he became Willie and just about everything in him had turned off; not even latent any more, but almost absolutely dead.

There are absolutes, even in a cartoon universe.

When they sat across from each other in the deli devouring sloppy sandwiches, Ron and Bill were almost mirror images. They both wore crisp white shirts with button-down collars, striped rep ties, and slacks with the proper creases. Their faces were smooth and framed with neatly styled light-brown hair.

"Pass the spice," Ron said.

Bill reached for the shaker of ground oregano and dried hot peppers, handed it to Ron.

Ron opened his sandwich and liberally sprinkled the spice over its steaming contents. "Great lunch."

"Think I'll have another iced tea."

"Should we have some dessert?"

"Sure," Bill said. "Let's try that cannelloni stuff."

The tips of Willie's fingers itched and his chest ached when he recalled the feel of warm flesh against his own, and, for a fleeting second, he thought he felt a little lead in his pencil.

Then he shut the feeling off, abruptly, deciding it was unseemly after all and that he had better things to worry about than the raw longing for a goddamn woman.

He didn't need a woman, neither to look at nor to touch. They were just too much trouble for what you received in return from them, and they wasted money that was better spent on a jug.

Wine never let you down like any female would, like every woman he'd ever known had done. Wine never broke its promise of sweet relief from the past, of numbing the senses for the present, and the surcease of sorrow from the already moribund future.

He continued down the block, seeking enough hard cash to buy the jug that now seemed especially important. Wine made all the difference in life. Sweet wine. Not women.

Goddamn *Penthouse* anyhow.

Goddamn women.

Pure evil is a potent force to be admired, and pure evil rode shapelessly on the wind, seeking something.

It had no words with which to think, no brain cells in which to store memories, no substance, no organs of any kind, nor any function to worry about.

It was an essence only. Pure. Driven. Its substance—that is, its absolute ethereal essence—was animated by a singular purpose: to find its ultimate victim.

And though the shapeless thing had no reason, it sensed some-how—in the striations of its invisible gossamer vapors—that there was poetry in its purpose.

Very few things, living or dead, purposeful or purposeless, have poetry in them.

"Yeah, you're right, that was a great lunch," Bill said as he and Ron left the deli.

"Okay, I guess," Ron said. "I think I ate too much, though. Those meatball sandwiches are real belly bombs. And, Lord, what was *in* that cannelloni?"

"A little bit of everything, but mostly sugar." Bill glanced at his watch. "Hey, it's already after one. We'd better get back to the office on the double, or we'll really get our asses chewed out."

"Hey, I'm not worried."

"We've been late getting back twice this week already."

"Oh, all right. Let's cut down this alley."

Willie stood in the alley, propping himself against the brick wall with one hand while urinating. He glanced down at himself and grimaced. His old wrinkled penis had no shine to it at all. It was a dull piece of meat that knew nothing and sensed only the most basic biological imperatives. Willie cursed at it, tucked it back in and zipped up; then he folded himself in a crouching position against the opposite wall.

He had a bottle of cheap wine, still in its brown paper bag, tucked under one arm. He had purchased it only a few minutes ago and had drunk almost all of it. Now he held the bottle up to his lips and finished it off, chugging it noisily. Then he hugged the empty to his body for a while, as if he might refill it with wishes, then sighed and tossed it away.

Damn.

It wasn't quite enough to wipe him out. At least it took the edge off his senses, which was all he needed to settle into his afternoon stupor.

"Life sucks," he mumbled through purple, wine-stained lips, then smiled crookedly.

The wind whipped through the alley, stirring up the little wads of trash, causing dust to whirl in tortuous little dances, and giving Willie a bit of a chill that was somehow soothing.

He spat out a whimpering little sound as something settled in him.

*   *   *

"Oh, hell," Ron said as they neared the end of the alley, "would you look at that? A goddamn wino."

"So just walk by him," Bill said. "He's harmless."

"Winos aren't harmless! They're a drain on society."

"Don't be so heavy, Ron. We have to get back to—"

"What purpose do they serve? None. Just derelicts. They occupy space, that's all. They ought to round them all up and *shoot* them!"

"Come on, Ron. The poor old guy will hear you."

"Let him."

Ron stopped directly in front of Willie and looked down with evident scorn. "What a mess." He started to turn away.

That was when Willie grabbed him.

"Hey, you old rummy, let go! Let go before I kick your teeth in."

"I'll handle this." Bill leaned down to pull the wino's hands from Ron's legs. He tugged at the bony fingers with all his strength, but he couldn't pry them away.

Then he found himself up in the air.

Then he was back on the pavement about ten feet away from his friend and the wino.

He tried to get up and discovered his left leg was broken. Strangely, it didn't hurt much.

Ron stared down at Willie. "What the hell did you do?" He turned. "Bill?"

"I can't move." A gasp. "Leg's broken, I think."

Ron snarled, "You old *bastard*. Now I *will* give you a going-over."

Willie's head snapped back abruptly. He glared up at Ron.

Ron desperately tried to look away, but couldn't. Willie's eyes were red with tiny yellow snake-slit pupils that tore into Ron's brain. Reflected in those eyes were miniature screaming things.

And tombstones.

Ron panicked, tried to pull away again and realized the wino's fingers had sprouted razorlike claws that were cutting into his calves. He bent over to beat the wino on the top of his skull, but some force shoved him back; the only thing that prevented him from falling was the claw grip on his legs.

Ron screamed—but the sound died quickly in the alley, as if muffled by an unseen force. Then he realized he could say or do nothing to escape what was happening. He was frozen in time for a moment, completely awestruck by the sudden transformation of the withered man, viewing it with a kind of fleeting detachment that reason could not alter:

The top of Willie's head had split open and become a huge mouth ringed with rows of pointed fangs, and out of this gaping red orifice came a stench of alcohol, blood, and piss that stung Ron's nostrils so badly they began to bleed.

The mouth-thing wasn't finished growing, though. It ripped down the center of Willie's body, stopping at his groin, and it grew more teeth and stank more and rippled obscenely.

Then it was feeding time.

Later, Bill couldn't remember if he had passed out because of the pain in his leg or because of what he had seen.

It didn't matter. No one seemed to believe his story and there was very little evidence of what had happened; only a few non-descript stains and an old wino's cap.

Perhaps people would be more inclined to believe Bill later. Later, when more guys like Ron disappeared. Later, when more absolutes met more ultimate victims.

Because there were more shapeless things in the wind, and a lot more Willies haunting the streets and alleys.

Soon all the Willies would have a purpose.

K. Marie Ramsland

THE DRINKING PARTY

AFTER writing her provocative psychological horror yarn "Nothing from Nothing Comes" for *Masques II* and the definitive chapter about "The Psychology of Horror and Fantasy Fiction" in a how-to book I edited, Dr. Ramsland moved with her husband—and her reputation as a Kierkegaard scholar—to a small town with a Lovecraftian name: Upper Black Eddy. There, she began to write horror novels.

But new tales chosen by Martin and Roz Greenberg for their anthology *Phantoms*, and a delectable number entitled "Ghost Crabs," in bloody *Gorezone*, altered Kathie's image as a "brain." Like all the gifted women it has been my joy to know, Katherine Marie Ramsland is probably more complex than most men. She loves costumes parties, paints at a professional level, sings with records. This is the lady who, in her how-to piece, wrote that we all want to "recall . . . our primordial selves."

Case in point, the slime-and-suspense-dripping "Drinking Party."

THE DRINKING PARTY

K. Marie Ramsland

AMNIOTIC. THAT'S HOW THE PLACE FELT. Warm and oozy, concealed in membrane—so damp it made your bones swell. I licked my lips, tasting salt, trying to focus on what we were there for.

We'd let ourselves in, which I thought odd; but Frank, who claimed to know our host well enough, had insisted. The odor of sodden earth assailed us at once, as if we'd entered the late summer lair of a listless newt. Candles burned on either side of several doorways in what appeared to be some sort of sparsely furnished waiting room. The windows were round, small and few, like portholes on a ship. A faint background bubbling reminded me of the job I'd once held and quickly lost at an oceanography lab. Glancing around, I shrugged against underwear that suddenly seemed too tight. Or too loose. Or something. I wanted to get out or get started—anything to slip out of the cloying skin of that unwelcoming room. But our host had not yet begrudged us an appearance.

Frank, younger than my forty years by half a decade, nudged me, pointing.

"Say, look at that!"

He walked toward a shadowy wall to our right. For the first time, I noticed a huge aquarium stretching across five feet of wall space—as tall from the floor as a man of average height. That explained the bubbling. Thrown back to the false but seductive promise of my days as a biology graduate student, I joined Frank beside it. Moments later, I was sorry I had.

The filmy glass container seemed more a captured swamp than an exotic aquarium. It smelled of stale neglect. Amid slimy, strangling weeds, a large frog straddled murky water at eye level. It stared, its eyes dull. I waved my hand but it didn't even blink. I felt invisible. Then I realized what had drawn Frank's attention. *The frog was disappearing—right there in front of us!*

Well, not disappearing exactly, but *changing*—as if it were being devoured from *inside*. The skin sagged and crumpled into something like the formless folds of a shirt dipped into a washtub. The amphibian flattened out. Something drained from its eyes, some life force bade farewell; blinked out. The frog dropped lower, shrinking, emptying backward into its former tadpole state. The once-taut skin drifted to the brackish surface, blending into tiny islands of curdled scum.

Frank looked at me. *What the hell. . . ?* his eyes asked.

I shrugged, bewildered, then glanced again at the gruesome, floating bag. It began to sink. That's when I saw the shadow.

A thing dark and oval scooted away, as if the frog's own astral projection were swimming free of its visceral cage! I stepped closer, squinted. I'd heard of this marvel but had never witnessed it: the feeding habits of a subaqueous beetle, paralyzing its prey before turning bones, muscles, and organs into a siphonable juice. I strained to recall the scientific name.

"A water bug," came a voice from behind us. I jumped as if I'd been swatted, and made my first visual acquaintance with our host.

"Oh, geez, Leth!" Frank exclaimed—"You scared the bejiminies out of us."

I was glad Frank'd spoken. I'd lost my voice.

Leth was unlike anyone I'd ever seen. A bald head of brownish skin and small watery eyes topped an obesely bulbous body. I'd heard from Frank that this guy was a former bartender who'd won enough money from outdrinking everyone who wagered on it to have quit his job altogether. He claimed he'd never lost.

That's why we were there, to take up Leth's challenge. But I saw immediately what such a degenerate life had done to the man: I could almost hear the liquid sloshing around inside him, and not just in his belly—in the whole, bloated trunk of his disgusting body.

He turned dark eyes on me. I stepped back, involuntarily touching the cold glass of the aquarium. I thought of the frog and drew away. Leth extended his hand, a stubby thing with several fingers cramped arthritically inward. Frank was introducing us, so I swallowed and allowed my palm to slip quickly across the one extended to me. I didn't quite catch his last name. It sounded Irish: O'Serus, or something like that. It didn't matter. He was clearly a foreigner.

"I'm glad you came, Victor," he said. "Frank has impressed me with your capacity to stay sober."

I swallowed. Suddenly the whole thing seemed like a bad idea, an adolescent game. But I couldn't back out—not with him looking at me like that, gloating, ready. I thought of my cut of the money we'd get if I stayed—and if I won.

"Let's begin," I said.

Leth gestured toward a doorway. I strode boldly into the next room, almost as dark and humid as the first save for two candles burning in the center of a splintering table, and two at each of three doorways.

I took a seat. Frank sat to my left, eyebrows raised. His fleshy chin quivered below pale lips. Clearly, I was not the only one who wished we hadn't come.

Leth set a bottle of Jack Daniels—my request—and three glasses on the table. Then he slapped down a shabby deck of cards. Poker was not the point, we all knew that; we simply had to pass the time somehow.

"Let's get one thing straight," piped up Frank. His voice was raspy, taut with nerves. "I'm betting on Victor here. Are we settled on the stakes?"

"We're settled," the brown man replied.

I glanced at Frank through narrowed eyes. I knew only what he

had to gain—a great deal of money with which to shovel himself
out of debt; Frank hadn't told me what he—*we*—had to lose. He
winked to reassure me. I shrugged and went along.

Leth filled our glasses equally, then handed the bottle to Frank,
who acted as referee. It didn't seem fair to Leth, actually. Frank
had something to gain by cheating. But the idea was that we'd all
be sober enough to recognize cheating if it happened; so it didn't
much matter who poured.

While Leth dealt cards, I studied him surreptitiously. He was an
odd one, no doubt. To boost my own confidence, I envisioned him
caught in a sticky web, bleating "Help me" in a pathetic voice. It
didn't work. The web would have to be enormous because he was
at least six feet tall. I glanced to Leth's misshapen hands—thick,
stubby paws, with hardened skin. It reminded me of a snake I'd
seen once, about to shed its lifeless shell. I grimaced.

Leth caught my eye. He grinned. Too much liquor had rotted his
teeth into a dark, cavernously empty mouth. I concentrated on my
cards.

The game went on as we continued to drink. Frank watched me
closely. He seemed nervous. I thought of his wife and two-year-
old son, hoped he hadn't gambled with their security the way I
had once with my own family, losing them with the house. Long
since, I had substituted a debilitating drinking habit for a promis-
ing career in science, but the work was a negligible loss compared
to never seeing my wife and two children again.

Scratching the back of my neck, my hand came away—
shockingly—with a live *roach!* I flung it to the stone floor, froze.

"I'm not much of a housekeeper," Leth said. "I suppose I like
having the critters around." He took another drink. I swallowed,
mentally nodded. The guy liked bugs? It made sense. People who
look like bulldogs bought bulldogs.

Frank filled my glass. I held the gaze of the brown man opposite
me, tried in vain to read his thoughts. If there was anything swim-
ming around behind those liquid eyes, it was neatly hidden from
my perception.

"You okay?" Frank asked. Beads of sweat had popped out on
his brow. I frowned, lit up a cigarette, casually replaced the pack
in my shirt pocket.

"I'm fine," I replied, "Got a long way to go."

But I didn't; not really. One had to stay in control to win such games, and I was getting rapidly digested in the stomach of apprehension. The third empty bottle quivered before me. Empty. I caught the hard, smirking eyes of my host.

Also empty.

Swollen air pressed my clammy shirt to my back. I took a deep breath, licked the sting of whiskey off my mustache. Frank poured another round. It struck me he was somehow acting out a part. The room seemed to brighten. I wanted to puke.

I'd experienced a similar sense of unanchored floating when my wife had announced her intention to divorce me, to leave me with my debts, my isolation, my habits. I'd gasped then for air too thin to sustain consciousness, swaying with the surreal force of her verbal blow: "You won't see me again."

Frank nudged me. My eyes had closed. I snapped to attention, a wayward schoolboy. The "teacher" across the table eyed me with a Mona Lisa grin.

"Shit, Victor," Frank exclaimed, "you done better than this before! What's with you?"

He was right. Something was seriously wrong. I filled my lungs, clenched my teeth for control.

Abruptly, I simply didn't care enough. I didn't need money *that* badly. I wanted out, no matter what it cost. It was Frank's fault if he'd gambled everything away. I pushed back from the table. "That's it." My tongue was thick, my brain battered seasick by booze. "I concede."

Frank jumped up. His chair crashed to the floor.

"Concede?" he screamed. "You *can't*! I *bet* on you!"

I shrugged. "Sorry. Y'win some, ya lose some." I needed a place to vomit.

Frank grabbed me by my jacket lapels. "You don't get it, Vic!" he shrieked, his control gone. "You lose *this* one, there won't be no chance to win *anything else!* Ever!"

I jerked away, urgently ill.

Leth leaned forward, his smallish head on crusty hands. His face was expressionless. Yet I had the distinct impression he was savoring his easy victory. I wasn't sober enough to be sure, but he seemed not the least bit affected by his own fast intake of alcohol.

Out of one eye, I saw Frank run to the door. Leth made no move to stop him.

The door was bolted.

"Let me out!" screamed Frank. He pounded on the solid wood, hysterical. I began to understand that Frank's fear implied more than financial collapse. He was trapped—*we* were trapped.

Frank groped his way along the darkened wall to another door and I stood up. "Frank, get hold of yourself!" I called shakily.

He pushed open the door. Flinging a desperate look toward me, he grabbed a candle and ran.

And turning to Leth, woozily, I got it through my head *that I was alone with him!*

Nausea braided into panic. I dared not look at Leth's face, sensing his expression would somehow be terrifying. Mumbling about assisting Frank, I staggered to the door through which he'd disappeared. I called out, heard nothing, then felt along a descending corridor so slick with moisture I surmised we'd meandered into an underwater tunnel. Outside, I hadn't noticed water, but it had been dark. Muggy, bubbling queasiness fused my senses.

Hearing a noise, I turned. The light from the room I'd just left was extinguished by the closing door. I gasped aloud. Had our repulsive host locked us in? *Why?* Did he intend to keep us there until we paid our debt, whatever it was?

I thought of the roach. Leth liked bugs. What would I encounter farther into his damned tunnel? Movie images of screaming people covered with ants, being devoured bite by little bite, crawled into my thoughts.

And then I realized a more horrifying possibility.

Perhaps Leth'd locked himself in with us!

I forced myself to stay calm. What could he do, anyway? I'd aged, yes, my belly was bloated—but I was fit enough to take on Leth, even with the disadvantage of inky darkness.

So I waited, listened, heard no sound, not even my friend somewhere ahead of me. Slowly, cautiously, I pressed numbed fingertips along the roughened stone wall, moving farther from the room where I'd drunk myself into the first stages of a perceptual haze. Toward what I moved I had no idea.

A sound. I stopped, listened with acute awareness. Something dragging, scraping, clawing. Did Leth have a weapon? Did he want to *kill* us?

I took a few more steps, found a doorknob, let myself noiselessly into an equally lightless room. I shut the door, moved to the side. If anyone opened it, then I'd have the advantage.

Nothing happened.

Something rotten stank nearby. Whatever it was, I hoped to God it wasn't alive. I remembered slipping a book of matches into my cigarette cellophane, safe and dry in my shirt pocket. Seconds later, holding the lit match high, I scanned the small room.

It was a cell of some kind, without furnishings, but it had the ubiquitous porthole window. A pile of rancid clothing lay in one corner, heaped against the wall. I went closer, but the match burned out.

A sound, outside the door, startled me. I waited. Then I lit another match. I moved closer to examine the lumpy, smelly material. I poked around gingerly. Several black shapes skittered out of the folds. It was not someone's discarded suit. Grayish in color, it looked more like a stiffened vinyl garment bag.

I don't think I understood that it had been human until I saw an eyeball dangling from a stiff, dark hole. It took me a moment to figure out, like a perceptual illusion coming into focus, that I was kneeling next to a sack of skin . . .

With a howl, I jumped back, burned my finger on the match, slammed myself against the wall. Breathing hard, I tried to steady my swimming senses. The gorge boiled into my throat. I had to get out, get away from that reeking thing. My God, what had *happened* here? Who was this Leth O'Serus?

I stopped, straightened. I knew at that moment where I'd heard the name. Yet it was no wonder I hadn't made the connection earlier. It had been part of . . . all *that*!

A piercing scream ripped into my slowly understanding brain. *Frank!*

I flew to the door, jerked it open. Frank's candle, thrown aside, illumined an expected but incomprehensibly freakish sight.

Frank struggled with our host, shrieking, his eyes turned to me, pleading. But there was nothing I could do, just as there'd been no way to assist the wretched frog back in the tank. I watched in stunned helplessness—unable even to run—as Leth held Frank in a vampire-like grip, his beetle mouth pressed to Frank's chest—injecting him, I knew, with paralyzing serum. *Preparing Frank for a grisly evening meal!*

Leth O'Serus; lethocerus. *Lethocerus americanus.*

I'd never thought of it before, never wondered how really huge they might get. *Giant water bugs.* I leaned against the frame of the door, laughing weakly at the ironic misnomer. Giant! They'd all been tiny in those oceanography tanks—mere specks compared to the one now munching on the shriveled neck of my friend.

Exactly like the frog, Frank went limp as his bones dissolved into edible mush. He lost the definition of his shoulders at once, then his rib cage; his face melted into an amorphous sack of loosened teeth and unsupported eyeballs. I watched for only a moment more as Frank's shoes fell from his dangling, flattened feet and the pants began to slide from his emaciated waist. Then I turned to flee back into my tiny cubicle.

There seemed only one means of escape: the window. I lifted the latch, pulled. But it wouldn't budge. I had no idea how long it would take that monstrous thing out there to devour Frank, but I thought I had precious little time. No doubt Leth's hunger was as voracious as his thirst. I tried again, wildly.

Water crashed into the room, slapping my face with a force that made me stagger. In moments, I'd lost the support of the floor and I was floating. Somehow I kept my wits enough to hold up my head and tread the water that was quickly filling the room. Something knocked against me. I pushed it away, realized it was the bag of human skin, almost vomited, reflexively. I dived under and kicked my way to the window. It had looked—if I hadn't drunkenly miscalculated—just large enough to pull myself through. I knew I might drown but I had to try.

I found a wall, pushed along it, banged my head, almost breathed in; mentally gasping, I pushed again. My fingers dipped into an unevenness, a depression! The water had balanced itself. I forced my shoulders through the small hole, squeezed up to my cursed beer belly.

But too many years of drinking had taken their toll. *I was stuck.*

I strained, desperately needing air, tightly maintaining control, thought of the supping water bug, perhaps finishing up—and still hungry. I gripped the outside wall and strained harder. Something tugged at my shoe. I kicked out, felt the sharp puncture of my toe. That was enough to send me through!

I awoke in daylight, half-submerged in a watery ditch. Sitting up was too quick for my expanding head and I turned, lost it. Vomited. Groaning, I tried to recall just how I had gotten there. I felt my swollen nose and it all came back.

Leth. Frank. The drinking party. I was sick again.

Somewhat composed, then, I sat up and glanced around. There was no sign of a lake, pond, or river, as I'd expected—nothing from which I might have emerged when I swam to freedom. Had I imagined the whole thing? For a long time I sat in muck, rocking myself against all the numbing possibilities, nauseous and uncertain, sliding between visions of Frank's shrinking, beseeching face and my own disgraceful alcoholic history.

My foot hurt. I'd lost a shoe. And I'd been bitten.

It could have been a snake, or a snapping turtle in the ditch. I might have banged my nose in another drunken tumble. There were simple explanations, if I wanted them. Perhaps the ditch water had nurtured a harrowing hallucination neurotically formed by deeply suppressed guilt over my lost career.

With some difficulty I got to my feet. The countryside looked perfectly normal. Stepping away from the muck, I heard *ker-plunk*. A frog, startled in its morning hunt. We peered fleetingly at one another, both hesitant, both wanting to go our own way and forget the other.

The frog. Frank. It all seemed too vivid for some pie-eyed delusion. I walked around all that day searching in vain for the dreadful house, Frank's remains, *anything* that might provide assurance that my mind hadn't simply snapped under the weight of boomeranging self-laceration.

No luck.

I've stopped drinking now. For good. I couldn't look a bartender in the eye without wondering whether he might have another life, another shape . . . whether he was eyeing me for some predaceous purpose. It seems ridiculously clear at times that I simply went too far, drank too much. Saw the dreaded "pink elephant." Perhaps that's all it was. I don't really know.

But the fact is, I never saw Frank again.

G. Wayne Miller

CHOSEN ONE

FLYING back from London and the 1988 World Fantasy Convention to Rhode Island, the author of the new William Morrow novel, *Thunder Rise*, heard the captain say, "We've lost our primary hydraulic system. Do not panic, but there *are* fire trucks waiting on the field."

Thunder, and the sun, are not the only things that rise. Try terror.

G. Wayne Miller, whose often-praised ghost story "Wiping the Slate Clean" appeared in *Masques II*, survived the perils of acquiring an agent, placing Novel One, *and* that landing. He wasn't asked what frightened him most, but this wry eastern journalist/Boston Celtics buff expressed the thought that he'd only *imagined* he understood horror in the past.

He knew plenty when he was writing the deceptive and chilling "Chosen One."

CHOSEN ONE

G. Wayne Miller

HER VOICE WAS SILKY. SO INCREDIBLY silky. That was the only reason she'd been able to come on to him successfully, that extraordinary voice.

He remembered how it used to be. Late at night—her time to rule the airwaves—he'd lie back, smoke a joint, close his eyes and listen to that voice, fantasizing what she looked like. Blond, he imagined. A Nordic face, with high cheekbones and ice-blue eyes. Blush-red lips that pursed perfectly for every word. A body to make a man a kid again, like the first time in the backseat of his daddy's car. If he felt bad about anything, that was it: that some-one with a voice so magical, so powerfully seductive, had to be destroyed.

But it was a fact of life now. Her blood had to be splattered, pooled in pretty red patterns across the floor. Maybe before it dried he would dip his finger into it, then put his finger to his mouth, savoring victory at last. Maybe that would be most fitting.

He hadn't set out to be a hero. He'd only meant to survive.

That's why, early on, he'd lined the walls of his apartment with aluminum foil. That's why he'd bricked up the windows, sealed the bathroom ceiling vent, disconnected the phone, pulled out the wall switches, the TV cable, those two tiny wires that went to the doorbell. Anything—anything at all—that might conduct electromagnetic radiation, the means she used to get inside his head.

How silly it had been. He knew that now.

Because nothing kept her away, not for long. Such meticulous precautions and her voice was still strong and clear inside his head. Cajoling him to surrender, pleading with him to give in and join her in conquering the world . . . before drastic steps became necessary.

Only now was he in true awe of her power.

No question, he thought, feeling his bulletproof vest, fingering the .44-caliber Magnum he'd bought from a sunglassed dude who did business out of a Cadillac trunk. *It's past the crisis stage. Stop her tonight, or there will never be another chance.*

Mankind will be lost.

Already it may be too late.

It had taken almost a year to get to tonight.

In the beginning, there was only a new show, a new disc jockey, an exciting new voice. It was inevitable they'd get together. He was a late-night person, a Pink Floyd fan, a thinker, philosopher, a loner with a master's in computer software. She was a companion. A *friend.* She understood the cruel things girlfriends and bosses had done. She understood the terrible odds men like him labored under, making their way through the heartless world.

More than that, she *agreed.*

It's not you, she assured him on an early visit inside his head. *It's them. Let's be friends. Us together, the rest be damned.*

Beguiled by that audio silkiness, he welcomed her. And at first, they got along swimmingly. A purely platonic relationship, two soulmates helping each other through the long, lonely night. Even when she was off the air, she'd sometimes seek him out. In the company men's room, on the subway, on his noontime walks through Central Park, she would drop in to chat. How thrilling, being singled out like that. How special he felt.

He remembered the first danger sign.

It was a Saturday, the day she discovered the Dirty Thoughts he'd begun to have. There he was in the privacy of his own bathroom, kneeling by the mirror, towel in one hand, violent erection in the other. He was thinking about her. Thinking about having her from behind, where you wouldn't have to look into the depths of those ice-blue eyes. Thinking how he would blindly cup her breasts, kiss her neck, ease slowly inside, the passion escaping like steam . . .

In the sharpest of terms, she'd told him how disappointed she was, finding those Dirty Thoughts. He tried to explain that his thoughts were meant as tribute. What higher compliment was there than showing how desperately he wanted to merge their flesh, their souls, by taking her from behind?

Get rid of them, she ordered, her disgust tearing through him like shrapnel.

He had tried. For a day or two, they were gone. But the Dirty Thoughts always came back, stealing into his head like rats through a darkened alley. She began to use the power of her voice to nudge them out. Sometimes—most times—she succeeded. The thoughts faded. In their place was black, hollow pain that Tylenol with codeine couldn't touch.

It wasn't long before he understood: she was no different than the rest. She didn't want to share; she wanted to control. A simpleton could see the distinction.

Of course, Krystal discovered *that* thought, and when she did, she came clean: *Perhaps sharing secrets is better than angry tirades to make an ally out of such a fine, strong man. I am not a DJ,* she admitted. *I am an extraterrestrial, beamed down to begin my species' takeover of the world.* The first phase, she informed him, was subjugation; that would be followed by colonization. Electromagnetic radiation—a refinement too complex for humans to comprehend—was their secret. And while it took time to deploy such an awesome weapon, Central Control had no doubt victory would be theirs.

Once Krystal clued him in, he had seen things in a whole new light. Where once he was scornful of his fellow humans, he saw them now as innocent victims, deserving of pity and salvation. Through no fault of their own, they were being conscripted into Krystal's army—an army of zombies. Now he understood that you

didn't have to tune in to her show to be taken over. If that were
the case, you could simply have turned your radio off. No, she was
infinitely more clever. Electromagnetism—in the air, passing
effortlessly through walls, silent, damn near inescapable—was
how she worked.

Now do you comprehend the true nature of her threat? he wrote in
the diary he prayed would be cherished someday by millions.
Now do you understand why I had to act so drastically?
Now will you thank me?

Over the next week, he did what any good citizen would do: he
called the police. He typed long, fact-filled letters to the White
House, the governor, Congress, NASA, the FBI, the Air Force. "For
humanity's sake," he ended each letter, "Krystal must be
stopped."

He received several responses. Someone identifying himself as
an agent of the Secret Service called, asked a stream of highly
personal questions. Someone else in the governor's office chatted
amicably for over ten minutes. But nothing changed. No one ar-
rested her or canceled her show or blew up her station or set out
to find her spaceship. It made him realize how deeply she'd infil-
trated the fabric of society.

It was only then that Apocalypse occurred. One night, alone in
his apartment, another voice—a voice he'd never heard before,
would never hear again—announced that he had been Chosen.

"Go on and laugh," he wrote the next morning to the editor of
The New York Times. "Get it out of your system, then listen care-
fully. The hour is late. But there's still hope. I am Chosen . . ."

The letter wasn't published.

His arrest was next.

It came comparatively late in the game, but before he under-
stood what radical measures had to be taken. He was still leaving
his apartment, making the rounds of politicians and agencies, try-
ing desperately with a sandwich board, a bullhorn, and pamphlets
to get his message out. That is not to say he was entirely reckless.
He knew enough to wear a lead bib he'd stolen from a hospital. To
protect his head, he wore a football helmet customized with as-
bestos and foil.

He was dressed that way the afternoon he attacked a remote-broadcast van belonging to Krystal's station. He spotted it there in Washington Square, a crowd of zombies gathered around. Wielding a baseball bat, he'd smashed through the windows and was bloodying a zombie-technician by the time the cops dragged him away.

In jail, a zombie-cop gave him a tranquilizer, a zombie-sergeant read him his rights, a zombie-matron tried to make him eat zombie food. He was taken in handcuffs to district court, where a zombie-judge released him to the custody of a mental health center.

Why you? one bespectacled little zombie-turd wanted to know.

It wasn't ego, he explained calmly. It was part of a larger plan. He had been anointed, if you wanted to look at it like that. Chosen. No one might ever know why it had been he and not, say, a gas jockey from Perth Amboy or Larry Bird. If you knew anything, you knew that was sometimes how it happened. Look at Joan of Arc. Who, back then, would ever have guessed a milkmaid would be a Chosen One?

Why can't she conquer you as easily as other people?

He almost laughed, that was so stupid.

But he didn't. Patiently, he explained that it was a tribute to his strength of character that she couldn't succeed behind his back. *He* had to be faced. *He* was the enemy, her most formidable enemy.

By now, almost certainly, her final one.

Because I am anointed. I am The Chosen One.

That's what The True Voice said.

Praise The Voice.

Hallelujah.

In the end, he was no fool. He allowed them to give him an intramuscular shot of Thorazine. He signed the form agreeing to return voluntarily in two weeks for another one.

He didn't, of course.

He vowed not to leave his apartment until he had a plan. How long that might take, he had no idea. He'd devote every waking hour, but it could be days . . . months. An awesome responsibility, saving his people.

In the meantime, there was no choice but to go full battle alert. He stockpiled food and bottled water. He lined his apartment with a second layer of aluminum and brick, and a third, and a fourth. He started drawing a half-pint of his blood every day, storing it in bottles in his refrigerator, which he kept packed with dry ice. The blood was for contigencies; exactly which contingencies, he didn't know yet. But it was better to be overprepared than caught short. Any soldier worth his salt would tell you that.

It was 2:15 A.M. now. A Tuesday morning. Twelve floors below him, the streets of lower Manhattan slumbered.

Krystal had been on the air two hours and a quarter.

He hadn't been listening.

He'd learned, through the most incredible concentration, that he could keep her out of his head for as much as an hour or two. He'd been very careful in drafting his plan. Careful never to think of the great task ahead of him without first blocking her out. He prayed it had worked.

He fingered his handgun, patted his bulletproof vest and ammo belt. It might get very ugly in there. Krystal had confided that twenty-four hours a day she surrounded herself with security forces armed with Uzis. The standing orders were shoot first, ask questions later—if any were to be asked.

Again, he thought of the risk. There was every chance he was going to get his guts sprayed all over the walls before the night was done. Any other man would say it was 99.9 percent certain that's how it was going to go down. What gave him strength was knowing that any other man would have backed out by now.

Suddenly, a knock on the door. A voice said he was from the mental health center's mobile crisis team. Could it possibly be coincidence? Or had Krystal succeeded in reading his thoughts after all? Was closing in at the zero hour?

"We know you're in there," the voice repeated. "Neighbors have been calling."

He didn't move.

"We only want to talk."

He didn't answer.

"You missed your appointment. Can't we just talk? We won't harm you. I promise."

Any second he expected the firing to start. He fingered his gun. They wouldn't get him without a fight.

"If we have to come back with the police, we will."

No answer.

And then, retreating footsteps. A trap? Minutes passed. The pounding in his head built to thunder level. He felt dizzy, hot.

Finally, he had no choice. The night was getting away from him. He cracked the door and peeked up and down the corridor. It was deserted. Gingerly, he stepped outside.

It must have been luck.

Finally, a well-deserved stroke of luck! Using alleys, he made it to the station without being seen. Jimmied the lock to the door without being seen. Up the elevator without being seen. Past corporate offices without being seen.

He was crouched outside her studio now, squinting through the glass door. From somewhere, he heard a janitor vacuuming.

She was alone.

She doesn't know, he dared think, giddy with the thought. *I've been able to keep her out!*

He stared, transfixed. She was smaller than expected, but in every other respect exactly what he'd imagined. Her hair was blond, straight, sweeping down over her shoulders. High cheekbones. Steely blue eyes. Perfectly round lips.

And her body . . . The sight of that body took his breath away.

He walked on sneaker-silenced feet through the glass door.

"Krystal," he said.

She turned but didn't answer. For a moment, her face was blank; then an expression—a mixture of surprise and fear—crossed it.

"Who are you?" she demanded. "How did you get in?"

"You know who I am," he said.

"I've never seen you before in my life."

"Don't play games with me," he shouted. "You *know* me. You've been inside my *head.*"

"I . . . I don't know what you're talking about."

"No games, Krystal." He moved toward her. "It's over."

"W-what do you want?"

"You know what I want."

"Is it money?" She reached for her pocketbook. "Here, take it all, take the credit cards, take—"

"DON'T MOVE!" he shouted. He was too supercharged to notice her foot, making contact with the emergency button under the console.

"Please don't hurt me," she whimpered.

"Back away from the console!"

Trembling, she did.

"Put your hands on your head."

She did. Her hands were shaking; she could not control them.

"Now walk toward me. *Slowly.*"

She started toward him.

"Turn around. Back into me."

She hesitated.

"AGAINST ME OR I SHOOT."

She made contact. Her body recoiled in disgust. He ran his fingers through her hair and the first tears fell.

"I wouldn't have thought it was possible anyone could be so beautiful."

"Please . . ."

He was tempted. The Dirty Thoughts eddied and swirled, beating against the inside of his skull. She was in there with them, stoking them. He felt her then, her last-gasp shot at defeating him. Such sweet promise, taking her from behind, she allowing him, encouraging him . . . His head began to pound.

"Please don't hurt me," she pleaded.

Grunting, he pushed the Dirty Thoughts away. "Before I end it," he said, "I want you to apologize. Apologize to the people."

He forced her to the boom mike. She began sobbing.

"Apologize and set them free!"

He didn't see the back door open. He didn't see the guard come in. He didn't see the guard draw a bead on him with an Uzi.

"Say '*I'm sorry.*'"

"I . . . I'm sorry," she cried.

"*. . . for enslaving my people.*" He squeezed her violently. "Go on—say it."

"F-f-for enslaving my—"

The bullets traveled through his head on a line between his ears. Blood gushed. His grip on Krystal loosened. She wriggled free as the gun tumbled harmlessly to the floor. No more Dirty Thoughts now, nothing about salvation, only a kaleidoscope of white noise and pain. He collapsed to the floor as if deboned.

The only sound was the turntable, spinning emptily.

Krystal slumped into her chair. The tears were flowing freely. With effort, she brought herself to look at him.

There was nothing left of his ears or the sides of his head, just mangled gray tissue and matted strands of hair. His body spasmed and a crimson froth decorated his lips. His chest heaved as he drew his last breath. His eyelids fluttered and were still. She noticed a sudden purplish tinge to his cheeks, and wondered if that was normal under the circumstances.

She stared up at the security man. "I don't know how to thank you," she said. "You saved my life."

"It's my job," he answered.

The tension started to drain away. Krystal would have nightmares for ages, but life would go on.

Her show would, too.

She gazed at his body again. She couldn't help herself. The final death twitches had passed. The joints already were stiffening, his temp dropping. Around the studio, his blood was splattered in pretty red patterns. Krystal dipped her finger into it, then brought her finger slowly to her mouth. She hesitated, then licked it.

Then smiled.

It was an irony Krystal knew wouldn't have escaped him.

She wiped her finger on her pants, then bent over the console to punch up the right frequency. She leaned into the microphone.

"Central Control," she said. "Colonization may begin."

Joseph A. Citro

THEM BALD-HEADED SNAYS

ON the phone, Joe Citro doesn't remind you of the characters dropping by Bob Newhart's inn. But he's a Vermont native nevertheless and *does*—in this, his first published short fiction—exhibit some of the flavor of Larry, Darryl, and Darryl. The woods, you know. Critter-company.

Author of the novels *Shadow Child* and *Guardian Angel*, and two more sold to Warner's, Citro is moving fast now (Up East-wise) with film options, a Horror Writers of America post, and projects too premature for discussion. He's a long way from the "wispy family with sparse, cornsilk hair" that Joe says was the inspiration for his initial story; "dumb and poor and always picked on." There're those *woods* in the back of his mind, you see—and soon to be in the back of yours, after you've met the extraordinary "Snays." (Can *critter du jour* be far behind?)

THEM BALD-HEADED SNAYS

Joseph A. Citro

AFTER THE CANCER GOT MOM, DAD took me way out in the Vermont countryside to live with my grandparents.

"I'll come back for you, Daren," he said. His eyes looked all glassy and sad. I bit my top and bottom lips together so I wouldn't cry when he started home without me. Sure, he'd come back, but he didn't say when.

Before that day I'd never seen too much of my grandparents. They'd come to visit us in Providence once, right after Mom got sick. But that was years ago, when I was just a kid. I remember how Dad and Grampa would have long, quiet talks that ended suddenly if Mom or me came into the room.

After that they never came to visit again. I don't think Mom liked them, though she never said why. "Their ways are different from ours," that's all she'd say.

And they sure weren't the way I remembered them! Grampa turned out to be sort of strange and a little scary. He was given to long, silent stretches in his creaky rocking chair. He'd stare out the window for hours, or read from big, dark-covered books. Sometimes he'd look through the collection of catalogs that seemed to arrive with every mail delivery. My job was to run to the bottom of the hill and pick up the mail from the mailbox. There were always the catalogs, and big brown envelopes with odd designs on them. There were bills, too, and Grampa's once-a-week newspaper. But there was never a letter from Dad.

"Can we call Dad?" I asked. Grampa just snorted as if to say, *You know we ain't got a phone.* Then he turned away and went back to his reading. Sometimes he'd stand, take a deep breath, and stretch, reaching way up toward the ceiling. Then he'd walk— maybe to the kitchen—bent over a little, rubbing the lower part of his back.

Grampa didn't talk to me much, but Gram was the quiet one. She'd move from room to room like a draft. Sometimes I'd think I was all alone, then I'd look over my shoulder and Gram was sitting there, watching me. At first I'd smile at her, but soon I stopped; I'd learned not to expect a smile in return, only a look of concern.

Sometimes she'd bring me a big glass of greenish-brown tea that tasted of honey and smelled like medicine.

"How you feeling today, Daren?" she'd ask.

"Good," I'd say.

"You drink up, now." She'd nod, pushing the glass toward me. "You'll feel even better."

When I'd take the glass away from my mouth she'd be gone.

Every other Friday, Grampa went into town to get groceries. After I'd been there about a month, he took me along with him. And that was another odd thing about him: he had a horse and buggy when everybody else had cars. I felt embarrassed riding through the downtown traffic beside an old man in a horse-drawn wagon.

Grampa said his back was acting up real bad, so he made me carry all the bags to the wagon. Then he told me to stay put while he made a second stop at the liquor store.

I didn't, though. I took a dime from my pocket and tried to make a collect call to my father. The operator said our number was no longer in service.

Grampa came back with his bottle before I'd made it back to the wagon. He yelled at me, told me he'd tan me brown if I ever disobeyed him again.

I'd lived in Stockton, Vermont, about two months before I saw Bobby Snay.

I was playing in the barn, upstairs in the hayloft, looking out the loading door toward the woods. I saw him come out from among the trees. He swayed when he walked, moving with difficulty, as if a heavy wind were trying to batter him back to where he'd come from.

He continued across the meadow, weaving through the tall grass and wildflowers until he came to the road that ends in Grampa's dooryard. When he got closer I saw how funny he looked. His skin was the color of marshmallows, his eyes so pale it was impossible to say if they were blue or brown.

And it looked like his hair was falling out. Maybe it wasn't really, but it wasn't very plentiful. It looked limp and sparse and stuck out here and there in little patches, making his head look like it was covered with hairy bugs.

Back home he would have been the type of nerdy kid we'd pick on in school. But here, well, he was the only other kid I'd seen for a long time.

"Hey!" I called, "hey! Wait up!"

I dodged back into the barn and jumped down into the pile of hay below. I sneezed once, then made for the door, ran after him. But I didn't need to; he was in the barn waiting for me.

All of a sudden I wasn't so eager to say hi. In fact, I was kind of scared of him. He was taller than I, but he was spindly, weak-looking. I wasn't afraid he was going to beat me up or anything. It was something else. Maybe it was the way he had crossed the dooryard and entered the barn in less time than it took me to jump out of the loft. Maybe it was the way he stared at me as if there was no brain behind his washed-out eyes.

Or maybe it was the smell.

I didn't realize it at the time, but now I think that strange odor was coming from him.

It was like the odor of earth, the strange scent of things that were once alive—like rotting squirrels and leaves mixed with the smell of things that would never live. Like water and stones.

"I . . . I'm Daren Oakly."

"Bobby," he said. "Bobby Snay." His voice was windy-sounding, like air through a straw.

"Where you going?" I couldn't think of anything else to say.

"Walkin', jes' walkin'. Wanna come?"

"Ah . . . No. Grampa says I gotta stay here."

"You don't gotta. Nobody gotta. Nobody stays here."

It was warm in the barn. The smell seemed to get stronger.

"Where d'ya live?"

He pointed with his thumb, toward the woods.

"You *live* in *the woods*?"

"Yup. Sometimes."

"How old are you?"

He blinked. I hadn't noticed till then, but it was the first time he'd blinked since we stood face to face.

"I gotta go now," he said. "But I'll come again. I always come 'round when ya need me."

I watched him walk away, lurching, leaning, zigzagging through the field. He had no more than stepped back into the woods when I heard Grampa's wagon coming up the hill.

"You ain't to do it again!" Grampa raged. "I won't have it. I won't have you keepin' time with them bald-headed Snays! Not now, not till I tell ya. You don't know nothin' about 'em, so you stay clear of 'em, hear me?"

"But—"

"You see them around here again, you run an' tell me. That's the long an' short of it."

"But Grampa—!"

It was the fastest I'd ever seen him move. His hand went up like a hammer and came down like a lightning bolt, striking my cheek.

"An' that's so you don't *forget*."

Anger flared in me; adrenaline surged, uselessly. Then fear settled over everything. I couldn't look at Grampa. My nose felt warm. Red drops splatted on the wooden floor like wax from a candle. I bit my lips and fought away the tears.

Later, I heard him telling Gram, "They're back. The boy seen one of 'em just today." Grampa sounded excited—almost happy.

*   *   *

I woke up to the sound of shouting. Outside my bedroom window, near the corner of the barn, two persons were fighting. One of them, the one doing the hollering, was Grampa.

"I don't care *who* you come for, I'm the one's got you now!"

Grampa pushed the other away, butted him with his shoulder against the open barn door. The door flapped back, struck the side of the building like a thunderclap.

I could see the other person now. It was Bobby Snay.

Grampa hit him in the stomach. Bobby doubled up. Puke shot out of his nose and mouth.

Grampa lifted a boot and Bobby's head jerked back so hard I thought his neck would snap. He tumbled sideways, slid down the barn door and curled up on the ground.

Grampa stomped hard on his head, once, twice. Every time his boot came down he'd yell, "YEH!"

There was a big rock near the barn. Grampa kept it there to hold the door open. It was about the size of a basketball, yet Grampa picked it up like it were weightless.

I was surprised how easily Grampa lifted that rock all the way to his shoulders. Then he did something crazy: he let it drop. Bobby lay still after it had smashed against his head.

Grampa turned and walked toward the house. He was smiling.

All the rest of the day I tried to pretend I hadn't seen anything. I knew I couldn't tell Gramma, so I actually tried to forget how weird Grampa was acting. But I couldn't forget; I was too scared of him.

It was then I decided that staying clear of him wouldn't be enough. I'd have to sneak off, run away. Then I'd find my father and things would be pretty much the way they used to be.

Gramma watched me force down a bowl of pea soup at the silent dinner table. Then I got up and started toward the back door. My plan was to run through the woods to the main road, then hitch a ride.

When I opened the door, Grampa was in the yard. He stood tall and straight, hands on hips. That arthritic droop to his shoulders was gone now. His face, though wrinkled as ever, seemed to glow with fresh, pulsing blood. He was still smiling.

I knew he could tell by the terror on my face that I'd seen everything. "Get dressed," he said, "you got some work to do."

I thought he was going to make my bury Bobby Snay's body. Instead, he made me go down to the cellar to stack firewood he handed to me through a window. We did that all afternoon. After about an hour my back was hurting something awful, but Grampa never slowed up. Now and then he'd stand straight and stretch his arms wide. He'd smile; sometimes he'd laugh.

I didn't dare say anything to him.

I could hardly eat supper. I was tired and achy and I wanted to take a nap. Grampa wasn't tired at all. He ate lots of beans and biscuits, even carried on a conversation with Gramma. "I feel ten years younger," he said.

The next day Grampa went into town again. I asked him if I could go too. I wanted to get at least that far in the wagon, then . . . well, I wasn't sure. I'd go to the police, or run away, or something.

He said, "No. I'm goin' alone. I want you *here.*"

I was sitting on the fence by the side of the barn, trying to decide what to do, when Bobby Snay stepped out of the woods.

I couldn't *believe* it.

As he got closer, I saw what was really strange: he wasn't bruised or cut or anything. I mean, I was sure Grampa had killed him, but here he was, without any trace of that awful beating.

He walked closer, weaving this way and that, as if one of his legs was shorter than the other. When he was near enough to hear me, I forced myself to ask, "Are you okay?"

He stopped walking. His eyes were pointed in my direction but I didn't feel that he saw me. "Yeah," he said, "yeah, sure, 'course I am."

Then he lurched to the right as if someone had shoved him, and he continued on his way.

I watched him go, not believing, not knowing.

Should I tell Grampa Bobby was okay? Should I talk to the law? Keep quiet? Or what? I had to decide; I had to do something.

*   *   *

Friday at supper Gramma had a heart attack.

She was spooning stew onto Grampa's plate when she dropped the pot. Grampa's hand went up like he was going to smack her. Then he saw what was happening.

She put both her hands on the tabletop, trying to steady herself. Her knuckles were white. Sweat popped out all over her face. "I . . . I . . . I . . . ," she said, as if her tongue was stuck on that one word.

Then her knees folded and she dropped to the floor.

Grampa said, "Jesus, oh Jesus . . . oh *God.*"

But instead of bending over and helping Gramma, he did something awfully weird: he grabbed his shotgun and ran out the door.

Left alone with Gramma, I didn't know what to do. I knelt over her and tried to ask how I could help. I was crying so hard I was afraid she couldn't understand what I was saying.

Now her skin turned completely white; her lips looked blue. Her whole face was shiny with sweat. She whispered something: "Go get me a *Snay,* boy. Go quick."

I didn't argue. I ran toward the door.

Maybe Mr. Snay was a doctor, a preacher, or something, I didn't know. Whatever he was, Gramma seemed to need him. Somehow, I guessed, he'd be able to help her.

Quickly finding the path Bobby Snay had taken earlier, I entered the woods. Almost at once I heard noises. Grunting sounds. Soft *thupps.* Cracks and groans.

It was Grampa and one of the Snays—*not* Bobby this time, but surely one of his relatives. It was a girl. She had the same tall, frail body, the same mushroom-white complexion, the same patchy growths of hair.

Grampa was smashing her with a piece of pipe that looked like a tire iron. The Snay didn't fight back, didn't scream, she just stood there taking the blows. I saw Grampa jab at her with the flattened end of the metal rod. It went right through her eye, sinking halfway into her skull. She fell backwards, sat on the ground. Grampa jerked the rod up and down just like he was pumping the blood that spurted from her eye socket.

I couldn't look and I couldn't run away. "Grampa," I shouted, "stop it! You gotta *help Gramma!*"

Grampa finished what he was doing and looked up. His eyes

were bright, fiery-looking. Then he took a step toward me, squeezing the bloody pipe in his slimy red hand.

He looked wild.

I backed away from him, thinking, He's going to brain me with that thing.

Then my heel hit something.

The shotgun!

I picked it up from where Grampa must have dropped it. I guessed he wanted to do his job by hand. I guessed he enjoyed it.

I pointed the gun at him.

"Put that down, boy!" His voice was as gruff as I'd ever heard it. When he stepped toward me I stepped backward, almost stumbled. I had the gun but that didn't keep me from being afraid.

"Put it *down.*" He waved the tire iron, gesturing for me to drop the shotgun. Tears blurred my vision; the gun shook in my hands.

"Listen to me, boy . . ." His hand was reaching out.

I looked around. The Snay wasn't moving. There was no one to help me.

Grampa took another step.

"I'm *tellin'* you, boy—"

Closer.

I cried out and pulled the trigger.

If I hadn't been shaking so much, I might have killed him straight off. As it was, his shirt tore away and red, slimy skin exploded from his left side.

We both fell at the same time, me from the recoil, Grampa from the shot.

I stared at him. A white, red-glazed hipbone showed through his mangled trousers. Broken ribs bit through the shredded flesh.

"Daren," he said. This time his voice was weak.

I couldn't move. I couldn't go to him. I couldn't run away.

"Daren, you don't understand nothin'."

I could barely hear him. "The Snays," he said, "you gotta give 'em your pain. You gotta give 'em your troubles. You *can't* hurt 'em. You can't *kill* 'em. They jest keep comin' back . . ."

I found myself on my feet again, moving closer to Grampa dragging the shotgun by the barrel.

Suddenly, I was standing above him.

"You shot me, boy—but you can make it right. You gotta *do* one of 'em. You gotta do jes' like you're killin' one of 'em. Then I'll be all right. You gotta kill one of 'em, for me."

"But what about Gramma?"

"Please, boy . . ." His voice was weak. I could barely hear him. He lifted his finger toward the Snay with the ruined eye. "See that? I got to her in time. Your gramma's all right."

I needed proof, wanted to run back to the house to see for myself, but there was no time. And Grampa was dying.

The mangled Snay was moving now. She was using the tree trunk to work her way back up to her feet.

"See there, boy," Grampa wheezed. "*Get* her, boy, shoot her. Hit her with the gun!"

I lifted the shotgun, braced my shoulder for another recoil.

"Hurry, Daren, 'fore she gets away."

My finger touched the trigger. I was shaking so much the metal seemed to vibrate against my fingertip.

"*Please*, boy . . ." Grampa was propped up on his elbow. He watched the Snay lurch, stumble toward the shadowy trees—

"Now, boy, *NOW!*"

—and disappear.

Grampa collapsed on the ground. He was flat on his back, head resting on an exposed root. Now his eyes were all cloudy-looking. They rolled around in different directions.

I was still posed with the gun against my shoulder. When he tried to speak again, I just let it fall.

I had to kneel down, put my ear right up next to his mouth, to hear what the old man was saying.

"You shoulda *shot*, Daren . . ."

"I couldn't, Grampa." I was blubbering. "I can't shoot nobody . . ." My tears fell, splattered on his face.

"You *gotta*, son. Your daddy, he never had no stomach for it neither. Couldn't even do it to save your mama. That's why he brung you here. He knew old Gramp would know what to do. That cancer that got your mama, boy—that cancer that killed her? Well, Daren . . . you got it, too."

His words stopped in a gag, his eyes froze solid, and he was dead.

I looked up. Looked around. The Snay was gone. The birds were quiet. I was alone in the woods.

Steve Rasnic Tem

MOTHERSON

COLORADO-based, like Dan Simmons (what *do* they put in the water out there?), Steve Tem is that rare pro whose work is generally welcomed for almost any sort of horror mag or anthology. He places craft ahead of other considerations and has the talent to shift from one fantastic attitude to another while sustaining quality and speaking in his own clear voice.

When the Bearded One made this uncommon and powerful story available last summer, he appended a note saying he had yarns coming out "in the anthologies *Tropical Chills, Post Mortem, Graystone Bay #3, Hot Blood, Pulphouse #1, The Book of the Dead,* and *Halloween Horrors II.*" That means Steve has virtually blanketed the grimacing face of horror. For the second time, a *Masques* anthology peeks out from under a corner of that coverlet. Smiling.

MOTHERSON

Steve Rasnic Tem

JOEL FOUND SAMSON IN A FREIGHT car. Or Samson found him. In any case, both would have been hard to miss.

Joel was a runaway. One of his many social workers said he was becoming a "chronic" runaway, whatever that meant. All he knew was he had to run away all the time. *Had* to. How else was he going to find his own true mother?

Joel's mother had abandoned him when he was just a year old. Or at least that's what the social workers told him. But everybody knows social workers are liars, so he had no idea if that story was true or not. The social workers really liked to tell the story, though, and that made him suspicious. They made it sound like an adventure.

A woman from their agency had just gotten off the plane from a two-week vacation in the Bahamas. She was in the airport rest room when she heard a soft crying sound. She looked everywhere, even in the toilets, but she couldn't find a thing. But she knew that somewhere a baby must be in terrible trouble, so she kept looking.

Finally she thought to lift the lid of the trash can, and there was Joel, all wrapped in a blanket. They said he must have been crying for a very long time because his face was bright red and he had trouble catching his breath. He'd even thrown up on the blanket, he'd been crying so hard.

So she called the police and brought Joel to the agency. The social workers were always telling him how cute he was then, and how all of them wanted to take him home with them, especially the lady who had "saved" him, but unfortunately it was against agency policy to place a child with someone who worked there.

That was a big lie. None of them had really wanted him. Joel was ugly. His face wasn't red just from crying. He had a big strawberry birthmark covering the right side of his face. It looked as if he had been left under a sunlamp too long on one side. And when he got mad the mark got redder and redder, until it almost looked like his face was on fire, that he'd burn you if you touched him. He'd watched himself in the mirror, made himself get mad just to watch the birthmark flame. That wasn't hard; there were a lot of things that made Joel mad, and all he had to do was think about any one of them.

He'd been in six or seven foster homes, and three "adoptive placements." They hadn't wanted him either—they just said they did so they could brag to their friends and neighbors about what good people they were. Nobody wanted a kid with that kind of face, and Joel made sure that the families who took him in finally realized that fact.

He remembered the first place they'd sent him to. He had a little brother, five years old. The kid had a white puppy. The parents didn't want Joel to feel jealous, so they let him feed the puppy sometimes. Joel didn't feel jealous at all, but adults always thought they knew everything you were thinking. So he went along with them and fed the dog. Except one day he just added a little broken glass to the high-priced dog food they always bought.

Joel used to tell the social workers he only wanted to find his *real* mother and go back to her. They always told him she must not have been able to take care of him because she'd just abandoned him like that, but they didn't know that. They'd never even talked to her.

Sometimes Joel imagined his mother must be somewhere crying over him, wondering what could have possibly happened to him. Maybe she'd been sick, or knocked unconscious. Or maybe someone had kidnapped him and left him in that bathroom. Maybe even that social worker who said she had found him had actually stolen him out of his mother's front yard. Maybe the whole agency had been part of the crime. *Anything* might have happened.

Sometimes Joel could hear his mother inside his head, telling him to get out of whatever house and family the social workers had put him into and go find her. She needed him; they belonged together. Joel wondered if she had a big red mark on her face, just like his.

But that wouldn't be right. His own true mother was beautiful.

This last time Joel had run away from a foster home. They were nice-enough people; at least they didn't bother him with a lot of family-togetherness crap. But his mother told him it was time to leave. She told him to go to the railroad yards, where the freight trains go through. Maybe she was going to meet him, or tell him which train to take when he got there.

His mother told him to crawl into a certain freight car. *Go to sleep,* she said. That wasn't hard to do—Joel always felt tired when his mother was talking to him. And the steady rocking of the train was about the finest thing Joel had ever felt.

When he woke up, the car was all red inside. Without thinking, he touched his face, wondering what was wrong. He'd been dreaming of fire, of burning up, and for a moment he wondered if he might still be dreaming. He turned his head in nervous little jerks.

The freight car was full of straw and empty cloth sacks. Most of the sacks were gathered in a big bundle at the shadowy other end of the car. The sliding door to the car was cracked a little, and it was there all the red was coming from. Joel staggered to his feet and went to take a look outside.

It was the most beautiful dawn Joel could remember. The sky was a gorgeous crimson, like it was on fire; but a nice fire. It warmed his birthmark pleasantly. He touched his face, helpless to prevent the smile he felt coming.

Nice, huh?

Joel stiffened. "Mother?" He turned and peered back into the darkened interior of the car. His eyes had to adjust again; he could barely see.

The bundle of empty sacks began to rise on two enormous legs. "What you mean, boy?" The sacks parted to reveal the wide, bearded face. "You lost or something?"

Joel stared at the man standing among the discarded sacks. He was incredibly tall, with matted black hair and beard, and he wore a huge black overcoat that hung past his knees. It was hard to judge the man's width because of the bulk of the coat, but Joel figured he must have weighed well over three hundred fifty.

"I asked you a question, son."

Whoever he was, he was an adult, and not to be trusted. "I'm *not* your son," Joel said. "And I'm not lost."

The man tilted his head awkwardly, like as if he was stiff or something. Joel had a thought that the man might be crippled, but he couldn't imagine where that idea came from. The man coughed a little, and Joel wondered if the man might be laughing at him.

"Well, you must be somebody's son," the man said. "I heard you asking for your mama."

"Don't you talk about my mother!" Joel felt his birthmark beginning to burn.

It's all right, son. Don't upset yourself so.

"What, what did you say?" Joel raised his fists. He suddenly felt confused, like he wasn't fully awake yet.

"I didn't say anything . . . uh . . . what's your name, anyway?"

Joel just looked at him. "Joel," he finally said, not sure why he was telling him.

"No last name?"

"No. Not one that belongs to me, anyway."

"Well, that's okay. My name's Samson. No last name for me, either." They stood like that awhile, awkward with each other. "Nice sunrise," Samson said a couple of times, and Joel simply nodded. After a while Joel sat down, watching the countryside roll past the door. "You hungry . . . Joel?" Samson held out something wrapped in brown paper.

Joel took it, examined it. It was a candy bar. "Thanks," he said, feeling a little more relaxed.

"No problem." Samson was squatting now. Joel stared at the big man's coat. It creased funny. He turned away again, afraid to look too closely.

They said nothing for several miles. The train seemed to change direction in a switching yard. For some reason Joel felt nervous. He didn't know why. "I've never done this before," he said. "I don't even know where this train is going."

It's all right, baby. Everything's going to be fine.

Joel stared at Samson's beard, searching for signs of movement.

"Nothing to worry about, Joel," Samson finally said, facing him, his mouth moving distinctly between the rolls of greasy dark beard. "I've been doing this for years. Perfectly safe. Where you off to, anyway?"

"I'm looking for my mother." Joel felt foolish for having told him, but he was scared now, he needed for this man to help.

I'm here. I'm here, baby.

Joel shook. He rubbed his hand back and forth in the hay, wishing she would stop, wondering where she was.

"Well, that's just fine. Mothers are *real* important. Ol' Samson *knows.*"

Joel couldn't understand how the man could look so calm.

It's me, baby. Mama's right here.

Joel closed his eyes tightly, then opened them again. Samson was staring right at him. He wondered if his birthmark was glowing. It burned his face just thinking about it. "What you looking at?" he muttered between clenched teeth.

"Nothing, Joel. Not one thing. We gots lots in common, you know?"

Joel felt like laughing. "Like what?"

"Mothers, for one. We're both our mother's son and that's real important. And we ain't got no last names. My mama never told me hers."

Come here, baby.

Joel bit the inside of his mouth. "Where is your mother now?"

Samson grinned. He had no teeth. "Oh, here, there, everywhere."

Everywhere . . .

Joel started to cry.

Don't cry . . .

"Oh, don't cry, Joel. I didn't mean nothing."

Baby, don't cry . . .

"I want my mama."

"I know. We all want our mamas. And it's like . . . it's like all mamas are the *same*, even when they're not the same person, you know?"

"She didn't mean to leave me behind. They're all liars!" Joel began to wail.

"That's a fact, son. They'll lie every chance they get. You don't have to tell ol' Samson about social workers."

"But how did you know . . ."

"I tell you, I've had more than my share of social workers in my time."

Baby . . .

Joel felt something. Joel felt inspired, and he risked a silly, crazy question: "Is your mother my mother?"

Samson chuckled. "No, no, that's not it at all. You're looking for your mama. My mama understands that, and she just appreciates how you feel. Yes, indeedy, she *does* appreciate it. That's what got her interested in you; that's what brought you here. Like a moth to a burning fire." Samson's head fell back and the close air filled with his deep-throated laugh.

Joel hesitated. Then he felt it all rush out of him. "She must have been sick. Something *bad* must have made her leave me!"

"I believe you." Samson crawled across the rocking floor and looked Joel in the face. "Mamas go through a lot. My mama got her belly *cut open* giving birth to me. And she *died* for her trouble!"

I did it for you, baby. I'd do anything for you.

Joel stared at Samson. The huge man looked even more grotesque, splayed across the shaking, rocking floor of the freight car. The vibrations of the moving car made his loose overcoat move and bend in strange ways, as if it had a life of its own.

Come to me, son. I'm here *for you.*

Joel scooted back until he was leaning against the metal wall. Samson looked exhausted, his mouth open and eyelids half-lowered. He turned over awkwardly, lumping the straw together to make a cushion for his back.

"I'll help you find her, Joel. Least I can do. 'Cause I know how you feel."

One of the shiny black buttons holding Samson's coat together had pulled off.

"You owe it to your mama to keep looking."

Something gray was falling into the gap in the coat left by the missing button.

"I thank my own mama every day for what she did for me— giving me life like that."

More buttons popped from the coat as the gray skin pressed away from Samson's body. Joel could see hair, and white bone.

My baby . . .

Joel rose up on his knees, leaned forward to get a closer look.

"Your mama'll do anything for you, you know that?"

Joel rose to unsteady feet. The coat was almost completely open now. Something was dropping from its hidden folds to the freight-car floor.

"My mama, now, she suffered *bad*."

For you, son . . .

Joel bent over, his hand on Samson's overcoat.

My baby . . .

Joel began to lift one side of the heavy coat.

"They shouldn't have cut her open like that! Weren't even a proper hospital!"

Something flopped forward onto the floor, grinning up at him.

My son . . .

"Why, that woman was just a midwife! Not no proper doctor! The operation just didn't work out!"

Joel stared down at the shriveled woman's corpse.

Mama's boy . . .

"But she never left me, my mama. That ol' midwife couldn't keep us apart. So that crazy ol' midwife just kept us together. Raised me up, all by myself in that little attic room, still in my mama's arms. My mama dearly loved me. Couldn't give me up."

Mother's son . . .

Joel stared down at Samson's hips, where the emaciated man's body joined his mother's broken frame. The woman's empty eye sockets stared up at him, her mouth fallen open.

Joel could barely contain his rage. He wanted to kick through
the twisted joining of mother and son, shatter the point where
Samson's narrowed, deformed torso emerged from female, skel-
eton thighs. He wanted to smash apart all the marbled surfaces
where living flesh and old bone had blended into one. It wasn't
fair.

Joel had never had his mother. Samson had never lost his.

Motherson . . .

John Keefauver

KILL FOR ME

LIKE Adobe James and Paul Dale Anderson, John Keefauver is a living secret editors should want to expose. To acclaim. I knew of neither John nor "James" before Ray Russell confided their existence. But "Kill for Me" was (like "Motherson") once meant to be part of an anthology I edited to advance new and "undersung" greats, like this Californian whose book appearances include several *Hitchcock Presents* anthologies, Joe Lansdale's *Best of the West,* and *Shadows 4.* John's fiction and humor have also made *OMNI, Playboy, National Review,* and *Twilight Zone.* Whereas my other anthology never made it into print, the tales by the likes of McCammon, Kisner, R. C. Matheson, Winter, Paul Olson, Castle, Tem, and Wiater *have*—
And now, at last, this existential corker too!

KILL FOR ME

John Keefauver

Now, THE GUN IS AIMED AT him as he sleeps so peacefully there, and all I have to do is pull the trigger and the whole horrible thing will be finished. Finally finished. Years of it, over. And I'll be the only one left. Not that I deserve to be the one surviving. But if Irene had told me what she was going to do, there would have been two of us left. I would have killed him then instead of now.

In a way, of course, she's the one who will be killing him. Not that she would want it that way. Still, there's the irony of it. Her note to me after I found her: "Tell him you did it, that it was your idea. He will think I'm the 'somebody' and he will stop. He will be satisfied . . ."

Satisfied? *Him?* Him, stop? Whatever possessed her to think that he'd stop! Why should he stop after all these years? To my mind he's just getting started. A bullet will be the only thing that will stop him.

She was always the optimist, though, Irene. She always said he would grow out of it. From the very beginning, she was the one who gave in to him, thinking he'd stop. And what she has just done was her final giving-in. Not that I didn't think the same way she did, too, at first, that it was simply a baby thing on his part. After all, don't all babies go into a tantrum at some time or another, at least once, in order to get their way? Like holding their breath until you give them whatever they want. Like he did, although I don't remember what it was he wanted anymore. But that was the beginning. And I suppose if we hadn't given in to him then, and all the childhood years afterward, I wouldn't be standing here now in his bedroom with a gun aimed at his head, my finger on the trigger. Can I really do it? If I hadn't lived through it, I would think of myself now as a monster. Can I really do it?

It's not a matter of whether I can, but that I must do it. For Irene's sake. And for all the others he will destroy if I don't destroy him. I won't give in to him again. If I—and Irene—had only stopped years ago. If we'd let him hold his breath until he turned blue. He couldn't hurt himself—we knew it then—but he scared us and we gave him what he wanted. Scared us . . . Little did we know.

That time when he was six or seven and he wanted to see that movie and we wouldn't let him and he said he was going to jump out of a tree if we didn't let him go. We wouldn't, and we found him not long afterward with a broken leg at the foot of the elm in the backyard. He hadn't made a sound. No screaming or crying, lying there I don't know how long with a broken leg. Just lay there until we found him. All he said then was "I demand to be allowed to go to all the movies I want to go to." Demand. Allowed. That was the way he talked, even then. As if he was reading the words out of a book.

So from then on we let him go to the movies he wanted to. Wouldn't you? No?

That started it, anyway. We were afraid, although Irene for a long time didn't entirely come to stop believing that he simply had fallen out of the tree. She asked him more than once about it, at first: "Now, Billy, you *must* have fallen out of that tree." He'd simply say, "I jumped. I deliberately jumped." I believed him. After all, hadn't he been building up to it with his other threats from the time he'd learned to talk? The time he said he was going to burn himself with the birthday candles if he didn't get a bicycle for his birthday. Not a small boy's bike; a big one, one he couldn't possibly ride. Of course, he didn't get it—and he deliberately waited until it was time to blow out the candles, and we were all watching, to stick his hand over the flames and hold it there until Irene jerked it away. I felt sorry for the kids at his party. Of course, that was before we stopped inviting his friends to the house. He didn't mind. It wasn't long after that that he didn't have any friends, not at school or anywhere. He didn't care.

Even Irene had to admit that he had deliberately burned himself, since it happened right in front of her eyes that way. I think he did it in front of her to make her understand that it couldn't possibly have been an accident—especially when, about a year earlier, he'd fallen down the cellar steps after we wouldn't let him go ice-skating one day. (He had a bad cold.) Even I thought it had been an accident. He was furious with us for thinking he had simply fallen. "I told you I was going to do it!" he kept yelling. When he jumped out of the tree, I guess he just got tired of waiting for us to come out and watch him. He claimed he had yelled for us to "come see." We didn't hear him.

He got his bike, and when he eventually asked for another one, an expensive racer type, we gave it to him, even though he couldn't possibly ride it. He told us he would drown himself if he didn't get it. What would you have done? Irene was very frightened. She kept saying that he "might accidentally drown himself." I argued against it because I could see what was going to happen to us for the rest of our lives if we didn't take a strong stand, although I admit I never thought it would come to this. I told her there wasn't any body of water large enough for him to drown himself in for miles around. How could he get to it? (He was only seven or eight.) Then she mentioned our bathtub . . .

When I heard him running the water for his bath that night, on his own, I gave in. Especially considering that we'd always had to drag him to the tub.

From then on we gave in to all his demands that were halfway reasonable. When we balked on some of the more outlandish ones, he threatened to do himself bodily harm. Always bodily harm. I began to dread hearing him open his mouth for fear of another demand. He got everything he wanted.

Three or four years went by like this. Why didn't we take him to a doctor, a psychiatrist? We tried to. We told him he was going to the "doctor for a checkup." He thought he was going for a physical examination—until, unfortunately, he saw the word "psychiatrist" at the entrance to the doctor's office as we walked up to it. He darted from us, pulled a penknife out of his pocket, and told us he would stick it in his stomach if we didn't promise never to try to make him see a psychiatrist again. Or any kind of a doctor. Or—he was a smart one—if we ourselves ever tried to see a doctor *about* him.

The worst thing, for then, was when a year or so later he told us he was going to jump in front of a car if we didn't buy him one—a VW. "A car!" I yelled at him. "You're only twelve years old!"

"I *demand* a car. Do you think I'm only a child because I'm twelve?"

We argued about it until he made me so mad that I told him he could jump in front of cars for the rest of his life before I'd ever buy a twelve-year-old kid an automobile.

I had no sooner said that than he ran out of the house. I went to the door, but I didn't realize he was running toward the highway until he was too far away to hear me. I screamed then that he could *have* a car and began to run after him. From a distance, still screaming, I saw him reach the highway, wait a moment, then jump right in front of an oncoming sports car.

I had the VW waiting for him when he got out of the hospital— a new one. That's what he'd demanded.

I'd hoped that he'd be content just to own the car, to sit in it, to pretend he was driving it. But as soon as he was recovered enough, he demanded that Irene or I drive him wherever he wanted to go whenever he wanted to. We did. Wouldn't you? I was particularly anxious not to displease him. Irene had told me that if I ever did anything again that might cause him to do something on the order of jumping in front of a car, she would leave me. I also felt guilty about causing his injuries, if you can believe it.

He soon tired of being driven, though, and demanded that we buy him some property, a field large enough for him to drive the car in himself. He wasn't old enough to drive legally on public streets, of course, and the fact that he insisted on not breaking the law amused me in an ironic way—until I came to the conclusion that he was not really interested in not breaking the law, or even in driving. His interest lay in making another, a larger, demand on us. He well knew that I couldn't afford to buy a field. But I did it.

He'd had the VW less than a year when he told us that he'd cut his finger off if we didn't buy him a Porsche. I borrowed on the house for it.

I thought he was tiring of the game when he didn't make a major demand—there were many minor ones—for more than a year. Then out of the blue he said that unless we swore to give him anything he wanted for the rest of his life—*anything*—he would kill himself.

We agreed—what else was there to do?—and he said the first thing he wanted was for us to kill somebody for him.

He said this at dinner. Sitting at the head of the table, saying it very calmly, as if he were asking for the mashed potatoes (which he liked very much and which we therefore had every day), very composed, his face calm. He's a skinny, pimply kid, hardly someone who looks forceful. Yet right then he spoke with the assurance of a President of the United States—a mad president. And very seriously, just as he always was, incidentally, in asking for the potatoes.

In the morning, I thought, I'd go to the authorities and commit him to a mental institution. He was still a minor.

"Kill somebody for you?" I was afraid to look at Irene.

"That's what I said."

"Why?"

"Because I demand it."

"Well, then, who?"

"Anybody. It makes no difference. I demand that you kill for me."

"When?" I had to have until morning.

"Within twenty-four hours. If you don't, I'll kill myself."

There was no doubt in my mind that he would carry out his threat. And there was also no doubt in my mind that if we killed once for him, he would demand that we kill again—and again. How far could he go? To, indeed, the President of the United States?

With that, he rose and we were dismissed.

That night in our bedroom I told Irene about my plan to go to the authorities in the morning. In fact, I told her a number of times; she seemed so numb, so uncomprehending, so withdrawn, that I didn't seem to be getting through to her. She never answered me. She made no reply—except for a low moaning sound. As I tried to go to sleep I kept hearing her moan. She wouldn't let me hold her. And she wouldn't take a sleeping pill.

Toward dawn I awoke to find her gone from the bed. There was a light coming from our bathroom, and when I went in, there she was lying on the floor, dead, an empty bottle of sleeping pills beside her. The bottle had been nearly full.

Beside the bottle was a note: "Tell him you did it, that it was your idea. He will think I'm the 'somebody' and he will stop. He will be satisfied. It will shock him into sanity." And then a P.S.: "Hide the pills. Say you suffocated me with a pillow. Put me in bed."

Wild grief first. Then a fury. Calling the police simply wasn't enough.

I went into our bedroom and got my gun. Then, into his bedroom.

The gun, aimed at his head. What could be more fitting than that he be the 'somebody,' that within the time specified his last demand be fulfilled?—by me, as always.

Now that the police and everybody else have gone, I suppose I ought to tidy up a bit. If nothing else, clean up the blood. That's what Irene would do, God bless her soul. (Oh, God, how will I ever get along without her?) At least I got her into bed before the police saw her—she wouldn't have liked to be seen on the floor—although I didn't do anything else for the rest of the day except wait for dinnertime. I wasn't up to it. I thought a lot, though—about not killing "somebody" for him, putting it into the right words. And once more I thought about all of his threats, especially the last one, and how he'd followed through on every one of them. Had I made the right decision? Including telling him the truth about Irene, that she had committed suicide?

I had. He'd done exactly what I knew he was going to do. As

soon as the twenty-four hours were up, at dinnertime, and I'd
said, I-don't-know-how-many times, that I hadn't killed "some-
body" and that I wasn't about to, he'd taken the gun I'd offered
him—the same one I was going to shoot him with until I came to
my senses, and thinking of his final threat, changed my mind just
before I pulled the trigger—and he'd blown his own brains out.

Dan Simmons

SHAVE AND A HAIRCUT, TWO BITES

I found *Song of Kali* in an airport just a few hours after watching Colorado author Dan Simmons win the 1985 World Fantasy Award for that novel. That wasn't, however, the first time I'd heard of it. Phoning to cite some of the fine novels of horror, fantasy, and science fiction for a book I was editing, Harlan Ellison had insisted that *Kali* was "probably the finest novel in the last decade." Then Dean Koontz urged me to read it. Enjoying periodic rational moments, I did. At last.

And in galleys for my "how to" book I replaced on my Top Ten list a wonderful novel by a respected chum of mine—with *Song of Kali*. I hadn't been that totally absorbed by a book of fiction since the masterworks of Bradbury, Matheson, Bloch, Koontz, Ira Levin, Paul Wilson's *The Keep*, Steve King's *Pet Sematary*, or Peter Straub's *Ghost Story*. The first writer I wanted for *Masques III* was Dan Simmons; like Robert R. McCammon's classic "Nightcrawlers" in the original *Masques*, this was the last story in. I was twice-blessed.

Dan's first yarn won the Rod Serling Memorial Award for previously unpublished authors; it appeared in an issue of *Twilight Zone* that "came out on the day our first and only child was born," he says, "so no one in the family noticed that I was published for some time." After appearing in *OMNI* and

Asimov's, he had new tales in *Night Visions 5* (Dark Harvest); he is now working on a story collection *(Eyes I Dare Not Meet in Dreams)*, the SF novels *Phases of Gravity* and *Hyperion* for Bantam, and his massive novel *Carrion Comfort—co-illustrated* by Simmons—will be out when you read this.

Brace yourself for a shocking treat.

SHAVE AND A HAIRCUT, TWO BITES

Dan Simmons

OUTSIDE, THE BLOOD SPIRALS DOWN.

I pause at the entrance to the barbershop. There is nothing unique about it. Almost certainly there is one similar to it in your community; its function is proclaimed by the pole outside, the red spiraling down, and by the name painted on the broad window, the letters grown scabrous as the gold paint ages and flakes away. While the most expensive hair salons now bear the names of their owners, and the shopping-mall franchises offer sickening cutenesses—Hairport, Hair Today: Gone Tomorrow, Hair We Are, Headlines, Shear Masters, The Head Hunter, In-Hair-itance, and so forth, ad infinitum, ad nauseam—the name of this shop is eminently forgettable. It is meant to be so. This shop offers neither styling nor unisex cuts. If you hair is dirty when you enter, it will be cut dirty; there are no shampoos given here. While the franchises demand fifteen to thirty dollars for a basic haircut, the cost here has not changed for a decade or more. It occurs to the potential new customer immediately upon entering that no one could live on an income based upon such low rates. No one does. The potential customer usually beats a hasty retreat, put off by the too-low prices, by the darkness of the place, by the air of dusty decrepitude exuded from both the establishment itself and from its few waiting customers, invariably silent and staring, and by a strange sense of tension bordering upon threat which hangs in the stale air.

Before entering, I pause a final moment to stare in the window of the barbershop. For a second I can see only a reflection of the street and the silhouette of a man more shadow than substance—me. To see inside, one has to step closer to the glass and perhaps cup hands to one's temples to reduce the glare. The blinds are drawn but I find a crack in the slats. Even then there is not much to see. A dusty window ledge holds three desiccated cacti and an assortment of dead flies. Two barber chairs are just visible through the gloom; they are of a sort no longer made: black leather, white enamel, a high headrest. Along one wall, half a dozen uncomfortable-looking chairs sit empty and two low tables show a litter of magazines with covers torn or missing entirely. There are mirrors on two of the three interior walls, but rather than add light to the long, narrow room, the infinitely receding reflections seem to make the space appear as if the barbershop itself were a dark reflection in an age-dimmed glass.

A man is standing there in the gloom, his form hardly more substantial than my silhouette on the window. He stands next to the first barber chair as if he were waiting for me.

He is waiting for me.

I leave the sunlight of the street and enter the shop.

"Vampires," said Kevin. "They're both vampires."

"Who're vampires?" I asked between bites on my apple. Kevin and I were twenty feet up in a tree in his backyard. We'd built a rough platform there that passed as a tree house. Kevin was ten, I was nine.

"Mr. Innis and Mr. Denofrio," said Kevin. "They're both vampires."

I lowered the *Superman* comic I'd been reading. "They're not vampires," I said. "They're *barbers*."

"Yeah," said Kevin, "but they're vampires too. I just figured it out."

I sighed and sat back against the bole of the tree. It was late autumn and the branches were almost empty of leaves. Another week or two and we wouldn't be using the tree house again until next spring. Usually when Kevin announced that he'd just figured something out, it meant trouble. Kevin O'Toole was almost my age, but sometimes it seemed that he was five years older and five years younger than I at the same time. He read a lot. And he had a weird imagination. "Tell me," I said.

"You know what the red means, Tommy?"

"What red?"

"On the barber pole. The red stripes that curl down."

I shrugged. "It means it's a barbershop."

It was Kevin's turn to sigh. "Yeah, sure, Tommy, but why *red*? And why have it curling down like that for a barber?"

I didn't say anything. When Kevin was in one of his moods, it was better to wait him out.

"Because it's blood," he said dramatically, almost whispering. "Blood spiraling down. Blood dripping and spilling. That's been the sign for barbers for almost six hundred years."

He'd caught my interest. I set the *Superman* comic aside on the platform. "Okay," I said, "I believe you. Why is it their sign?"

"Because it was their *guild sign*," said Kevin. "Back in the Middle Ages, all the guys who did important work belonged to guilds, sort of like the union our dads belong to down at the brewery, and . . ."

"Yeah, yeah," I said. "But why *blood?*" Guys as smart as Kevin had a hard time sticking to the point.

"I was getting to that," said Kevin. "According to this stuff I read, way back in the Middle Ages, barbers used to be surgeons. About all they could do to help sick people was to bleed them, and . . ."

"*Bleed* them?"

"Yeah. They didn't have any real medicines or anything, so if somebody got sick with a disease or broke a leg or something, all the surgeon . . . the barber . . . could do was bleed them. Some-times they'd use the same razor they shaved people with. Sometimes they'd bring bottles of leeches and let them suck some blood out of the sick person."

"Gross."

"Yeah, but it sort of worked. Sometimes. I guess when you lose blood, your blood pressure goes down and that can lower a fever and stuff. But most of the time, the people they bled just died sooner. They probably needed a transfusion more than a bunch of leeches stuck on them."

I sat and thought about this for a moment. Kevin knew some really weird stuff. I used to think he was lying about a lot of it, but after I saw him correct the teachers in fourth and fifth grade a few times . . . and get away with it . . . I realized he wasn't making things up. Kevin was weird, but he wasn't a liar.

A breeze rustled the few remaining leaves. It was a sad and brittle sound to a kid who loved summer. "All right," I said. "But what's all this got to do with vampires? You think 'cause barbers used to stick leeches on people a couple of hundred years ago that Mr. Innis and Mr. Denofrio are *vampires?* Jeez, Kev, that's nuts."

"The Middle Ages were more than five hundred years ago, Niles," said Kevin, calling me by my last name in the voice that always made me want to punch him. "But the guild sign was just what got me thinking about it all. I mean, what other business has kept its guild sign?"

I shrugged and tied a broken shoelace. "Blood on their sign doesn't make them vampires."

When Kevin was excited, his green eyes seemed to get even greener than usual. They were really green now. He leaned forward. "Just think about it, Tommy," he said. "When did vampires start to disappear?"

"Disappear? You mean you think they were *real?* Cripes, Kev, my mom says you're the only gifted kid she's ever met, but sometimes I think you're just plain looney tunes."

Kevin ignored me. He had a long, thin face—made even thinner-looking by the crew cut he wore—and his skin was so pale that the freckles stood out like spots of gold. He had the same full lips that people said made his two sisters look pretty, but now those lips were quivering. "I read a lot about vampires," he said. "A *lot.* Most of the serious stuff agrees that the vampire legends were fading in Europe by the seventeenth century. People still *believed* in them, but they weren't so afraid of them anymore. A few hundred years earlier, suspected vampires were being tracked down and killed all the time. It's like they'd gone underground or something."

"Or people got smarter," I said.

"No, *think*," said Kevin and grabbed my arm. "Maybe the vampires were being wiped out. People knew they were there and how to fight them."

"Like a stake through the heart?"

"Maybe. Anyway, they've got to hide, pretend they're gone, and still get blood. What'd be the easiest way to do it?"

I thought of a wise-acre comment, but one look at Kevin made me realize that he was dead serious about all this. And we were best friends. I shook my head.

"Join the barbers' guild!" Kevin's voice was triumphant. "Instead of having to break into people's houses at night and then risk others' finding the body all drained of blood, they *invite* you in. They don't even struggle while you open their veins with a knife or put the leeches on. Then they . . . or the family of the dead guy . . . *pay* you. No wonder they're the only group to keep their guild sign. They're vampires, Tommy!"

I licked my lips, tasted blood, and realized that I'd been chewing on my lower lip while Kevin talked. "All of them?" I said. "Every barber?"

Kevin frowned and released my arm. "I'm not sure. Maybe not all."

"But you think Innis and Denofrio are?"

Kevin's eyes got greener again and he grinned. "There's one way to find out."

I closed my eyes a second before asking the fatal question. "How, Kev?"

"By watching them," said Kevin. "Following them. Checking them out. *Seeing* if they're vampires."

"And if they are?"

Kevin shrugged. He was still grinning. "We'll think of something."

*   *   *

I enter the familiar shop, my eyes adjusting quickly to the dim light. The air smells of talcum and rose oil and tonic. The floor is clean and instruments are laid out on white linen atop the counter. Light glints dully from the surface of scissors and shears and the pearl handles of more than one straight razor.

I approach the man who stands silently by his chair. He wears a white shirt and tie under a white smock. "Good morning," I say.

"Good morning, Mr. Niles." He pulls a striped cloth from its shelf, snaps it open with a practiced hand, and stands waiting like a toreador.

I take my place in the chair. He sweeps the cloth around me and snaps it shut behind my neck in a single fluid motion. "A trim this morning, perhaps?"

"I think not. Just a shave, please."

He nods and turns away to heat the towels and prepare the razor. Waiting, I look into the mirrored depths and see multitudes.

Kevin and I had made our pact while sitting in our tree on Sunday. By Thursday we'd done quite a bit of snooping. Kev had followed Innis and I'd watched Denofrio.

We met in Kevin's room after school. You could hardly see his bed for all the heaps of books and comics and half-built Heath Kits and vacuum tubes and plastic models and scattered clothes. Kevin's mother was still alive then, but she had been ill for years and rarely paid attention to little things like her son's bedroom. Or her son.

Kevin shoved aside some junk and we sat on his bed, comparing notes. Mine were scrawled on scraps of paper and the back of my paper-route collection form.

"Okay," said Kevin, "what'd you find out?"

"They're not vampires," I said. "At least my guy isn't."

Kevin frowned. "It's too early to tell, Tommy."

"Nuts. You gave me this list of ways to tell a vampire, and Denofrio flunks *all* of them."

"Explain."

"Okay. Look at Number One on your stupid list. 'Vampires are rarely seen in daylight.' Heck, Denofrio and Innis are both in the shop all day. We both checked, right?"

Kevin sat on his knees and rubbed his chin. "Yeah, but the barbershop is *dark*, Tommy. I told you that it's only in the movies that the vampires burst into flame or something if the daylight hits them. According to the old books, they just don't *like* it. They can get around in the daylight if they have to."

"Sure," I said, "but these guys work all day just like our dads. They close up at five and walk home before it gets dark."

Kevin pawed through his own notes and interrupted. "They both live alone, Tommy. That suggests something."

"Yeah. It suggests that neither one of them makes enough money to get married or have a family. My dad says that their barbershop hasn't raised its prices in years."

"Exactly!" cried Kevin. "Then how come almost no one goes there?"

"They give lousy haircuts," I said. I looked back at my list, trying to decipher the smeared lines of penciled scrawl. "Okay, Number Five on your list. 'Vampires will not cross running water.' Denofrio lives across the *river*, Kev. I watched him cross it all three days I was following him."

Kevin was sitting up on his knees. Now he slumped slightly. "I told you that I wasn't sure of that one. Stoker put it in *Dracula*, but I didn't find it in too many other places."

I went on quickly. "Number Three—'Vampires hate garlic.' I watched Mr. Denofrio eat dinner at Luigi's Tuesday night, Kev. I could smell the garlic from twenty feet away when he came out."

"Three wasn't an essential one."

"All right," I said, moving in for the kill, "tell me *this* one wasn't essential. Number Eight—'All vampires hate and fear crosses and will avoid them at all cost.'" I paused dramatically. Kevin knew what was coming and slumped lower. "Kev, Mr. Denofrio goes to St. Mary's. *Your church, Kev.* Every morning before he goes down to open up the shop."

"Yeah. Innis goes to First Prez on Sundays. My dad told me about Denofrio being in the parish. I never see him because he only goes to early Mass."

I tossed the notes on the bed. "How could a vampire go to your church? He not only doesn't run away from a cross, he sits there and stares at about a hundred of them each day of the week for about an hour a day!"

"Dad says he's never seen him take Communion," said Kevin, a hopeful note in his voice.

I made a face. "Great. Next you'll be telling me that anyone who's not a priest has to be a vampire. Brilliant, Kev."

He sat up and crumpled his own notes into a ball. I'd already seen them at school. I knew that Innis didn't follow Kevin's Vampire Rules either. Kevin said, "The cross thing doesn't prove . . . or disprove . . . anything, Tommy. I've been thinking about it. These things joined the barber's guild to get some protective coloration. It makes sense that they'd try to blend into the religious community, too. Maybe they can train themselves to build up a tolerance to crosses, the way we take shots to build up a tolerance to things like smallpox and polio."

I didn't sneer, but I was tempted. "Do they build up a tolerance to mirrors, too?"

"What do you mean?"

"I mean I know something about vampires too, Kev, and even though it wasn't in your stupid list of rules, it's a fact that vampires don't like mirrors. They don't throw a reflection."

"That's not right," said Kevin in that rushy, teacherish voice he used. "In the movies they don't throw a reflection. The old books say that they avoided mirrors because they saw their *true* reflection there . . . what they looked like being old or undead or whatever."

"Yeah, whatever," I said. "But *whatever* spooks them, there isn't any place worse for mirrors than a barbershop. Unless they hang out in one of those carnival fun-house mirror places. Do *they* have guild signs, too, Kev?"

Kevin threw himself backward on the bed as if I'd shot him. A second later he was pawing through his notes and back up on his knees. "There was one weird thing," he said.

"Yeah, what?"

"They were closed Monday."

"Real weird. Of course, every darn barbershop in the entire *universe* is closed on Mondays, but I guess you're right. They're closed on Mondays. They've got to be vampires. 'QED,' as Mrs. Double Butt likes to say in geometry class. Gosh, I wish *I* was smart like you, Kevin."

"Mrs. Doubet," he said, still looking at his notes. He was the only kid in our class who liked her. "It's not that they're closed on Monday that's weird, Tommy. It's what they do. Or at least Innis."

"How do you know? You were home sick on Monday."

Kevin smiled. "No, I wasn't. I typed the excuse and signed Mom's name. They never check. I followed Innis around. Lucky he has that old car and drives slow, I was able to keep up with him on my bike. Or at least catch up."

I rolled to the floor and looked at some kit Kevin'd given up on before finishing. It looked like some sort of radio crossed with an adding machine. I managed to fake disinterest in what he was saying even though he'd hooked me again, just as he always did. "So where did he go?" I said.

"The Mear place. Old Man Everett's estate. Miss Plankmen's house out on 28. That mansion on the main road, the one the rich guy from New York bought last year."

"So?" I said. "They're all rich. Innis probably cuts their hair at home." I was proud that I had seen a connection that Kevin had missed.

"Uh-huh," said Kevin, "the richest people in the county, and the one thing they have in common is that they get their haircuts from the lousiest barber in the state. Lousiest *barbers*, I should say. I saw Denofrio drive off, too. They met at the shop before they went on their rounds. I'm pretty sure Denofrio was at the Wilkes estate along the river that day. I asked Rudy, the caretaker, and he said either Denofrio or Innis comes there most Mondays."

I shrugged. "So rich people stay rich by paying the least they can for haircuts."

"Sure," said Kevin. "But that's not the weird part. The weird part was that both of the old guys loaded their car trunks with small bottles. When Innis came out of Mear and Everett's and Plankmen's places, he was carrying *big* bottles, two-gallon jars at least, and they were *heavy*, Tommy. Filled with liquid. I'm pretty sure the smaller jars they'd loaded at the shop were full too."

"Full of what?" I said. "Blood?"

"Why not?" said Kevin.

"Vampires are supposed to take blood *away*," I said, laughing. "Not *deliver* it."

"Maybe it was blood in the big bottles," said Kevin. "And they brought something to trade from the barbershop."

"Sure," I said, still laughing, "hair tonic!"

"It's not funny, Tom."

"The heck it isn't!" I made myself laugh even harder. "The best part is that your barber vampires are biting just the rich folks. They only drink premium!" I rolled on the floor, scattering comic books and trying not to crush any vacuum tubes.

Kevin walked to the window and looked out at the fading light. We both hated it when the days got shorter. "Well, I'm not convinced," he said. "But it'll be decided tonight."

"Tonight?" I said, lying on my side and no longer laughing. "What happens tonight?"

Kevin looked over his shoulder at me. "The back entrance to the barbershop has one of those old-style locks that I can get past in about two seconds with my Houdini Kit. After dinner, I'm going down to check the place out."

I said, "It's dark after dinner."

Kevin shrugged and looked outside.

"Are you going alone?"

Kevin paused and then stared at me over his shoulder. "That's up to you."

I stared back.

There is no sound quite the same as a straight razor being sharpened on a leather strop. I relax under the wrap of hot towels on my face, hearing but not seeing the barber prepare his blade. Receiving a professional shave is a pleasure which modern man has all but abandoned, but one in which I indulge myself every day.

The barber pulls away the towels, dries my upper cheeks and temples with a dab of a dry cloth, and turns back to the strop for a few final strokes of the razor. I feel my cheeks and throat tingling from the hot towels, the blood pulsing in my neck. "When I was a boy," I say, "a friend of mine convinced me that barbers were vampires."

The barber smiles but says nothing. He has heard my story before.

"He was wrong," I say, too relaxed to keep talking.

The barber's smile fades slightly as he leans forward, his face a study in concentration. Using a brush and lather whipped in a cup he quickly applies the shaving soap. Then he sets aside the cup, lifts the straight razor, and with a delicate touch of only his thumb and little finger, tilts my head so that my throat is arched and exposed to the blade.

I close my eyes as the cold steel rasps across the warmed flesh.

"You said two seconds!" I whispered urgently. "You've been messing with that darned lock for *five minutes!*" Kevin and I were crouched in the alley behind Fourth Street, huddled in the back doorway of the barbershop. The night air was cold and smelled of garbage. Street sounds seemed to come to us from a million miles away. "*Come on!*" I whispered.

The lock clunked, clicked, and the door swung open into blackness. "*Voilà,*" said Kevin. He stuck his wires, picks, and other tools back into his imitation-leather Houdini Kit bag. Grinning, he reached over and rapped "Shave and a Haircut" on the door.

"Shut up," I hissed, but Kevin was gone, feeling his way into the darkness. I shook my head and followed him in.

Once inside with the door closed, Kevin clicked on a penlight and held it between his teeth the way we'd seen a spy do in a movie. I grabbed on to the tail of his windbreaker and followed him down a short hallway into the single, long room of the barbershop.

It didn't take long to look around. The blinds were closed on both the large window and the smaller one on the front door, so Kevin figured it was safe to use the penlight. It was weird moving across that dark space with Kevin, the penlight throwing images of itself into the mirrors and illuminating one thing at a time—a counter here, the two chairs in the center of the room, a few chairs and magazines for customers, two sinks, a tiny little lavatory, no bigger than a closet, its door right inside the short hallway. All the clippers and things had been put away in drawers. Kevin opened the drawers, peered into the shelves. There were bottles of hair tonic, towels, all the barber tools set neatly into top drawers, both sets arranged the same. Kevin took out a razor and opened it, holding the blade up so it reflected the light into the mirrors.

"Cut it out," I whispered. "Let's get out of here."

Kevin set the thing away, making sure it was lined up exactly the way it had been, and we turned to go. His penlight beam moved across the back wall, illuminating a raincoat we'd already seen, and something else.

"There's a door here," whispered Kevin, moving the coat to show a doorknob. He tried it. "Drat. It's locked."

"Let's *go!*" I whispered. I hadn't heard a car pass in what felt like hours. It was like the whole town was holding its breath.

Kevin began opening drawers again. "There has to be a key," he said too loudly. "It must lead to a basement; there's no second floor on this place."

I grabbed him by his jacket. "Come on," I hissed. "Let's get out of here. We're going to get *arrested.*"

"Just another minute . . ." began Kevin and froze. I felt my heart stop at the same instant.

A key rasped in the lock of the front door. There was a tall shadow thrown against the blind.

I turned to run, to escape, anything to get out of there, but Kevin clicked off the penlight, grabbed my sweatshirt, and pulled me with him as he crawled under one of the high sinks. There was just enough room for both of us there. A dark curtain hung down over the space and Kevin pulled it shut just as the door creaked open and footsteps entered the room.

For a second I could hear nothing but the pounding of blood in my ears, but then I realized that there were *two* people walking in the room, men by the sounds of their heavy tread. My mouth hung open and I panted, but I was unable to get a breath of air. I was sure that any sound at all would give us away.

One set of footsteps stopped at the first chair while the other went to the rear hall. A second door rasped shut, water ran, and there came the sound of the toilet flushing. Kevin nudged me, and I could have belted him then, but we were so crowded together in fetal positions that any movement by me would have made a noise. I held my breath and waited while the second set of footsteps returned from the lavatory and moved toward the front door. *They hadn't even turned on the lights.* There'd been no gleam of a flashlight beam through our curtain, so I didn't think it was the cops checking things out. Kevin nudged me again and I knew he was telling me that it had to be Innis and Denofrio.

Both pairs of footsteps moved toward the front, there was the sound of the door opening and slamming, and I tried to breathe again before I passed out.

A rush of noise. A hand reached down and parted the curtain. Other hands grabbed me and pulled me up and out, into the dark. Kevin shouted as another figure dragged him to his feet.

I was on my tiptoes, being held by my shirtfront. The man holding me seemed eight feet tall in the blackness, his fist the size of my head. I could smell garlic on his breath and assumed it was Denofrio.

"Let us go!" shouted Kevin. There was the sound of a slap, flat and clear as a rifle shot, and Kevin was silent.

I was shoved into a barber chair. I heard Kevin being pushed into the other one. My eyes were so well adjusted to the darkness that now I could make out the features of the two men. Innis and Denofrio. Dark suits blended into black, but I could see the pale, angular faces that I'd been sure had made Kevin think they were vampires. Eyes too deep and dark, cheekbones too sharp, mouths too cruel, and something about them that said *old* despite their middle-aged looks.

"What are you doing here?" Innis asked Kevin. The man spoke softly, without evident emotion, but his voice made me shiver in the dark.

"Scavenger hunt!" cried Kevin. "We have to steal a barber's clippers to get in the big kids' club. We're sorry. Honest!"

There came the rifle shot of a slap again. "You're lying," said Innis. "You followed me on Monday. Your friend here followed Mr. Denofrio in the evening. Both of you have been watching the shop. Tell me the truth. *Now!*"

"We think you're vampires," said Kevin. "Tommy and I came to find out."

My mouth dropped open in shock at what Kevin had said. The two men took a half-step back and looked at each other. I couldn't tell if they were smiling in the dark.

"Mr. Denofrio?" said Innis.

"Mr. Innis," said Denofrio.

"Can we go now?" said Kevin.

Innis stepped forward and did something to the barber chair Kevin was in. The leather armrests flipped up and out, making sort of white gutters. The leather strops on either side went up and over, attaching to something out of sight to make restraining straps around Kevin's arms. The headrest split apart, came down and around, and encircled Kevin's neck. It looked like one of those trays the dentists puts near you to spit into.

Kevin made no noise. I expected Denofrio to do the same thing to my chair, but he only laid a large hand on my shoulder.

"We're not vampires, boy," said Mr. Innis. He went to the counter, opened a drawer, and returned with the straight razor Kevin had been fooling with earlier. He opened it carefully. "Mr. Denofrio?"

The shadow by my chair grabbed me, lifted me out of the chair, and dragged me to the basement door. He held me easily with one hand while he unlocked it. As he pulled me into the darkness, I looked back and caught a glimpse of my friend staring in silent horror as Innis drew the edge of the straight razor slowly across Kevin's inner arm. Blood welled, flowed, and gurgled into the white enamel gutter of the armrest.

Denofrio dragged me downstairs.

The barber finishes the shave, trims my sideburns, and turns the chair so that I can look into the closer mirror.

I run my hand across my cheeks and chin. The shave was perfect, very close but with not a single nick. Because of the sharpness of the blade and the skill of the barber, my skin tingles but feels no irritation whatsoever.

I nod. The barber smiles ever so slightly and removes the striped protective apron.

I stand and remove my suitcoat. The barber hangs it on a hook while I take my seat again and roll up my left sleeve. While he is near the rear of the shop, the barber turns on a small radio. The music of Mozart fills the room.

The basement was lighted with candles set in small jars. The dancing red light reminded me of the time Kevin took me to his church. He said the small red flames were votive candles. You paid money, lit one, and said a prayer. He wasn't sure if the money was necessary for the prayer to be heard.

The basement was narrow and unfinished and almost filled by the twelve-foot slab of stone in its center. The thing on the stone was almost as long as the slab. The thing must have weighed a thousand pounds, easy. I could see folds of slick, gray flesh rising and falling as it breathed.

If there were arms, I couldn't see them. The legs were suggested by folds in slick fat. The tubes and pipes and rusting funnel led my gaze to the head.

Imagine a thousand-pound leech, nine or ten feet long and five or six feet thick through the middle as it lies on its back, no surface really, just layers of gray-green slime and wattles of what might be skin. Things, organs maybe, could be seen moving and sloshing through flesh as transparent as dirty plastic. The room was filled with the sound of its breathing and the stench of its breath. Imagine a huge sea creature, a small whale, maybe, dead and rotting on the beach for a week, and you've got an idea of what the thing itself smelled like.

The mass of flesh made a noise and the small eyes turned in my direction. Its eyes were covered with layers of yellow film or mucus and I was sure it was blind. The thing's head was no more defined than the end of a leech, but in the folds of slick fat were lines which showed a face that might have once been human. Its mouth was very large. Imagine a lamprey smiling.

"No, it was never human," said Mr. Denofrio. His hand was still firm on my shoulder. "By the time they came to our guild, they had already passed beyond hope of hiding amongst us. But they brought an offer which we could not refuse. Nor can our customers. Have you ever heard of symbiosis, boy? Hush!"

Upstairs, Kevin screamed. There was a gurgle, as of old pipes being tried.

The creature on the slab turned its blind gaze back to the ceiling. Its mouth pulsed hungrily. Pipes rattled and the funnel overflowed.

Blood spiraled down.

*   *   *

The barber returns and taps at my arm as I make a fist. There is a broad welt across the inner crook of my arm, as of an old scar poorly healed. It is an old scar.

The barber unlocks the lowest drawer and withdraws a razor. The handle is made of gold and is set about with small gems. He raises the object in both hands, holds it above his head, and the blade catches the dim light.

He takes three steps closer and draws the blade across my arm, opening the scar tissue like a puparium hatching. There is no pain. I watch as the barber rinses the blade and returns it to its special place. He goes down the basement stairs and I can hear the gurgling in the small drain tubes of the armrest as his footsteps recede. I close my eyes.

I remember Kevin's screams from upstairs and the red flicker of candlelight on the stone walls. I remember the red flow through the funnel and the gurgle of the thing feeding, lamprey mouth extended wide and reaching high, trying to encompass the funnel the way an infant seeks its mother's nipple.

I remember Mr. Denofrio taking a large hammer from its place at the base of the slab, then a thing part spike and part spigot. I remember standing alone and watching as he pounded it in, realizing even as I watched that the flesh beneath the gray-green slime was a mass of old scars.

I remember watching as the red liquid flowed from the spigot into the crystal glass, the chalice. There is no red in the universe as deeply red, as purely red as what I saw that night.

I remember drinking. I remember carrying the chalice—carefully, so carefully—upstairs to Kevin. I remember sitting in the chair myself.

The barber returns with the chalice. I check that the scar has closed, fold down my sleeve, and drink deeply.

By the time I have donned my own white smock and returned, the barber is sitting in the chair.

"A trim this morning, perhaps?" I ask.

"I think not," he says. "Just a shave, please."

I shave him carefully. When I am finished, he runs his hands across his cheeks and chins and nods his approval. I perform the ritual and go below.

In the candlelit hush of the Master's vault, I wait for the Purification and think about immortality. Not about the true eon-spanning immortality of the Master . . . of all the Masters . . . but of the portion He deigns to share with us. It is enough.

After my colleague drinks and I have returned the chalice to its place, I come up to find the blinds raised, the shop open for business.

Kevin has taken his place beside his chair. I take my place beside mine. The music has ended and silence fills the room.

Outside, the blood spirals down.

Amanda Russell

THE ORCHID NURSERY

Amanda Russell has had her prose appear in the *Los Angeles Times* and *The Tibetan Review*. This is her first professionally published poem.

The oft-witty, oft-charming Ray Russell book of poetry, *The Night Sound* ('87), was dedicated to "my daughter, Amanda, the other poet in the family." Editorially and personally, I feel that the world is ready, at last, for *two* Russells.

THE ORCHID NURSERY

Amanda Russell

In this humid artificial tropic,
Images of lust are grown in pots.
For sixty-five dollars,
One can buy a leering maniac
With a greasy green face
Spotted in bloody purple.
"An excellent breeder," says the tag.
He has the prognathous jaw
Of a later Hapsburg emperor,
But his line will grow stronger
With each succeeding generation.
On the next table
His courtesans await him,
Tiny and delicate beauties
Of pure white, yellow, and lavender.
Their waxen faces
Reveal only a hint of insane passion,
Like a women in a Goya tapestry.

Ray Bradbury

OF ABSENCE, DARKNESS, DEATH: THINGS WHICH ARE NOT

ELEVEN days after Halloween 1988, writers Jim Kisner, Dennis Hamilton, and I, along with our wives Carole, Jan, and Mary, saw the world premiere of a brilliant musical drama, *Fahrenheit 451*. We also welcomed its author, Ray Bradbury, to Indiana and listened to a different kind of music when—after the last curtain—Bradbury, flu and all, walked from the wings and took center stage.

It was a music of awe, of wonder—a word Ray sometimes seems to have invented—and it was full of other emotions such as joy, appreciation, and love. It was the first time I have heard the sound of memory being reawakened, restored, relived. We speak warmly of melodies we listened to when we gave our hearts first; we shriek within when we recall where we were when wars began, and when Presidents fell. We *sing*, our bodies electric, when we remember our own first readings of Bradbury stories, novels, poems—and it is a song from our skin and bones, of the inner mind and from the starved cells of our souls, when we see the man in our midst.

Here he is, again among us, to close this book.

OF ABSENCE, DARKNESS, DEATH: THINGS WHICH ARE NOT

Ray Bradbury

Of absence, darkness, death: things which are not
Each unshaped shape resembles
Some midnight soul
That "with Nothing trembles."
Blind skies, cloudless dimensions;
Do smother souls
Whose nameless apprehensions
Go unborn; all's diminution;
No spirit-fire flares, no apparition
Leans forth its faceless face from looking-glass
Or windowpane.
The rain wears only wind, while wind wears rain,
And when the wind with winter-white bestows
A-spectral ice, there no ghost goes.
All attics empty, all breezeways, bare,
No phantom, prideless, restless, drifts his dustprints there.
The autumn round all dreamless goes; no seamless shrouds,

No palaces of callous stars, no marble clouds,
The earthen basements drink no blood,
All is a vacuumed neighborhood,
Not even dark keeps dark or death hides death,
And sightless pulse of panics keep their breath.
Nor does a ghostless curtain pale the air
All absence is, beyond the everywhere.
Then why this unplumbed drowning-pool of fear?
My soul dissembles
Like unlit candles blown down-wind where nothing trembles
With bloodless, lifeless snowchild's seed
Miscarried by nobody's blood and need,
No moans, no cries
No blizzard mourns of silent celebration
Whose tongueless population
Stays unborn-dead.
But in my mindless marrow-bed:
Fears unremembered
How then forgot? Yet:
Absence, darkness, death: things which are not.